'It is an enormously exciting story—one which must captivate not only every modern punter, but also those who don't know one end of a horse from another. The unvarnished facts, the high society setting and the higher racing drama are splendid material enough. But the skill with which Mr Blyth tells the story matches its content.' OXFORD TIMES.

'Magnificent.' TIMES LITERARY SUPPLEMENT.

'Dramatic and impressive.' EVENING STANDARD.

THE POCKET VENUS
A Victorian Scandal

To Sophie

The picture on the cover is a detail from William Powell Frith's painting DERBY DAY, *reproduced by kind permission of The Tate Gallery, London.*

THE POCKET VENUS

By

HENRY BLYTH

SPHERE BOOKS LIMITED
LONDON

FIRST PUBLISHED IN GREAT BRITAIN BY
WEIDENFELD AND NICOLSON IN 1966

COPYRIGHT © HENRY BLYTH, 1966
FIRST SPHERE BOOKS EDITION, 1968

AFRICA: Kenya, Uganda, Tanzania, Zambia, Malawi:
Thomas Nelson & Sons Ltd., Kenya
South Africa, Rhodesia: Thomas Nelson & Sons (Africa) (Pty) Ltd., Johannesburg
Ghana, Nigeria, Sierra Leone: Thomas Nelson & Sons Ltd., Nigeria
Liberia: Wadi M. Captan
Angola, Mozambique: Electroliber Limitada, Angola
Zambia: Kingstons (North) Ltd.
AUSTRALIA: Thomas Nelson (Australia) Ltd.
AUSTRIA: Danubia-Auslieferung
BAHAMAS: Calypso Distributors Ltd.
BELGIUM: Agence et Messageries del la Presse, S.A.
CANADA: Thomas Nelson & Sons (Canada) Ltd.
CARIBBEAN: Roland I Khan (Trinidad)
DENMARK: Sven Gade, Scandinavian Book Wholesale
FRANCE: Librarie Etrangere, Hachette
GERMANY: Distropa Buchvertrieb
GIBRALTAR: Estogans Agencies Ltd.
GREECE: Hellenic Distribution Agency Ltd.
HOLLAND: Van Ditmar
HONG KONG: Western Publication Distribution Agency (HK) Ltd.
ISRAEL: Steimatzky's Agency Ltd.
IRAN: I.A.D.A.
IRAQ: Dar Alaruba Universal Distribution Co.
KUWAIT and GULF STATES: Farajalla Press Agency
LEBANON: The Levant Distributors Co.
MALAYSIA SINGAPORE and BRUNEI: Marican & Sons (Malaysia) (Sdn) Berhad
MALTA: Progress Press Co. Ltd.
NEW ZEALAND: Hodder & Stoughton Ltd.
PORTUGAL: Electroliber Limitada
SOUTH AMERICA—Colombia: Libreria Central
Chile: Libreria Studio
Mexico and Central America: Libreria Britanica
Peru: Liberias ABC
Venezuela: Distribuidora Santiago
SPAIN: Commercial Atheneum, S.A.
SWEDEN: Importbokhandeln
SWITZERLAND: Friedr. Daeniker
THAILAND: The Pramuansarn Publishing House
TURKEY: Librarie Hatchette
WEST INDIES—Barbados: Wayfarer Bookstore

Conditions of Sale—This book shall not without the written consent of the Publishers first given be lent, re-sold, hired out or otherwise disposed of by way of trade in any form of binding or cover other than that in which it is published.

Any similarity or apparent connection between the characters in this story and actual persons, whether alive or dead is purely coincidental.

Printed in Great Britain by Richard Clay (The Chaucer Press), Ltd., Bungay, Suffolk

CONTENTS

	Foreword	11
1	Star-cross'd Lovers	15
2	The Formative Years	33
3	The Salad Days	65
4	The Call of the Turf	90
5	The Pocket Venus	102
6	The Birth of Rivalry—1865	135
7	Ebb and Flow—1866	160
8	The Crisis—1867	183
9	The Final Reckoning	212
10	The Road to Kensal Green	244
11	Epilogue	266
	Bibliography	272
	Index	277

ILLUSTRATIONS

Between pages 144 *and* 145

Harry Hastings: 'The perfect Cocker'

Henry Chaplin: 'Magnifico'

Florence Paget: 'The Pocket Venus'

'The rage of the park, the ball-room, the opera and the croquet lawn'

Harry Hastings

(*Above*) The Prince of Wales as an Oxford undergraduate, 1859. Henry Chaplin

(*Below*) The Bullingdon Cricket Club, 1859

Florence Paget: 'Deprived of a mother's care . . .'

Donington Park, Leicestershire;

Blankney Hall, Lincolnshire

Hermit, with J. Daley

FOREWORD

I AM not greatly in favour of a Foreword, since I believe that an author should set down all he has to say in the main body of his book, but when a writer is presented with a difficult subject, a Foreword does give him an opportunity for explaining what he has tried to achieve.

I have been conscious, throughout the writing of *The Pocket Venus*, that it must always be the first consideration of a biographer, and of the historian in general, to assemble and to present facts. But since historical events are largely the outcome of human behaviour, it is also often necessary to leave the field of fact and enter that of conjecture. The flow of history has often been substantially altered by those who have acted precipitously and unpredictably. The results of such actions are usually not difficult to assess; but the causes of them can lie deep within the character of the persons concerned, and may not be easy to discover.

The story of Harry Hastings, the fourth and last Marquis of Hastings, and of his rivalry with Henry Chaplin over the hand of Lady Florence Paget, 'The Pocket Venus' of the title, is only a small part of Victorian history, but it is of interest not only because it mirrors the affluent world in which they lived, but also because it presents a curious example of an unpredictable action which drastically altered the course of three young lives. Lady Florence's sudden elopement with one suitor at the expense of the other presents her biographer with a number of questions that cannot easily be answered. Thus the field of conjecture becomes wide open for both author and reader to explore.

There are other aspects of the Hastings drama which are hard to explain. During the year and a half which it has taken me to write this book, I have often told its story to friends and to casual acquaintances in whose company I have found myself, with the purpose of testing out their reactions. The incidents have invariably aroused discussion, and the cause of Lady Florence's behaviour has been variously interpreted. But one point that has always both perplexed and intrigued me is that the majority of those who have been told this story (and certainly the majority of the women) have seen Harry Hastings as its hero. I thought at first that this was because I was telling the story badly and was giving it the wrong emphasis. Thereafter I was careful to enlarge upon Harry's faults, and to dwell upon Henry Chaplin's virtues, but the result was the same. To the majority of my listeners, Harry remained the hero.

In my own assessment of these three young people, I have sought objectivity and tried not to take sides. I have emphasized Harry's many failings, and throughout the book I have condemned his weakness of character. But I have not attempted to hide the fact that Harry had panache. It is a word which I have used frequently in connection with him and is derived from the plume which the French knight at arms used to wear on his helmet. Somerset Maugham, in his short story, *Appearance and Reality*, has interpreted the word as signifying 'dignity and bravado, display and heroism, vainglory and pride', and these are exactly the qualities which I have sought to portray.

As for Harry's rival, Henry Chaplin, I have done all in my power to present him fairly. In the past he has been labelled smug, which he was not; and dull, which the facts of his life strongly contradict. He was an admirable personality in many ways, but perhaps some of the readers of this book may find this to his disadvantage. In life, and indeed in literature, it is a man's faults which make him interesting and attractive and not his virtues. Many of the faults from which Harry suffered were shared by Henry Chaplin; but Henry had the habit of cloaking them—quite unwittingly, I am sure—with an outward air of respectability.

Florence Paget remains largely an enigma. One cannot be wholly objective about her because too many of the basic facts are missing from her story. I imagine that men, for the most part, will tend to make allowances for her, as I have done, and that women probably will not. If I seem at times to be defending her, it is because I feel that she has been in need of someone to speak up for her. At the time when this Hastings story was enacted she was all too readily censured. That Victorian middle-class morality to which Alfred Doolittle took such exception was just beginning to envelop the country, and Florence's behaviour provided it with what, at the time, must certainly have seemed to be a heaven-sent opportunity for pointing a moral.

There are other characters in this Hastings story who have,

I think, been unjus iably condemned in the past. And so I have even tried to make out a case for the money-lender, Henry Padwick, who has invariably been branded as the villain of the piece. He certainly provided the young bucks of Victorian society with a service of which they were much in need, but it can reasonably be argued that, if he ruined a number of them, they were anyway of the type who had dedicated themselves from the outset to self-destruction.

As for the horses which play so important a part in this Hastings story, I have tried to present them as creatures of flesh and character, and not simply as racing machines. It may well be that the reader, when he reaches the end of *The Pocket Venus*, may form the opinion that Hermit is the real hero of the story, and that Lady Elizabeth is its tragic heroine.

And when the reader does reach the end of this story, I hope that he will leave the company of these characters, whether human or equine, with regret, as I have done, and will feel, with me, that, although they were often wanton and unpredictable and were frequently flamboyant and undisciplined, they at least shared the grand manner and that their lives were never dull.

I acknowledge with gratitude all those people who have, by their several efforts, supplied me with many of the pieces which have gone to the compilation of this particular jig-saw puzzle. In particular, I should like to thank my research experts, Dr Sylvia England at the British Museum, Mrs Saunders and her staff at The Writer's and Speaker's Research, and the staff in the reference department of the Brighton Public Library. Together they delved into many obscure and curious corners, and came up with some fascinating information.

I should also like to thank the Marquess of Anglesey for supplying me with pictures of both Lady Florence Paget and the Marquis of Hastings, and for giving me what information he could about Lady Florence. There was no one whom I could find to speak up for Harry Hastings, but I am greatly indebted to Mr J. G. Shields, the owner of Donington Hall, for all that he did for me during the day when we explored Harry's ancestral home together and tried to recapture something of its past.

When dealing with Henry Chaplin, I have leant heavily on the late Marchioness of Londonderry's biography of her father, *Henry Chaplin, a Memoir*, and I would like to thank her daughter, Lady Mairi Bury, and her publishers, Messrs Macmillan, for permission to reproduce some of the illustrations, and several of the letters which passed between Henry Chaplin and Harry Hastings and between Henry Chaplin and Lady Florence.

I should also like to thank the Tate Gallery for their permission to reproduce details of Frith's *Derby Day,* and the British Museum for permission to reproduce the cartoon entitled 'Home from the Derby' from the magazine *The Tomahawk.* I must also mention my most reliable typist, Colleen Wilby, who has lived with this book without protest for eighteen months, and must certainly have typed twice the number of words it now contains—with unfailing accuracy.

Biographical research can be rather like criminal research; a vital clue may turn up at the last moment, and quite unexpectedly. For a year and a half I tried to discover the date of birth of Lady Florence Paget. No book of reference gave it, and the Marquess of Anglesey could not find it in the records of his family. One of my last acts before sending the manuscript to the publishers was to visit her godson, Major Allott, at Lymington, who had kindly supplied me with information about her previously; and the last scrap of paper which he gave me was a cutting which described her burial, and referred to the inscription on her coffin, which gave the date—18 August 1842.

Finally I should like to acknowledge my debt to the works of a writer who has been dead for nearly a century, and who originally aroused in me the desire to tell the story of Lady Florence and of 'the man who belonged to The Duke and little Lecturer'. The obituary notice which Henry Hall Dixon, better known as 'The Druid', wrote in *The Daily News* after Harry's death has provided my book with its central theme; and the reader will discover that I come back to this obituary notice again and again. For this I make no apology. It has always seemed to me to be a wise and compassionate piece of writing, and an example of sporting journalism at its best.

CHAPTER ONE

STAR-CROSS'D LOVERS

THE chief criticism levelled by Victorian Society against Lady Florence Paget and the young Marquis of Hastings was that each came of a noble line and should therefore have known better than to do what they did. There were very few who could find it in their hearts to excuse them.

As is only to be expected, the woman was blamed more than the man. She who was hailed as 'The Pocket Venus', because of her beauty and the exquisite symmetry of her tiny figure, was condemned for the heartlessness of her conduct. There were, it is true, a handful of sentimentalists who saw in them 'a pair of star-cross'd lovers' whose destinies were inevitably entwined; and some of the young bucks of Mayfair, dazzled by Florence's radiance and impressed by Harry Hastings' unfailing panache, did attempt to make out a case for them. But the Victorians as a whole would have none of it. It was not simply a question of morality. It was a matter of principle—of failing to live up to a traditional standard. Florence was cold-shouldered in Mayfair, and in the little villages surrounding Harry Hastings' country estate at Castle Donington they christened him 'the Wicked Marquis'. They still speak of him thus to this day.

A modern generation can form a more objective judgment, and today it is more constructive to view this Hastings story as a part of the Victorian picture and to allow the facts to speak for themselves. In essence it is perhaps no more than a commentary on the effects on young people of extreme wealth allied to extreme boredom. It is certainly throughout a story of extremes. The characters are extravagant in their behaviour, and some of the incidents are scarcely credible. It is a story which follows the traditional pattern of the eternal triangle, and to it are added the classic ingredients of tragedy, revenge and retribution. It has all the makings of a popular novel, because its central characters are rich, carefree, handsome and debonair, but many of its events are too melodramatic for fiction, and it lacks a happy ending. But the Victorians were able to find in it a most salutary moral, for the worthlessness of profligacy is exposed, and wantonness and immodesty are suitably punished.

A modern generation can read more into it than this. The three central characters may have been wanton, impetuous and undisciplined, but they never lacked either spirit or courage. Their misfortune was to have been born into the wrong age, and to have been brought up against a background which encouraged their excesses; and each demonstrated to a remarkable degree the traditional English virtue of being a good loser —an outmoded quality, perhaps, but one which is not altogether lacking in nobility.

As the story develops, each personality comes gradually into focus, although Florence is never quite clearly seen, nor are her motives ever fully revealed. But as an introduction to the three, they can first be glimpsed in a few brief, contemporary descriptions, which can serve to fill in the first outlines of each character. This, then, is how their contemporaries saw them.

> There he would stand smiling at the wild tumult below, wearing his hat jauntily on one side, a red flower in his button-hole, and his colours round his neck, and cool and calm. . . .

It is a portrait of a young man in his early twenties on his way to hell. That was the general verdict of Victorian England on Henry Weysford Charles Plantagenet Rawdon Hastings, fourth and last Marquis of Hastings, Earl of Rawdon and Viscount Loudoun, in the peerage of the United Kingdom; Baron Rawdon, of Rawdon, in the county of York, in the peerage of Great Britain; Baron Grey de Ruthyn, Hastings, Hungerford, Newmarch, Botreux, Molyns, and Moels, in the peerage of England; Earl of Loudoun and Baron Campbell of Loudoun in the peerage of Scotland; Earl of Moira and Baron Rawdon, in the peerage of Ireland; a baronet of England, a co-heir of the barony of Montague; and one of the three peers who enjoyed the dignity of a coronet in each of the three Kingdoms of England, Scotland and Ireland—the others being the Duke of Abercorn and the Earl of Verulam.

> For a time he was a perfect Cocker; but he fell at last in the unequal strife, and the men who had 'drawn' him most copiously were among those who set their faces most sternly against him. . . .

It was the epitaph written after his death, when his ultimate destination had presumably been reached. It was not one which would have displeased him, for when all was said and done, he had been, for a time, a perfect Cocker.

> Among the belles of our English aristocracy, few of late years created such a sensation on her début as Lady Florence Paget, the youngest daughter of the Marquess of Anglesey. Gifted with the hereditary beauty of her family to a rare extent, her petite figure and dove-like eyes caused her at once to become 'the rage of the park, the ballroom, the opera and the croquet lawn'. These personal charms were not a little enhanced by the unaffectedness of her manner and extreme good nature, which caused her to become the idol of her father and the household.

It is a portrait of a young girl in her early twenties who was also, by the common consent of her contemporaries, on the downward path to perdition.

> When our Henry is broke, which is only a matter of time, all the crowned heads of Europe ought to give him a hundred thousand a year in order that he may show them how to spend their money.

This, by way of contrast, is a portrait of a young man in his early twenties who is on the threshold of a long and honoured career of public service—service alike to his country as a politician, and to the community in which he lived as a revered and much-loved Squire. It is a comment on Henry Chaplin, the master of Blankney, and Harry Hastings' rival for the hand of Lady Florence.

There are certain points which should be borne in mind when considering this Hastings story. In the first place, the tragedy which overtook these three people occurred when they were still in their early twenties. The crisis which confronted Harry Hastings, Florence Paget and Henry Chaplin came at a time when they could scarcely be said to have reached an age of discretion—and discretion was anyway the one quality in which each was singularly lacking. This fact should always be remembered as the Hastings story is unfolded. For all their brave and extravagant actions, their wild expenditures and bold excesses, and for all their carefully preserved attitude of stoical indifference to misfortune and their worldly air of self-assurance, these central characters remain fundamentally young and immature. This can explain, and in part excuse, much of what they did.

In the second place, their upbringing and family history is also of importance when considering their subsequent behaviour, for only one of the three, Henry Chaplin, can be said to have enjoyed anything approaching a normal childhood. Harry Hastings lost his father when he was eighteen months old, and became an orphan at sixteen. His childhood was chaotic. Florence Paget lost her mother before she was two, and was brought up by an adoring but profligate father, and by elder brothers who spoilt her. Even Henry Chaplin, the least irrational of the three, lost his father when he was only eight, and was therefore deprived of that paternal control which is so essential to self-willed young males in early youth.

Thus the formative years of these three young people's lives saw many harmful influences at work. Harry Hastings had far too much money, far too much freedom and far too little discipline. Henry Chaplin had plenty of money and too much leisure. Florence Paget had too much admiration and was endowed with too much uncurbed spirit. Each of the three had exceptional good looks, and charm in abundance.

And finally there remains to be considered the period in which they lived. Each of these three was born in the early 1840s, and the drama of their lives was played out during the period of the mid-Victorian era—that is to say, between 1860 and 1868.

It was a period of extremes, and it bred extremism in many of the people who lived during it. The idea that the early or mid-Victorian Englishman was a creature of solemn and methodical habit, prosaic in manner and unemotional in temperament, was far from the truth. The prosperous middle-class had not yet established itself, with its rigid code of respectability and refinement; and the licence and immorality of the eighteenth century was still very much in evidence. This fact is of particular importance, because human character is always influenced by its background, and human conduct is largely controlled by the customs of its time.

In the 'sixties, criminals were still being hanged in public outside Newgate Prison, and the spectacle was still being looked upon as one of the city's most entertaining diversions. Huge crowds flocked to watch an execution, the front rows being reserved for women and young girls. Cock-fighting and the baiting of bears and bulls still occupied the attention of both rich and poor, townsman and countryman; and the cruelty and coarseness of the average Briton frequently shocked the sensibilities of visitors from the Continent. There were more brothels in London and Manchester than there were in Paris, Bordeaux or Marseilles. In London prostitution was practised not only openly and extensively, but—in the West End—was also organized on a lavish scale. Poverty was widespread and abject, especially in the towns. Drunkenness was a national vice. One sixteenth of the population were employed as domestic servants.

The backbone of England in the nineteenth century was the landed gentry—a solid phalanx of country squires, ultra conservative in thought and politics, stubborn, courageous and honest; men who believed in the divine right of the Lord of the Manor as devoutly as did the Stuarts in the divine right of kings. If Harry Hastings was a typical product of the old-fashioned and wildly improvident aristocracy, his rival, Henry Chaplin, was equally typical of the old-fashioned landed gentry. Not that Henry Chaplin was himself anything but wildly extravagant, but he could still believe passionately in the need for thrift in the lower classes. And if Harry Hastings represented a world of profligacy that was akin to the French aristocracy before the Revolution, Henry Chaplin, in the 'sixties, was equally representative of the England of the eighteenth century, for he saw society as being divided into two distinct sections—'a small, select aristocracy born booted and spurred to ride; a large, dim mass born saddled and bridled to be ridden'.

'In this country all is contrast,' wrote Greville in his diary, 'contrast between wealth the most enormous and poverty the most wretched, between an excess of sanctity and an atrocity of crime.'

This was the background to the Hastings story. Harry Hastings himself was born to wealth the most enormous, without any conception of the responsibilities which went with it. In the Hastings era it was by no means unusual for a gambler to lose or win up to a hundred thousand pounds over a sporting event such as the Derby. If one assumes that a pound in those days equalled in purchasing power at least ten pounds today, that means an equivalent of one million pounds won or lost on a single race. It is a staggering figure.

Florence Paget was not born to great wealth, but she was accustomed to associating with those who were. Henry Chaplin was rich without being wealthy. All three were friends with royalty. They mixed freely with the highest in the land. Thus these 'star-cross'd lovers' lived in a world which was peculiar to their age and station; a world very different from our own today. Just how far their destiny and stars influenced their lives is open to conjecture, and is a matter best left to the astrologists, although it is interesting to note, in this context, that uncertainty exists over the birth dates of two out of the three main characters. On one point, however, there can be no doubt. Each came of a long and honoured line; and the roots of each were buried deep in the soil of England.

It was said of the Paget family in the nineteenth century that all their men were heroes and all their women angels. The comment was justified. The family tradition for the men to serve their country in the armed forces of the Crown was long and glorious, and to this was added a further romantic tradition of both marrying and begetting beautiful women. To many, Lady Florence was the most beautiful of them all.

The Paget family were of ancient lineage, for they were descended from William Paget, one of the bright young men whom Henry VIII had discovered to help him run the new Tudor Britain, and whom he had created Baron Paget of Beaudesert in 1549. But the most illustrious of all the Pagets had undoubtedly been Wellington's right-hand man at Waterloo—the legendary 'One-Leg' who having had his right knee shattered by almost the last shot in the battle had then submitted to amputation of the limb without anaesthetic, without flinching and without complaint. This was Henry William Paget, the Earl of Uxbridge, whom the Prince Regent had dubbed Marquess of Anglesey five days after the battle. This was Florence Paget's grandfather. It was from this great soldier that the Victorian Pagets inherited their courage, their spirit and their independence of thought. 'The most perfect Hero that ever breathed' was one contemporary description of him. 'The cleverest cavalry officer in the British Empire' was another, a comment which emphasized that he was not only a man of bravery but also a fine leader of men, with a lively and original mind.

Florence Paget was the sixth child, by his second marriage, of Henry Paget, 'One-Leg's eldest son. Great men seldom have offspring of the same exceptional qualities as themselves, and the first Marquess was no exception. His two sons, Henry and William, were extravagant and undisciplined, and each brought much sorrow and anxiety to his father, whose life was anyway made difficult by the agony he so often suffered from the stump of his leg. Yet both were given every opportunity to make something of their lives, for the first Marquess was a devoted and conscientious father. It is true that he established another famous Paget tradition by siring a very large family, and by marrying more than once; but the number of his offspring in no way affected his love for them. He worried constantly about their future, and did all he could to promote their careers. It would be unjust to say that Henry and William between them brought their father's grey hairs in sorrow to the grave, for the first Marquess lived to a ripe age and overcame greater difficulties in his life than his prodigal sons, but both lacked his integrity and responsibility, and neither had any conception of the value of money.

Florence's father, Henry Paget, was born on 6 July 1797. He was the eldest child of a family of eight by his father's first marriage. His brother, William, born in 1803, was the sixth child. They had five sisters, so both were spoilt. The third brother died in 1825.

Their father, the first Marquess, who was to survive the battle of Waterloo and the loss of his leg by nearly forty years, played an active part in the affairs of the nation, and encouraged his elder son to do the same. Thus Henry, during the course of his life, was a Colonel of the 42nd Foot, a Whig MP for Anglesey (Pagets tended to be too independently-minded for die-hard Toryism), a Lord-in-Waiting to Queen Victoria for the first two years of her reign, Lord Chamberlain of her household from 1839 until 1841, and Lord Lieutenant of Anglesey from 1854 until his death in 1869.

On paper this looks to be a responsible and orthodox career, but Florence's father was neither responsible nor orthodox. He was a spendthrift, and even something of a rogue, and of him it can only be said that at least he neither spent money at quite the rate of his younger brother, William, nor submerged himself quite so heavily in debt, although at times it was a close thing between the two of them. Nearly all Paget males pursued women with enthusiasm, married at least once and reared exceptionally large families. They might also have had a mistress or two tucked away on occasions, for they were nothing if not ardent admirers of the opposite sex. Henry became involved in various escapades and scandals and, whilst Lord-in-Waiting to the young Queen, was rumoured to have found a post for his current mistress in the Royal establishment.

The first Marquess had married twice and had eighteen children. His son, Henry, married three times and had eleven. It was a remarkable record of productivity, although not all of them survived beyond childhood. Henry's first wife was Eleanora Campbell, a niece of the Duke of Argyll, whom he married in 1819 and who died in 1828. Five years later he married his second wife, Henrietta Bagot, the third daughter of the Rt Hon Sir Charles Bagot, and she was soon busily occupied in the traditional Paget occupation of having children. Henrietta was little more than a child herself when Henry married her, and the labour of constant child-bearing, added to the worry of watching her husband sink ever deeper into debt, finally proved too much for her. She died in the spring of 1844, three weeks after giving birth to her seventh child, a son.

Her sixth child had been a daughter, Florence Cecilia. Although a beautiful baby, Florence had not been welcome, for she had arrived at a most inopportune moment in the affairs of her father. She was born in the summer of 1842, and this was the year in which Henry Paget found himself in really deep financial waters, for no less than seven people were prosecuting him for failing to pay the annuities which he had promised them in return for substantial loans. The whole thing was suggestive of sharp practice, and since it was proved that the money had not been paid, he lost his case. His father, the Marquess, had to suffer the indignity of being brought to court as a witness, although there was little enough he could tell the Bench about his son's financial dealings. All he could do was to advise Henry and his wife, then pregnant with Florence, to retire discreetly into the country and there lie low until the scandal blew over, while he himself paid the bills. The settlement of these debts, coupled with those of William, nearly ruined them.

It is probably because of this scandal that no one today seems to know exactly when or where Florence Cecilia was born. The reference books on the peerage, whilst giving the date of birth of the remainder of Henry's children, only show 'August, 1842' against the name of his sixth child by his second wife. The records of the Anglesey family are also incomplete on this point. But on the brass shield on her oak coffin at the time of her burial in Grendon churchyard in 1907, the date was given as 18 August.

There is no record of where Florence was born, or of where she was christened. From all of which it must be deduced that Henry had gone to ground at the time, and, since he desired no attention to be drawn to himself, he made no official registration of her birth (none was compulsory at the time).

It was not a very auspicious start in life for Florence Paget. Throughout the Hastings story she remains something of an enigma, and this mystery surrounding her birth is in its way symbolic of her career.

The lineage of Harry Hastings was even more impressive than that of Florence Paget, but in many ways it closely resembled it. Each had a grandfather of heroic proportions—a soldier who devoted his life to the service of his country and won for himself the admiration of his country and his monarch; and each had a father who failed altogether to live up to this heritage and enjoyed a life that was unheroic.

At the time when 'One-Leg' was campaigning in the Spanish Peninsula with Wellington, Harry's grandfather, Lord Moira, who was shortly to become the first Marquis of Hastings, was in India, campaigning against the Gurkha State of Nepal. In 1812 he had been appointed Governor-General of Bengal and Commander-in-Chief of the British forces in India, and had landed in Calcutta to relieve Lord Minto in the autumn of 1813. 'One-Leg' had been born in 1768, Lord Moira in 1754. Both had proved themselves to be soldiers of exceptional courage and talent. Military men are often criticized for their lack of vision, and yet both were possessed of tactical brilliance and originality of mind.

Lord Moira had enjoyed an outstanding career, in the best traditions of a family which had woven its name into the very pattern of English history. He could trace his ancestry back to the Sir Henry de Hastings who was summoned to parliament as a baron by Simon de Montfort in 1264. Sir Henry, as a follower of de Montfort when he became leader of the barons in their revolt against Henry III, was entrusted with the leadership of the London contingent of the Battle of Lewes and was taken prisoner at Evesham. After de Montfort's death he assumed the leadership of the baronial party when they made their last stand on the Isle of Ely.

Thus began a family tradition for leadership, and for military and political service dedicated to the good of the

State. A tradition also of courage and defiance in the face of adversity.

William, Baron Hastings, became Master of the Mint and Chamberlain of the Royal Household after the accession of Edward IV in 1461, and was looked upon by the sovereign as one of his most trusted advisers. After Edward IV's death he was executed by Richard III in 1483.

He left a son, Edward, who died in 1508, and who was the father of George, Baron Hastings, who was born in 1488 and was created Earl of Huntingdon in 1529.

When Francis, the tenth Earl of Huntingdon, died in 1789, the barony of Hastings passed to his sister, Elizabeth, who lived from 1731 to 1808 and who married Sir John Rawdon.

The Rawdon family traced their descent to Paulyn, or Paulinus, de Rawdon, to whom William the Conqueror had granted large estates in Yorkshire and the North of England, some of which had remained in the hands of his descendants in an unbroken male line for century after century. One of the Rawdon family, who had taken an active part as a soldier in quelling the Irish Rebellion in the reign of Charles I, had been raised to a baronetcy by Charles II as Sir George Rawdon of Moira, in the County of Down.

Sir John Rawdon, the fourth Baronet, who married Elizabeth, was later created Baron Rawdon of Moira and afterwards Earl of Moira. Their son, Lord Rawdon as he then was and Lord Moira as he later became, was educated at Harrow and Oxford. He joined the Army in 1771 as an ensign of the 15th Foot, and distinguished himself in the American War of Independence. He saw action at the battles of Bunker Hill, Brooklyn, White Plains, Monmouth and Camden, took part in the attacks on Forts Washington and Clinton, and was among those prosecuting the siege of Charleston. At Philadelphia he raised a corps of Irish Volunteers, who flocked to serve the dashing young Irish peer, and under his leadership they won a reputation for fearlessness and initiative. In the Battle of Hobkirk Hill, the young Lord Rawdon showed both courage and tactical skill by holding a greatly superior force which was opposed to him. His potentialities as a soldier were already clearly apparent.

He was invalided home in 1781, but was captured by the French and carried into Brest. Fortunately, his release was quickly negotiated and he returned to England to receive the commendation of his sovereign, George III, who created him an English peer, Baron Rawdon, in March of 1783 for his services to his country.

In 1789 his mother succeeded to the barony of Hastings, and so the young Rawdon added the illustrious surname of Hastings to his own. Four years later his father died, and he succeeded him as Earl of Moira. It was in this year that he seemed to have decided that his growing prestige demanded a country seat worthy of his honours, and he therefore decided to pull down the old Donington Hall, in Leicestershire, which he had inherited from his uncle, the tenth Earl of Huntingdon, and to rebuild it again, utterly regardless of cost, in the new 'Strawberry Hill Gothic' style of architecture, with Gothic Hall, imposing dining-room and immense library, and an entrance designed by himself. It was a magnificent house of 203 rooms, costing far more than he could afford, and was pre-eminently a country seat for the founding of a family tradition. But he was then nearly forty—and unmarried. The years went by, his prestige increased and the Hall was the envy of his contemporaries, but there was no wife to administer it, and no children to play in its splendid parklands.

The new Hall was completed in 1795, and one of his first acts as host was to invite the Bourbon family, who were in exile from France, to stay as his guests for as long as they wished. His hospitality to his royal visitors was said to have been so lavish that it included an open cheque on Coutts' Bank laid discreetly on each bedroom dressing-table, with a little note requesting the occupier of the room to fill it in according to his or her needs. This was a typical Hastings gesture—an act which established not only his extreme liberality but also his panache, a quality which was later to be valued so highly by his grandson. For many years afterwards a portrait of Charles X and the Dauphin looked down upon the owners of Donington Hall from the walls of the great library, reminding them of their heritage of unrestrained generosity.

But although there were guests in plenty at the Hall, there was no hostess to welcome them. However, in 1803, Lord Moira was appointed Commander-in-Chief in Scotland, and while he was fulfilling these duties he met and fell in love with a Scottish heiress of noble birth—Flora Muir Campbell, who was then less than half his age and was the Countess of Loudoun in her own right.

Thus Lord Moira united his own illustrious family with that of another, which if not quite so ancient (the first Earl of

Loudoun had only been created in 1633) had traditions as distinguished as his own. He carried away his beautiful Scottish wife from the gloomy atmosphere of Loudoun Castle, and set her up as mistress of Donington Hall. By their mutual efforts they produced a son and heir, George Augustus Francis Rawdon Hastings, in 1808. He and his mother settled down to enjoy a tranquil life amidst the noble oaks and the rambling deer of Donington Park, but country life was all too quiet for Lord Moira. In 1812 he was given the Order of the Garter and a year later he was appointed Governor-General of Bengal and Commander-in-Chief of the British forces in India. In 1817 he was created the first Marquis of Hastings in recognition of his brilliant campaign in Nepal, which not only brought about a wise and peaceful settlement, but also won the allegiance of the warlike Gurkhas, who thereafter became loyal supporters of the British Raj. Two years later, he obtained for his country the cession, by purchase, of the island of Singapore, a further example of his foresight and mastery of strategy.

He died, aged seventy, when he was still in harness and acting as Governor of Malta. He might well have retired sooner, but—as ever—he had continued to live far beyond his income, and could not afford to settle down to a life of peace amongst his trees and deer at Donington Hall. He died heavily in debt, which was not surprising, and the East India Company, which had already voted him £60,000 during his lifetime, now added a further £20,000 to support his widow and son.

Death came to him on 28 November 1826, in Bala Bay, off Naples. He requested, in his Will, that his right hand should be severed from his body and preserved until the death of his wife, when it should be buried beside her.

George Augustus Francis, the second Marquis of Hastings, and Harry's father, inherited none of the warlike instincts of his sire—and none of his restlessness and wanderlust. He was educated at Harrow, as his father had been, but spent only eighteen months on the Hill. By the time he was fifteen he was back at home at Donington Hall, where his education was completed by a series of tutors, who found that he had no interest in knowledge, having only one passion in life and that was for fox-hunting. Donington was in the very heart of the fox-hunting country, and the Quorn, the most famous hunt of them all, would often meet in front of the Hall (they still do). In summer he idled away the hours in one of the loveliest settings in the Midlands. In winter he rode to hounds. This was his life, and this his world, and he left it when his second son, Harry, was still an infant.

In the matter of character, Harry inherited little from his father, whom he never knew. But from his grandfather he inherited the Rawdon recklessness with money, and the Rawdon panache. Foreign royalty never stayed at the Hall in Harry's day, but open cheques on bedside tables would have been a gesture very much after his heart. In this he was certainly a chip off the old block.

But the first Marquis, for all his recklessness with money, was never a gambling fanatic. This was a side to Harry's character which he inherited from his mother.

There were two major upheavals in the otherwise tranquil life of the second Marquis of Hastings. One was the scandalous treatment of his sister, Lady Flora, 'the white flower of the Hastings line', at the hands of Queen Victoria,[1] which led to a lasting split between the Queen and the Hastings family. The other was his meeting with the enchanting and irresponsible young Barbara, Baroness Grey de Ruthyn, whom he married in the summer of 1831 (he would certainly not have contemplated marriage and a honeymoon during the hunting season).

Solid and unimaginative Englishmen of Conservative outlook are often fascinated by feckless beauty. It is the attraction of extremes. George Augustus Francis was entranced by this dazzling young woman, who lived only for excitement and foreign travel, and who had a mania for gambling. It was a curious union, but by no means an unsuccessful one. The second Marquis took his young wife to the bridal chamber set immediately above the Hall's main entrance, which the first Marquis had had built to his own design, and there were conceived two sons and four daughters. An heir, Paulyn Reginald Serlo, was born within a year of the marriage. A younger son,

---

[1] Lady Flora Hastings, a member of Queen Victoria's household suffered from a serious liver complaint. This caused her stomach to swell, and the rumour grew that she was pregnant. The young Queen unwisely allowed herself to believe this. When Lady Flora died of the kidney complaint in July 1839, a post mortem revealed her to be a virgin. Public opinion was strongly expressed on the matter, and the Queen suffered a period of unpopularity which she deeply resented. Both Lady Flora's brother, the second Marquis, and her mother, the Dowager Marchioness, bitterly attacked the Queen and her adviser, Lord Melbourne.

Henry Weysford Charles Plantagenet, was not born until ten years later. Both were small and delicate.

Their father may have been stronger, but he was still not robust. He left his wife, now nicknamed 'the jolly fast Marchioness', to live very much her own life whilst he devoted himself once again to hunting. In common with most of his contemporaries, he ate too much, drank too much and took too much physical exercise in the saddle. The John Bull type of hunting squire survived this existence, but it proved altogether too violent for the second Marquis, and in the end it killed him. He died at the Dolphin Hotel, at Holyrood, on 13 January 1844, within a month of his thirty-sixth birthday, from 'a spasm of the Heart from Retrocedent Gout four months'. His mother, the Countess of Loudoun, had died four years previously and had been laid to rest in the family vault alongside the severed hand of her husband, the first Marquis. Now she and the hand were joined by their son and heir, and six young children were left fatherless at the Hall under the care of their erratic mother, and with no grandparents to supervise her indiscretions.

The beauties of Donington Hall held no special attraction for 'the jolly fast Marchioness'. She spent most of her time visiting the casinos and watering places of the Continent, and very little looking after her family of six. Widowhood also did not suit her temperament, and she married again a year later. The children were left to be brought up at, and, one might almost say, by, Donington Hall.

A house can prove a beneficial parent, for its rooms and gardens can build up a sense of security and comfort. But Donington, beautiful though it was, could not overcome in Harry that sense of insecurity which results from lack of parental control and lack of parental love. He was the fifth child of the marriage, and thus was given the doubtful advantage of having an elder brother and three elder sisters. A manly child will struggle against an excess of sisterly adoration and will overcome it, but Harry was never at any time really manly. He was a delicate and appealing baby, who not only invited petting and spoiling, but also revelled in it. His fragile appearance brought out all the maternal instincts in his sisters, who lavished affection upon him. Indeed his ability to arouse the maternal instinct in a woman remained with him throughout his life, and is a key to the whole Hastings story.

This was a very different state of affairs from that which

existed in the Paget family. Florence had also only one parent, and she also was spoilt. But Florence was a girl of spirit and resolution, as befitted a Paget, and was not a child whom spoiling and adoration could seriously harm. On the whole, spoiling only tended to make her wilful, but it made Harry's already weak character weaker still. There was a strong streak of femininity in Harry. There was a strong streak of masculinity in Florence, for all her lack of inches, or maybe because of it. This is also a key to the Hastings story.

And what of the third child in this story? The third corner of the eternal triangle, and Harry's ultimate rival for Florence Paget's hand?

Henry Chaplin, at the time when Harry and Florence were born in the summer of 1842, was already a sturdy yearling (and possibly even aged two);[1] a bouncing, cheerful baby with bright chestnut hair who was being reared in ideal circumstances at Ryhall Hall, in Rutlandshire. He was the eldest son of the Rev Henry Chaplin, who was the Lord of the Manor and the Rector of the Parish and thus earned for himself the traditional title of 'Squarson', being both Squire and Parson.

The Reverend Henry had been born in 1791, and had been married late in life—to Caroline Horatia, a daughter of William Ellice of Invergarry, who was the MP for Great Grimsby. She was very much younger than her husband, and in many ways a surprising choice for a matter-of-fact, middle-aged country parson, for she was pretty and gay. He may well have thought long before asking her to marry him, but of one thing he never had any doubt—she was unquestionably a woman who would make a fine mother for the children that might be born to them.

In fact, there were five—three boys and two girls. Of these, Henry was the eldest—a sturdy baby with an equable temperament, who laughed a great deal and seldom cried. He was a determined child, and to his resolution was added notable courage. Throughout his life, Henry would tackle anything. If he knew fear, he never showed it.

The Chaplin family had been squires of Lincolnshire since 1658, when John Chaplin of Wiltshire, having married

---

[1] It seems probable that he was born on 22 December 1841, and this is the date given in most official books of reference, including *Who's Who*, and was the date he himself favoured. But his Aunt Matty always maintained that he was born a year earlier, in 1840, and *The Times*, in its obituary notice of him, gave 1840 as well.

Elizabeth Hamby, only daughter and heiress of Sir John Hamby, of Tathwell in Lincolnshire, had decided to leave his own native country and to make his home in that corner of England which his wife loved so much.

They took up residence in the Hamby family seat at Tathwell, and John Chaplin became High Sheriff of the county. The Hambys could trace their descent back to Walter Hamby, who lived in the time of Edward I, and the union of Hamby and Chaplin stock was therefore of two ancient county families, and of the landed gentry as opposed to the aristocracy, but with a fine inheritance of wealth if not of high-sounding titles. The Chaplin heritage was as solid as an oak tree and equally English. They were a line of typical English country squires.

In the chancel of the Church of St Vedast, at Tathwell, there is a monument to Thomas Chaplin, who was born in 1684 and died in 1747, on which is inscribed in Latin:

Sacred to the memory of Thomas Chaplin, Esq, a kind and blameless man, who having enjoyed a happy fortune and living honourably performed all the duties of life...

The same might have been written of so many English country gentlemen, 'kind and blameless men' who inherited wealth and gave thanks for it, and who served their community with consideration and self-sacrifice.

Thomas Chaplin inherited the Tathwell estate in 1730, but eleven years before this he had bought for himself an ancient country seat in Lincolnshire. This was Blankney Hall, an imposing residence with a tradition of buried treasure hidden there by the previous owner during the rebellion of 1715. It was destined to become the ancestral home of the Chaplin family and to remain in their possession for nearly 200 years.

A powerful influence in the early life of Florence Paget was the reputation and the strength of character of her grandfather, the first Marquess of Anglesey. Harry was probably not influenced very much by any family tradition in his childhood, but he certainly basked in the prestige which he enjoyed as being the grandson of the first and great Marquis of Hastings. But with Henry Chaplin it was his uncle, Charles Chaplin, the Lord of the Manor of Blankney, who played an important part in his early and formative years, and on whom he modelled himself. The Pagets leaned towards Liberalism and the Hastings were by tradition Tories, but in the Chaplin family Toryism was the very mainspring of their life, and as important to them as their religion. Squire Charles played a prominent part in politics, and represented Lincolnshire in Parliament from 1818 to 1832. He was known and feared throughout the countryside of Blankney for his autocratic ways, and local lawbreakers who came up before him when he sat on the Bench used to shiver in their shoes as he thundered his denunciations of their sins, especially if these involved poaching on his lands.

Yet his was a benevolent despotism, for he was a kindly man, if somewhat narrow-minded, and the phrase *noblesse oblige* meant much to him. It was his tragedy that he remained childless, and as he grew older he became increasingly devoted to the three sons of his younger brother, the Rev Henry Chaplin, and above all to the sturdy little boy with the chestnut hair who would one day inherit all the wealth and traditions of Blankney. Even in childhood young Henry must have sensed that his beloved but rather awe-inspiring uncle was depending on him to carry on these family traditions and, being a courageous and resolute child, he must have squared his shoulders and prepared himself for the task. From his father he inherited the Christian outlook, but from his uncle he inherited the religion of Toryism, and an air of authority. There was more than a touch of the autocrat about Henry, even in early youth.

If one is to look upon the Hastings story as a play—whether drama or melodrama—then the setting for the first act is the tranquil one of the English country house, and the time is the early years of the young Queen Victoria's reign. Scene one is laid at Donington Hall, in Leicestershire, where a small boy is growing up against a background of idle luxury, fatherless and seeing little of his mother, and being spoilt and petted by his three elder sisters. Scene two shows another small boy, stronger and more self-reliant than the other, enjoying a normal and healthy life at Ryhall Hall, in Lincolnshire. And in scene three a small girl, motherless but petted and spoilt by an adoring father and elder brothers, and living a somewhat hand-to-mouth existence, is briefly glimpsed either 'somewhere in Hertfordshire' or else at one of her family's seats at Anglesey, Beaudesert in Staffordshire, Uxbridge in Middlesex or in Bruton Street, Mayfair.

Their paths are not destined to cross for several years, but childhood is already beginning to hold out its distant prospects of happiness and adventure. These are the formative years, when the character will be established, either for good or ill; and what happens in the future will be determined, in part at least, by the guidance and restraints which they are experiencing now. The climax of the second act and the tragedy of the third are scarcely to be foreseen. For the moment all is peaceful and serene as the curtain rises upon a panorama of Donington Hall.

Marquis with the closest attention, and were immensely proud of the family's history and its intimate connections with the Crown. (The first Marquis had not only been an intimate friend of the Prince Regent, but had also made him substantial loans.) When there was prosperity at the Hall, Castle Donington flourished; and if disaster struck the Hastings family, then there were many in the town who also suffered much. It was a charming and happy little hamlet, 'where Jane Austen might have lived agreeably and even Dr Grantly would have found life tolerable', to quote a contemporary comment.

The first Marquis loved Castle Donington, and Castle Donington loved him. His magnificent career thrilled them with patriotic pride. His son, George Augustus Francis, the second Marquis, was perhaps somewhat of a disappointment to them, but they shared his moments of excitement in the outside world, as when he fulfilled his duty as Bearer of the Golden Spurs at the Coronation of William IV in 1830, or when he went storming down to London in the early days of Queen Victoria to counter the baseless allegations which were being made at Court against the chastity of his sister, Lady Flora; and later watched over her like a faithful bulldog as she lay dying in Buckingham Palace. That had been a shameful business, indeed, and Castle Donington had burned with indignation, as he had done, over the monstrous treatment of an innocent woman, and the prevarication and dissimulation of the Court, and above all of the Queen and Lord Melbourne. He had thundered his accusations, it was true, but some felt at the time that the thunder might have been louder, and that he should have fought a duel, or at very least should have horsewhipped one of the scandalmongers within an inch of his life. But the second Marquis was a straightforward and uncomplicated character, and the duplicity of court life was something which he could not comprehend.

All he asked of life was that he should be allowed to live at Donington Hall and devote himself to fox-hunting. The memorial tablet to him which stands in Ashby-de-la-Zouch's ancient church declares with some pomposity that he was 'too pure for political ambition, too sensitive for party strife, and too manly for vain display' and that he lived 'in the unostentatious exercise of every private virtue'. It would be more accurate to say of him that he was just a genial host and a good rider to hounds.

The inhabitants of Castle Donington were taken aback by

his marriage to the captivating but unstable Barbara, Baroness Grey de Ruthyn. However, her love of gambling and her frequent visits to the Continent, did serve to furnish the little town with much exciting gossip. And if the second Marquis lived, on the whole, an uneventful life, the high and low lights of which were largely dependent on the vagaries of the fox, the atmosphere was nevertheless comfortingly humdrum and secure. There were not many opportunities for hanging out the bunting which every good villager kept in his attic, or for building the triumphal arches which were a Castle Donington speciality, or even for removing the Marquis's horses from his carriage and dragging it (and him) in triumph to the Hall, to celebrate some famous victory or escapade. Still, he had two sons to carry on the name, and the future looked rosy enough. So life, during the reign of the second Marquis, jogged happily along, and the Jane Austens of the little community were more than content.

The death of George Augustus Francis in 1844, and at the early age of thirty-five, was a blow to them all. He had been popular with everyone on account of his bluff and straightforward attitude, which was understood not only by his tenants and workers in Castle Donington, but also by the tougher and more outspoken colliers who laboured in the Hastings' coal mines at nearby Moira. The second Marquis had been a man who had called a spade a spade, who stood no nonsense from anyone and who talked to the Moira miners in a language they could understand. They were genuinely distressed when he died.

His death left six young children fatherless at the Hall, and there were many in Castle Donington who looked upon them as almost motherless as well, for the 'jolly fast Marchioness' was not thought likely to devote very much time to their upbringing in the future. It is true that they were given the benefit of an illustrious guardian, the first Earl Howe, who had been a close friend of the second Marquis, and had promised that he would look after their interests. Earl Howe knew the district and had strong local connections. He had become Viscount and Baron of Curzon on the death of his grandfather in 1820, and had assumed the name of Howe, and been created Earl Howe, in 1821. He was something of a lady's man, and was closely connected with court circles, being Lord of the Bedchamber to Queen Adelaide from 1837 to 1849, serving her both while she was Queen Consort and Queen Dowager.

Indeed his intimacy with the Queen was such that it aroused a certain amount of malicious gossip. How far this was justified is not certain, but his duties in London—whether or not they were closely connected with the bedchamber—were still such as to occupy most of his time, and he was unable to devote much personal attention to the care of his wards, although he was always alive to the need of protecting their inheritance, which was going to be substantial by the time they reached their majorities. Politically, he was an ardent Conservative, and was a highly respected member of the House of Lords.

'The jolly fast Marchioness' married again almost within a year of her husband's death, and became the wife of Admiral Sir Hastings Reginald Henry, GCB, an Irishman from County Kildare, who later assumed the name of Yelverton, which was the family name of the Grey de Ruthyns.

The six children left fatherless at the Hall consisted of two boys and four girls. The elder of these two boys, who became the third Marquis of Hastings and heir to the Donington estate, was Paulyn Reginald Serlo, who had been born on 2 June 1832, and was therefore only eleven-and-a-half when his father died on 13 January 1844. He was the eldest of the family and had been followed by Edith Maud, born on 10 December 1833; Bertha Lelgarde, born 30 April 1835; Victoria Mary Louise, born on 18 August 1837, and named after the Queen, who had ascended the throne two months previously; Henry Weysford Charles Plantagenet, born on 22 July 1842, in Cavendish Square, London, and christened at St George's Hanover Square; and finally Francis Augusta Constance, born in May 1844, four months after her father's death.

This family of six children were left very much to their own devices as they grew up at the Hall. They had a succession of tutors and governesses and very occasionally visited London, but their childhood was largely spent at Donington. Paulyn Reginald Serlo was sent off to Eton soon after his father's death, and remained there for three years, while Henry Weysford Charles Plantagenet—Harry to his adoring elder sisters and to his equally adoring nurses—was left to grow up in an atmosphere of feminine adulation.

Unfortunately for Harry, he was not very much of an outdoor type. He quite liked horses and had his own ponies, but the obsession for fox-hunting which had absorbed the life of the second Marquis had not been handed down to his younger son. But Harry found plenty of other things to keep him entertained and amused at Donington. He was a pleasantly-mannered little boy who made friends easily. He was fussed over and admired by the cottagers on the estate, and when he went down to see the old water-mills threshing and churning at Kings Mills, and trailed his bare toes in the Trent, there were always motherly souls who came hurrying out of the thatched cottages to admire this engaging little boy, and to give him fruit from their gardens or home-made cakes from their ovens. Thus Harry was spoilt from infancy. Had he been at heart a nasty little boy, this treatment would quickly have rendered him unbearable. But Harry was not a nasty little boy. There was nothing aggressive about him, and so flattery and adulation did not make him either autocratic or dictatorial. He had great charm of manner, and he could be as friendly and natural with a gardener's wife as he could with the wife of a lord. From his father he inherited this ability to mix freely with all classes. His charm no doubt came from his mother. Certainly this combination of friendliness and charm brought him a host of companions from all walks of life.

It was Harry's tragedy that he was no judge of character. From childhood he liked everybody, and at no time was he ever able to distinguish between his true friends and those who were seeking to ingratiate themselves with him. He basked in popularity, and his charm expanded under its hot-house warmth.

He mixed freely with the staff of the Hall, played with the gardener's boys and stable lads, and was friends with the ostlers, grooms and outdoor staff. Their influence was not always beneficial. They were honest enough countrymen, for the most part, but there was a rough element in Castle Donington and nearby Ashby who drank, fornicated, gambled and delighted in baiting bulls and in cock-fighting. Harry listened to their stories with interest; and he soon learnt the jargon of the tap-room and the cock-fighting ring. Inevitably the coarseness and the cruelty of these admittedly traditional English pastimes had in themselves a coarsening effect on a small boy's mind. Harry was neither cruel nor insensitive by instinct, but these influences tended to deaden the warmth of his nature— and certainly as far as animals were concerned.

It probably never entered his head during these childhood years that he might one day inherit the title. No doubt the thought, if it did cross his mind, was intriguing, but he was fond of his elder brother, and wished him well. It must therefore have come as a considerable shock to Harry when Paulyn Reginald Serlo died during a visit to Dublin at the beginning of 1851. He was then eighteen-and-a-half, and was an Ensign of the 52nd Regiment (the Oxfordshire Light Infantry). Various reports were circulated about his death, one of which stated that he had been drowned in Dublin Bay and that foul play was suspected, but it is more likely that he contracted a fever and was not strong enough to shake it off. But the sad fact remained. The Third Marquis had died before his coming-of-age, and the estate had to face another long minority, for the new Marquis of Hastings was then not yet nine years old.

Paulyn Reginald Serlo died on the 17th day of January 1851 and was buried in the family vault at Castle Donington a week later. On the day of his death his younger brother, Harry, ceased to be a relatively unimportant and inconspicuous child and became instead the fourth Marquis of Hastings.

Harry was never conceited, either as a child or a man, over his great inheritance. His attitude, even at this early age, was one of acceptance and casual indifference. It was never in his nature to think of the future, to worry about responsibilities or to assess his possessions and his wealth. He lived only for the present, and, once the sorrow over the death of his brother had eased, which it did quickly enough, he settled down once again to enjoying the pleasures of the moment. The future could take care of itself. To his surprise, he suddenly found himself the object of greatly increased servility and attention. Everyone around him now began to treat him with an added respect, and it was not long before he began to realize that the death of his brother had turned him into a very important person. This pleased him greatly. He enjoyed flattery, and he was receiving a great deal of it.

Now the numbers of his friends also increased. To those of the Hall's staff who were genuinely fond of the little boy were added those who were already looking to the future, and who curried favour with the young master for what this might bring them in the future. Harry accepted them all, without discrimination. He was friends with everyone.

His mother and his guardian met to discuss Harry's immediate future. The first problem was to decide upon his education. His father and grandfather had each been to Harrow, but his brother had been educated at Eton. Lord Howe himself had followed the standard pattern of education for the aristrocracy, and had been at Eton and then at Christ Church College, Oxford. It was therefore decided that Harry's education should follow that of his guardian. Eton, at the time, was a bigger school than Harrow, and numbered more of the peerage amongst its pupils. As for Oxford, it would provide the young Marquis with the necessary final polish, and knowledge of the world. Moreover, the Prince of Wales, it was rumoured, would probably be going up to Oxford himself, and would almost certainly be sent to 'The House', as Christ Church was known. Although he was a little older than Harry, they would be likely to overlap. The breach between the Hastings family and the royal family which had been caused by the quarrel over Lady Flora still existed, but by then it would probably have blown over. Anyway, Harry would meet other undergraduates of the same social standing as himself at both Eton and Christ Church so he would be ready to take his place in Mayfair society when the time came. As for a career in the army, that could be decided upon later. At that time it seemed unlikely that the delicate small boy at the Hall would ever follow in his grandfather's illustrious footsteps. Critics of Eton at that period were maintaining that it did no more than turn out 'Belgravian loafers'; but at least it could be said of Harry's future that he would be loafing in only the best company.

Thus the pleasant and idle life at the Hall was brought to an end in the summer of 1854, when he found himself at Eton, boarding with Miss Gulliver and having the Reverend Charles Wolley as his tutor.

Eton, at this period, was still in a period of transition. 'The Keate era' of headmastership, with all its outbreaks of riotous disorderliness, was over, and the College was settling down to a more organized existence. The Keate tradition, however, was still very much in everyone's mind, for the tempestuous little man had carved out a place for himself in Eton history with his birch and his flogging block.

Not that Keate was ever the monster of tyranny and sadism that later generations—of Etonians as well as of historians—have sometimes made him out to be. He was only trying to enforce authority upon the spoilt and undisciplined sons of the wealthy aristocracy and gentry; upon boys who—like Harry Hastings—had done very much what they pleased at home and had picked up bad habits from grooms and gamekeepers. When sternly admonished at school, they turned violent and rebelled; and so Keate flogged them into submission.

Hawtrey, who succeeded Keate as headmaster in 1834, and who had served under him as an assistant master, was another strong disciplinarian. He was also a dandy. He dressed fastidiously and elegantly, had exquisite manners and moved about Eton with an old-world courtliness and grace. In 1852 he was made Provost, and he left the school in the year in which Harry Hastings arrived there.

His influence, however, was still very much felt in Eton during Hastings' stay there. Perhaps he was responsible for a revival of the cult of the dandy and the elegant refinements of the perfect gentleman, as opposed to the mood of violence which had existed under Keate. The young 'swell' of Harry's time was very much after the Hawtrey pattern—though inadequately aping a man who had far more to offer than mere gentility and refinement.

Hawtrey was succeeded by Dr Charles Goodford, who was headmaster of Eton throughout the time that Harry Hastings was there. Goodford was a lesser personality than his two predecessors, which is hardly surprising, and was largely content to live in their shadow and to carry on with their traditions. He probably had little contact with Harry—a pleasant, friendly and ineffective small boy at the bottom of the school who was good at neither work nor games. Harry himself was probably more influenced by the stories told of Keate and Hawtrey; and it was not for many years that the memories and legends surrounding these two formidable characters faded away—if indeed they have ever done so at Eton.

By modern standards, the discipline existing at Eton at this time was at once lax and severe. Some seemingly unimportant restrictions were rigidly enforced, but in other ways the boys were allowed remarkable freedom. A contemporary of Harry Hastings was E. D. Stone, who, in his reminiscences, recalled a boy who appeared one Sunday evening 'reeling about the school yard, and another sent away for contriving to get drunk one morning before 9.15 absence'. Visits to country public houses were then the vogue, and beer was freely drunk both in and out of College.

The same writer goes on to remark of this period, 'I have always been grateful for the amount of leisure which we enjoyed, and the small amount of constraint which hampered our tastes. Games were not organized; there were no house colours and very few matches.'

The comment has a curiously modern ring to it. Today,

also, games are being enforced less and less in the public schools, and much more freedom is being allowed to the boys.

But in the 1850s, when Harry Hastings was at Eton, the freedom granted to the boys was often misused, and weak characters such as Harry were drawn into bad habits from which they should have been protected.

Certainly there was wildness in the air at Windsor in the early nineteenth century—much more so than at neighbouring Harrow-on-the-Hill—and it was more than the Keate tradition of a good flogging could do to eradicate it.

Then, and still to a certain extent today, a brilliant but unstable boy, if sent to Eton, had a good chance of ending up either as a cabinet minister or a rake; and this is not to decry the ultimate post of ministerial authority. Eton has never been an institution that encourages a slavish adherence to orthodoxy, or suppresses originality of thought.

On the credit side of this policy are the cabinet ministers. On the debit side are the rakes. In the 'fifties Eton produced Harry Hastings. In the 'sixties, the fifth Earl of Rosebery.

When Harry Hastings arrived at Eton, the mood, as a result of Hawtrey's influence, was less one of open defiance to authority and more one of bored indifference to it. This was in keeping with the young swells of Whyte-Melville's novels, then very much in fashion, who were so exquisitely relaxed and casual and who considered showing emotion of any sort to be such bad form.

Tout est perdu sauve l'honneur. Throughout the years it had become the motto of many an old Etonian rake, and they stood by it to the end.

Thus the mood of the young Victorian Etonian seemed to change, almost imperceptibly, from one of defiance to one of casual hauteur and of bored indifference. It was a pose, of course—but young men faced with the problems of life and of living have always adopted a pose in order to hide their sense of bewilderment and the fact that they are basically unsure of themselves. At Eton one did not wear one's heart, or one's emotion, on one's coat sleeve. Harry Hastings was always very conscious of this.

Harry Hastings left no mark on the annals of Eton College. His name cannot be found cut on 'the Boards', nor in any references to Eton sport. He was too easy-going to be rebellious, and probably careful enough never to be flogged.

Indeed, almost the only comment ever made about him during his short school career was that of Lord Redesdale who wrote in his *Memories*, 'The King of the Plungers was Harry Hastings—the last Marquis, who was my fag at Eton. He was an attractive little boy, and I think that everybody liked him, but his ideas when he grew up were on too large a scale. He had no health and burning the candle at both ends, as well as in the middle, sealed his fate.'

It is a passage that has been quoted many times in reference to the Hastings story, and like so many passages thus quoted, it does not stand close examination. Lord Redesdale (then Freeman-Mitford) was at Eton from the beginning of the Lent Half in 1846 to December 1854, and thus coincided with Hastings for two Halves. But he was in Evans' house and then in college, and his tutor was F. E. Durnford, so there seems no reason to suppose that Harry *could* ever have been his fag. However, Freeman-Mitford was in Pop, and it is possible that he may have occasionally given Harry some duty to perform.

The adjective 'attractive' may, perhaps, strike an ominous note to some ears. It is not one that is usually used about grubby little fags. But at least it emphasizes the point which recurs again and again in the Hastings story—that Harry had charm and gaiety and was always popular.

His stay at Eton was short—beginning with the Summer Half of 1854 and ending with that of 1855. There is no evidence as to why it was so short. Perhaps it had something to do with the adjective 'attractive'. Or it may have been that, like so many other rich and undisciplined young boys from broken homes, he refused to settle down to a controlled and ordered life.

Certainly the gambling habits which he inherited from his mother were already fully awakened by the time he reached Eton, and he was frequently to be seen during term-time at both Epsom and Ascot. It is possible that he was sometimes there legitimately—visits of parents and friends were encouraged at the school, and permission was often granted for boys to be taken out—but it is also probable that he often went racing without permission.

Money, of course, was no obstacle, as his allowance as a boy was liberal, and he must by then have already got in with the racing set, composed of young swells who drank, swore and gambled, and talked importantly of heavy betting and sensational successes. Several of these young bloods with whom he consorted were the sons of famous owners, whose colours were known on every racecourse in England, and the talk was always of secret trials and handicap certainties, whilst famous Old Etonians of the day, such as the fourteenth Earl of Derby, were doing their utmost to win the blue riband of the turf at Epsom.

One might almost say of this period that the course of life for the aspiring young aristocrat was to go to Eton, then to Christ Church College, Oxford, and then to the unsaddling enclosure at Epsom as owner of the Derby winner. And finally, to bring an illustrious career to its culmination by being elected a Steward of the Jockey Club. The fifth Earl of Rosebery, who followed this pattern exactly, was a few years junior to Harry Hastings, but he furnished the perfect example. The only really gentlemanly alternative to this programme was to go into the Army for a short time instead of Eton and Oxford; but the ultimate goal remained the same: the winner's enclosure at Epsom on Derby Day.

What, then, did Eton give to Harry Hastings? It certainly did not make him a snob, for he was never that, and this is a virtue amongst Old Etonians. It encouraged his gaiety, his friendliness and his charm, and it gave him character enough to become a good loser, if never character enough to resist temptations.

It handed on to him something of the dandyism of Hawtrey and of that most illustrious of Eton swells, Beau Brummell; and it certainly endowed him with what was destined to be his most memorable characteristic, and that was his indifference in the face of misfortune. Only once did he ever show his anguish in public, and that was at the end of his career when he had been finally broken by adversity. Until then, he was always able to laugh in its face.

There is rather a curious description of Harry at about this period, made by the Earl of Dunraven in his book *Past Times and Pastimes*:

> Hastings was a great friend of mine, and gay old times we used to have, more especially in Paris. Hastings was at a private school with me; he was a strange boy, and used to sleep with his eyes open, and in full glaring candlelight. He was a strange man, too. Very aristocratic, very charming—a good fellow, though somewhat provocative. We used in

those days to drive to Epsom, and the national holiday was conducive to much fun and chaff—good humoured to start with, but sometimes degenerating into a pretty lively scrap.

The passage throws a sidelight on some aspects of Harry's character. His gaiety, charm and aristocratic bearing have already been described. That he should have been somewhat provocative is interesting. It may have been the femininity in him that produced a desire sometimes to goad people. He could also be cruel at times, as he demonstrated in the practical jokes which he and other young bloods used to play on each other.

As to why he should have slept with his eyes open is a problem that may or may not have some significance. Medical opinion considers it improbable anyway. But that he should have fallen asleep 'in full glaring candelight' is in no way surprising. Harry Hastings was probably afraid of the dark.

What exactly was he like as a boy? To the writer of this book, searching to assess the changing image from boyhood to manhood, he can be seen twice in the canvas of Frith's picture of *Derby Day*.

It was in 1857 that W. P. Frith, in search of a new subject that would depict a typical aspect of Victorian life, visited Epsom Downs on Derby Day to witness the triumph of an immortal filly—Blink Bonny. Not that Frith cared twopence for racing, or for fillies of any sort, whether mortal or immortal, but the crowded and turbulent scene on a racecourse fascinated him. Some years previously he had attended a meeting at Hampton and there, in a booth that was being used as a dining-room, he had seen a racegoer, who had just been ruined, seize a carving knife and try to cut his throat. It had been enough to stimulate the imagination of an artist who was also a student of mankind.

The picture of Derby Day which was hung in the Royal Academy's exhibition of 1858 contained several recognizable faces; but those who years later imagined that the young swell in casual conversation with the gypsy girl in the right-hand corner of the canvas was Harry Hastings were making a mistake. The likeness, it is true, is remarkable; and the air of bored nonchalance exactly reflects the mood of Harry on occasions such as this. The girl in the carriage might also well be Florence Paget. But in fact this could not be so. Harry, at the time the picture was painted, would only have been fifteen, and so would Florence.

If Frith *did* have Harry Hastings in mind when painting this picture (he makes no mention of him in his *Memoirs*), then an equally representative figure is that of the young boy in the shiny topper who stands on the left of the canvas, his hands thrust deep into his pockets and a look of bewildered dejection on his face. Here might well be Harry as an Eton schoolboy, who has swaggered across the Downs on the great day and paused, as an elegant swell, to listen to the blandishments of the thimbleman and has then been tricked out of every penny in his possession.

These two figures are typcial of Harry at different periods in his life. Each repays careful study, for here is Harry in two stages of his career, against the background which was his world.

Harry left Eton in the late summer of 1855, when he was still only thirteen. He was not due to go to Oxford for another five years. The intervening time was spent being passed from tutor to tutor, each of whom no doubt found him amiable and engaging, friendly and generally co-operative, but without any interest in learning. Indeed during this time he can have learnt very little. However, his mother, now the wife of Admiral Yelverton, was in the habit of taking him with her on her trips abroad, and this must have broadened his outlook to a certain extent, although it also brought him into contact with new places for gambling and new aspects of vice.

Castle Donington saw little of their future Squire during this period. The Hall was let from 1856 to 1861 to a Colonel and Mrs Henry Daniell, and Harry spent much of his time staying with his sisters—and chiefly with Lady Edith at nearby Willesley Hall.

In the autumn of 1858 Harry accompanied his mother to Italy. Neither was in good health, and both were anxious to spend the winter in a warmer and drier climate than England could offer. Lady Barbara was then only forty-eight, but she died suddenly from apoplexy in Rome on 19 November. This sudden death must have come as a great shock to her son, who was then sixteen. He was forced to return precipitously to England, having added Baron Grey de Ruthyn to his already long list of titles.

Some two years later, at the age of eighteen, Harry Hastings arrived at Christ Church College, Oxford, as a freshman for the autumn or Michaelmas Term of 1860. Life stretched out before him—a life to be filled with the pleasures of the senses—but before he took up the role of man-about-town in London, there was this pleasant interlude at the university to be experienced.

The fact that in this same year he was appointed a Cornet in the Leicestershire Yeomanry Cavalry appears to have had no significance in his life at all. The appointment is shown in the records, and no more. There is no evidence to suggest that Harry ever commanded a body of men, attended a military manoeuvre or spent a night under canvas. It is doubtful if at this time he knew one end of a rifle from the other. His resignation in this military appointment was not long in forthcoming.

The Dean of Christ Church was Henry George Liddell, who had succeeded Canon Pusey, one of the most eminent of the nineteenth century divines, in 1855. The great Jowett, with his more modernist theology, was just beginning to make his reputation at Balliol, and at Christ Church itself Charles Dodgson was finding his feet as a distinguished mathematical don. Harry's arrival coincided with the publication of *A Syllabus of Plane Algebraical Geometry*, which was to be followed a few years later by *Alice's Adventures in Wonderland*.

It is doubtful if Harry ever looked at either, but in his first few terms he did make some effort to study. Dean Liddell had taken over from Pusey with the intention of restricting dissipation and indiscipline in the College and raising the standards of learning. To this end he gave the undergraduates some sharp lectures on their behaviour, and on the necessity of applying themselves to their books and lectures, and Harry—who was always easily impressed—must have taken some of this advice to heart. In his first term he read English History, and obtained a marking of *satis plus* from his tutor. In his second term the College records do not reveal that he read anything, but it is possible that he was ill. Then in his third term, the summer term of 1861, he specialized in English History from the Norman Conquest to John; and although this was hardly an ambitious undertaking, in view of the limited number of text books then available on this period, he won the verdict of *satis bene* from his tutor. This does not suggest brilliance, but it also does not imply indolence or lack of intellect.

However, Harry ran truer to form in the matter of gate

money, for in his first term his fines for being out late were the highest in the College (although they only amounted to 6s. 7d.).

Oxford, in the 'sixties, was a place that encouraged laxity and dissipation amongst those who were wealthy and had a leaning towards idleness. A college such as Christ Church, which was particularly patronized by Old Etonians, was largely dominated by its 'Fast Set'—wealthy sons of the aristocracy of the country gentry who had no leanings whatever towards scholarship and who had come to Oxford simply for a good time, and as a preliminary to sowing their wild oats in the West End of London.

The majority of them were 'Gentleman-commoners', who paid double fees, sat at a separate table with the dons in 'Hall', wore velvet caps and silk gowns, often had lodgings out of College and did very much as they pleased. They lived like lords, and many of them were.

All the fast set gambled extravagantly and talked racing interminably. They backed horses as being the done thing, and there were local bookmakers in plenty who were ready to accommodate them.

But bookmaking in those days was a much more hole-in-the-corner affair than today. The big bookmakers operated only in London or at Newmarket, there were no telephones on which to ring through bets, and the sporting intelligence carried by the newspapers was sparse and inaccurate. So the fast set swaggered down to some dingy office off the 'Corn', or the 'High', and were there received by some ferret-faced little rogue who treated them with the obsequious deference that they received from all the university tradespeople.

At Eton Harry had played at gambling and had stolen away to Ascot and Epsom because he was fascinated by the excitement of it all. But at Christ Church, amongst the fast set, he began to look upon gambling as something which was more than a momentary thrill and more satisfying than sex. It was a means for showing off and proving himself a man.

Unexpectedly, it was the theory of gambling which now began to intrigue him. This brought certain fundamental aspects of his character into conflict. One side of Harry adored flattery, adulation and admiration, and these, he soon discovered, could easily be commanded by his extravagance and his utter recklessness as a gambler. For even by the fast set standards Harry was a fearless plunger. The amounts which he was prepared to wager staggered even his wealthiest friends, who were also amazed—and impressed—by his willingness to gamble on anything, from the turn of a card to a race between flies crawling up a wall.

Another side of Harry's nature craved an excitement and exhilaration out of life which neither women nor drink could provide. Had he been stronger, and considerably less rich, he might well have found this exhilaration in courting danger, either as a soldier or even in the hunting field. But as he was weak and a little effeminate, only gambling could provide him with the supreme thrill—and the ultimate challenge to Fate.

But there was a third side to his nature which has seldom been appreciated by his biographers. Harry could be both shrewd and calculating; and he was by no means the fool that his wild extravagances implied. Robbed of his vanity, he might well have become an astute and successful backer. His judgment of racing form had both knowledge and insight.

At Oxford, an undergraduate was allowed to own horses for hunting or riding purposes, but not for racing. This was always a sore point with the fast set. Ownership could be contrived *sub rosa*, so to speak, but once colours had been officially registered with the Jockey Club (and half the excitement of ownership was to see one's colours being carried) then no secrecy about the matter could be maintained.

In 1835 John Bowes had won the Derby with Mundig when he was only just twenty-one, and thus became the youngest winning owner in the history of the race. The supreme ambition of a member of the fast set was therefore to own a Derby runner whilst still an undergraduate, but this the University regulations would not permit.

But although Harry, as an undergraduate at Christ Church, had already revealed his mania for gambling, he had not as yet envisaged the glories of ownership of a racehorse, let alone a Derby winner. Such an ambition was to blossom more slowly. It is possible that he held back from it, fearing the excesses into which it might lead him.

Harry Hastings drank a great deal and was not strong. These two points in themselves suggest that he was not a confirmed seducer. Everyone requires a stimulant in life, and with some it is sexual excitement, but the basic stimulant in Harry's life was gambling, as he began to realize while he was at Oxford. Gambling gave him all the exhilaration which he needed. He was a vain young man, and this made him susceptible to feminine flattery. He was also a gay and cheerful companion, who was always surrounded by women. But Harry probably had no strong physical desire for them; and he was never, as the French have it, in constant need of a bed.

But his attraction for women was undeniable. He had a fresh complexion and a slim figure. He had dark, silky hair which he wore rather full; a small, sensitive and slightly petulant mouth that would have looked well on a girl; a delicate, well-shaped nose; and the sad brown eyes of a spaniel dog. He dressed elegantly, even foppishly, and was always neat and trim in his appearance. His body was slender, his hands were white and slim, like a woman's, and he had small feet, which were always encased in expensive and well-fitting shoes or boots. His manner was a mixture of shyness and sociability, he had a youthful and infectious gaiety of manner; and he was generous to a fault. He did not flatter women, but he was always charming to them; and it was this charm—this wistful friendliness with its suggestion of a little lost boy who was longing to be loved—which they found so irresistible. He was conscious of his power to arouse their maternal instincts, and was certainly not above using it, but this they did not resent. They realized that he was spoilt and selfish, but they still found him excellent company. He stood out in marked comparison with the hearty, aggressive and muscular undergraduate who hunted or rowed. His casual air of indifference was tantalizing and intriguing. Women never quite knew what he was thinking.

No woman had it in her power to break his heart, and this they realized at once. It did not render him less attractive. On the contrary, he became that much more of a challenge to them. Each believed secretly that she might one day be able to rescue him from his loneliness, and save him from himself.

This, then, was Harry Hastings as a young man at Oxford—still carefree, eager and unsophisticated at heart, despite his worldly bearing, and still uncertain as to what he should make of his life. But the formative years were over, and the seeds already sown were waiting to blossom. The tenants who had taken Donington Hall in 1856 gave up their lease in 1861. Now, when Harry returned to his ancestral home in the vacations, he was welcomed no longer as a boy, but as a man of the world, and those who had flattered and fawned on him in the past now increased their attentions towards him. He was old enough now to take an active part in the cock-fighting which was carried on in an old barn off Featherbed Lane, in Ashby-de-la-Zouch, and his cronies included an unfrocked clergyman from Lockington named Storey, an ex-prizefighter named Bendigo, and his butler from the Hall—each of whom encouraged the young Marquis in these 'manly' pastimes, and helped him to act as host when the company afterwards repaired to the White Horse Inn or The Calais.

Now, when cricket was played on the lawn in front of the Hall, the whole purpose of the game was to allow Harry to display his prowess as a hitter, with each innings consisting of a series of mighty swipes to the boundary, for he was far too indolent to add to his score by running a single. The crowd would cheer and clap, Harry would stride from the wicket, flushed and delighted, and pint upon pint of ale would be consumed by the spectators and players at his expense. Sometimes he would pull out a handful of gold sovereigns from his pocket and scatter them with carefree indifference; and it was typical of his growing insensitivity that he would do this on occasions when he was surrounded by those who were suffering from poverty and privation.

Still, all these incidents could be magnified into heroic occasions when he returned to Oxford and regaled the fast set with tales of the high life that was being led at Donington Hall now that its young master had once again taken up residence there and was adopting the traditional Hastings role of benevolent Squire and lavish host. The fast set at Christ Church contained many such wealthy young bloods, and one story was capped by another, while the talk was of what each would do when he came into his inheritance and could set the night life of Mayfair alight.

But Harry, for all his attempts at bravado and wild living, was by no means the most distinguished personality whom the College produced in this period. Compared with some, alas, he was rather small fry, for he lacked the presence and the strength of personality to become a dominating figure in the College life. Moreover, he had the misfortune to arrive at Christ Church at the end of what might almost be described as its era of magnificence, when undergraduate life had been brought to the peak of sophisticated self-indulgence under the leadership of a young man who had earned for himself the title of 'Magnifico' on account of the lavish style in which he lived.

There is no evidence to suggest that Harry Hastings and Henry Chaplin had met before they were brought together at

Christ Church. And it is probable that they were never intimates while they were there. Henry Chaplin had come up to 'The House' in January 1859 and he left in the December of 1860, and so the two only overlapped by one term. Henry Chaplin had established himself as the leader of the fast set in the College almost from the moment of his arrival, and by the time that Harry Hastings arrived, a shy and rather nervous young freshman, Henry was looked upon with some awe.

He was certainly everything that Harry Hastings would have loved to have been himself. He had presence and self-confidence, and commanded authority. In face and figure he was strikingly good-looking. He was tall and strongly-built, and his body still retained the slimness of youth. As he grew older, he was destined to become burly in appearance, but in his undergraduate days this was still only hinted at in his physique. Constant exercise and many hours spent in the open air had given him a fresh complexion which spoke of abundant good health. He had bright chestnut hair, good teeth, a firm, masculine jaw, broad shoulders and strong hands. His eyes were blue, and reflected his gaiety and good humour. His charm lay in his friendliness and his sympathy; and in his innate courtesy and good manners. He believed devoutly in the distinctions of class, but like a true gentleman his manners were perfect towards all women, no matter what their station in life. In disposition he was even-tempered and seldom moody. He was cheerful, and always the best of company at any party which he attended. At twenty he was still a schoolboy at heart, and remained so throughout his life, although already mature in his character and outward manner. He was not an intellectual and indeed was rather slow of thought. He was always immaculately dressed, and even as a young man there was about him a certain stateliness and dignity. His enemies, of which he had few enough, found him pompous. His friends, who were many, smiled tolerantly at the solemnity with which he set about the daily task of getting dressed.

His nickname was 'Magnifico'. It described him perfectly, for he not only lived in the grand manner, but also possessed it. He had excellent taste in both food and wine, patronized only the best tailors and shirtmakers, rode only the best hunters, admired only the loveliest women and mixed quite naturally in only the very best company. 'No one,' said Lord Willoughby de Broke, 'was half such a country gentleman as Henry Chaplin looked.' The comment was made without malice. Henry Chaplin was born to the grand manner and it fitted him like a glove.

He lived in the grand manner, and he spent money in the grand manner. In this, he, too, followed the Whyte-Melville attitude to life. Money was vulgar but necessary, and a gentleman rose above it. And no gentleman who lived in the grand manner could be expected to adopt a policy of thrift or caution. Thrift was something which a Squire did his utmost to encourage in the poor on his estate, as being a most admirable quality; but it was not the sort of quality which he cultivated in himself.

He had arrived at Oxford a year before the Prince of Wales, and had at once impressed that rather timid and down-trodden young man by his effortless assurance. There was no question of the Prince taking up with Henry Chaplin. It was Henry Chaplin who, as the social leader of the College, extended his patronage to the future heir to the throne. And the Prince was as over-awed by Henry's magnificence as were the rest of Christ Church.

Henry Chaplin had four hunters of his own in the town, which was remarkable in itself even for a leader of the fast set, and had, in his own phrase, 'command' over nearly twenty more, which belonged to his cousin and were stabled at Bicester. During the season he hunted six days a week, and was only seen in College at breakfast, and occasionally for dinner. When he appeared in the College Chapel, as he was sometimes required to do by the College regulations, he was liable to appear with a surplice over his hunting clothes.

How different was the character of his admiring friend! Albert Edward, Prince of Wales, had arrived at Oxford after a period spent at Edinburgh University and before going on to Cambridge. His had been a dull life up to then, and the forbidding shadow of his austere father lay over him. He had been made well aware that the purpose of his university education was solely for intellectual advancement, and despite the protests of the Dean at Christ Church, he was not allowed to occupy rooms in college, and was discouraged from fraternizing with his fellow undergraduates. Dean Liddell took a great liking to Bertie, and described him as 'the nicest fellow possible; so simply, naif, ingenuous and modest'.

Bertie was not a scholar, and he noted with growing envy how enjoyable was the life of the average undergraduate. For most of the day a team of private tutors kept the royal nose close to the grindstone, but there were a few occasions when he was allowed off the lead. His mother, the Queen, strongly disapproved of the lax and dissipated habits of many of the young aristocracy, but members of the hunting set were just permissible. Bertie was therefore allowed occasionally to hunt, and it was while he was spending one of his rare days with the South Oxfordshire pack that he first met his fellow undergraduate at Christ Church, Henry Chaplin.

Henry at once took the Prince under his wing. It was probably not snobbishness that encouraged him to do so, although Henry Chaplin was fully alive to the social distinctions which existed in his life. But he was a considerate young man, and a kind one, and he must have taken pity on anyone who was living so dull a life as poor Bertie. Bertie, for his part, was deeply impressed by 'Magnifico'. His worldly manner, his air of authority, his splendid presence, his extensive knowledge of horses and of hunting and his considerable skill as a horseman together made him an excellent companion in the hunting field. And during moments of inactivity, when scent was poor or as they were on the way to a meet, Bertie would no doubt give his companion depressing accounts of his long and arduous days of study, whilst Henry Chaplin, in his turn, would describe the many gay and abandoned ways in which the fast set at Christ Church spent their days and nights.

Henry Chaplin's closest friend at Oxford was Sir Frederick Johnstone, an Old Etonian and the eighth Baronet. He was a cheerful and reckless companion, who was himself descended from a long and honourable line of country squires; who was equally devoted to hunting and the horse; and whose main interest in life was the turf. The two of them quickly took Bertie in hand, and although the strict supervision under which the Prince lived forbade any major excesses, it was they who taught him to smoke—an indiscretion which would have horrified the Queen had she discovered it.

Both Henry Chaplin and Sir Frederick Johnstone were at that time prominent members of the exclusive Bullingdon Club, and a photograph taken of a Bullingdon cricket team in 1859 shows the heir to the English throne seated in the centre of the group, with Henry Chaplin on his right and Sir Frederick standing at the end of the row. This friendship between the three undergraduates was no passing phase of youth. They remained on intimate terms for the rest of their lives, and there were to be few occasions in the future when the Prince of Wales's party to Epsom or Ascot did not include both Henry Chaplin and Frederick Johnstone amongst its members.

Harry Hastings was never a member of this exclusive Christ Church circle. In the first place, he only overlapped with the Prince and Henry Chaplin by one term, when he was an insignificant freshman and 'Magnifico' was the acknowledged social leader of the College. In the second place, Harry Hastings was not a hunting man, despite the traditions of his father, and violent physical exercise on the back of a horse was not his idea of pleasure. And thirdly there was the unfortunate matter of his aunt, Lady Flora. The memory still rankled with Queen Victoria, and Bertie would *not* have been encouraged to make friends with a member of the Hastings family. And so Harry, in whom there must always have existed the seeds of an inferiority complex, despite his position and numerous titles, must have resented Henry Chaplin's magnificence, and the Prince's aloofness. Moreover, the fact that Henry Chaplin represented so much of what Harry would have liked to have been himself, and was not, probably increased this feeling of resentment. Harry was never orthodox in his behaviour, but Henry Chaplin always was. Even his dissipations and excesses followed the orthodox pattern of the period. His passion for quality in everything may well have irritated someone like Harry, who had no real judgment in food, wine, women—or indeed in the artistry of loose living.

Harry Hastings may not have realized it at the time, but one of the things which he must have resented most strongly about Henry Chaplin was his complete normality. Henry's background had been normal and his childhood had been normal, and together these had succeeded in producing a normal and healthy young Englishman. To Harry, who was a tangle of complexes and inhibitions, the sight of 'Magnifico' moving majestically across the Quad as if he owned the College must have been both frustrating and infuriating. Henry Chaplin, for his part, may scarcely have noticed the slim young freshman who took no part in the organized games of the College, did not hunt and was not a member of the Bullingdon Club. Had anyone then told him that Harry Hastings was destined to be the major adversary of his life, he would have no doubt been surprised—and unimpressed. He can hardly have foreseen Harry as a serious rival in anything.

In the May of 1859, when Henry Chaplin had just started on his second term at Christ Church, news had reached him that his uncle, who had brought him up as his own son, had died. Thus Henry inherited not only Blankney Hall, but all the traditions which went with it. He was ready, and more than willing, to accept the honour and responsibilities of an important country squire.

It has already been noted that Henry Chaplin's father, the Reverend Henry Chaplin, of Ryhall Hall, in Rutlandshire, had died in 1849 when his son was only eight, and that thereafter Henry's uncle, Charles Chaplin, Lord of the Manor of Blankney, had made himself responsible for his brother's family and, being childless himself, had groomed the eldest boy, Henry, to be his successor.

Henry had already lost his mother six months before he went up to Oxford for his first term in the January of 1859. She had proved herself a devoted parent, and a woman of exceptional character, sensible and responsible, and a very different type of person from Harry Hastings' mother, 'the jolly fast Marchioness'. 'Mrs Henry', as she had always been called at Blankney to distinguish her from her sister-in-law, had been much younger than her husband, and was therefore that much closer to her children in both age and understanding. She endowed her eldest son, Henry, with an honest and honourable character, but the best of all the qualities which she imparted to him was her own ability to accept misfortune without bitterness. The Chaplin story has often been described as one of revenge by historians of the turf. Nothing was further from the truth. Henry Chaplin, due to the influences of his mother, was never either bitter or revengeful. He never found it in himself either to bear malice or to hate.

Life for the Chaplin family, before the death of their father in 1849, was happy and uneventful. For the most part it was spent in the country, and although Mrs Chaplin did rent a house in Montague Square, in London, and the children spent a few weeks in the year there, by far the greater part of their time was spent either at their home at Ryhall Hall or with their beloved uncle, Charles, at Blankney.

Some form of education for the boys was held necessary, and so Henry was packed off to a 'Dame's school' at Brighton, where—under the surveillance of a certain Mrs Walker—he was taken for walks across the Downs to see the old smock Mill standing guard above Rottingdean, or along the Chain Pier which, together with the Royal Pavilion, was then the pride of the town.

The Chaplin family used also to spend their summer holidays in Brighton, and it was here that he suffered his first real tragedy in life when his elder sister, Harriet, died suddenly in 1847. Two years later his father died.

Henry Chaplin was deeply hurt by these two losses. The family was the bulwark of his life, and it needed all the love and sympathy of his mother to help him to endure, and finally to accept, these bereavements.

But against these sorrows in early childhood was set the happiness of life at Blankney for, after their father's death, the children and 'Mrs Henry' spent more and more of their time with their uncle Charles. The old Squire, who was so feared by his tenants and who was such a martinet in the hunting field and on the bench, was accepted with an easy intimacy by his young nephews and nieces, who seem to have had no fear of him at all. They accompanied him on his rounds of the estate, and on his visits to his tenants, and quickly won both the respect and the affection of the many people who looked upon the old Squire with awe.

It soon became apparent that the young Henry was a good mixer. He was neither shy nor aloof; and his friendliness and his genuine sympathy with those in trouble or in pain was a feature of his character even in childhood. He had the priceless gift of being genuinely interested in people, and he was an understanding and sympathetic listener.

Young Henry imitated his old uncle. It would have been remarkable if he had not. And early in life he revealed a consciousness of his superior standing. But he was not aggressively autocratic, and although he inherited an air of authority the country folk of Blankney did not object. He knew his place and they knew theirs. He was but a chip off the old block. They felt that they could trust him.

Needless to say, riding and hunting were the chief pastimes of all who spent their leisure hours at Blankney, whether young or old, and the children of the Reverend Henry were placed on ponies almost as soon as they could walk. Henry was both strong and courageous, and he would have happily spent every hour of every holiday in the saddle. This delighted the old Squire, who soon realized that although he was himself childless, he had just the heir that he could have wished for in his brother's eldest son. This was the consolation of his life in the twilight of his days.

A close friend of the Squire's was Lord Henry Bentinck, the

younger brother of Lord George and the fourth of the four sons of the fourth Duke of Portland. He was at that time Master of the Burton Hunt, of which the Squire was an ardent supporter.

Lord Henry and the young Henry Chaplin became close friends and the elder man did much to help formulate the character of the younger. At first the friendship was no more than that of an elderly man taking a promising youngster under his wing, but as the years went by, Henry Chaplin found himself turning more and more to Lord Henry for advice and guidance.

There was a strong streak of eccentricity and stubbornness in the character of Lord Henry Bentinck, and this always fascinated the orthodox Henry Chaplin. Lord Henry was an egotist. He went his own way, and many people looked upon him as a bit of a crank. He lived at this time a vagabond life of his own with a small suite of rooms at The White Hart Inn, in Lincoln, where he had a private cook and kept his own private cellar.

But whatever the eccentricities of character which Lord Henry revealed, he was a good friend and wise counsellor to the young Henry Chaplin, who learnt a great deal from him not only about horses, but also about life.

As Henry was left fatherless when he was only eight, the responsibilities of guardian and adviser to him fell upon the old Squire, and these included the choosing of a suitable school for his nephew. There were really only two alternatives—Eton or Harrow—and the old Squire's choice fell on Harrow.

Harrow in the middle of the nineteenth century was altogether a smaller and less ambitious school than Eton. Like Eton, it catered in particular for the sons of the well-to-do and specialized in turning out politicians and men who devoted their lives to the service of their country, but it was altogether a rather less aristocratic establishment than its neighbour at Windsor.

Henry Chaplin was therefore entered for Harrow. He arrived there for the autumn term of 1854 and was placed in E. H. Vaughan's house, West Acre, which had only recently been opened.

The Headmaster of Harrow at that time was Dr Charles John Vaughan, who had been one of Dr Arnold's favourite pupils at Rugby. Indeed, on Arnold's death in 1842, he had been a candidate for the Headmastership of Rugby, even though he was at that time only twenty-six, which was remarkably young for him even to have been considered for so responsible a position. Vaughan was a man of strong character and great determination, and he understood boys. He was, of course, imbued with the great Rugby traditions of Arnold, but in many ways he was the more practical of the two. His more recent biographers have emphasized certain flaws in his character, but nevertheless Harrow, during his period of headmastership, turned out boys of honesty and worth. Eton was still wrestling with the system which tended to produce extremes, with its boys either benefiting from its liberal freedom or else abusing it. Harrow was less vulnerable. It can certainly be argued that Harry Hastings should never have been sent to Eton, but Harrow was an admirable choice for the future Squire of Blankney. It is true that Henry Chaplin's character was already basically formed by the normality of his family life before he ever went to Harrow, but the school served him well. It is possible that the Hastings story might have been substantially altered had Harry gone there as well for his youthful education.

The fact that Henry Chaplin was an Old Harrovian and Harry Hastings an old Etonian may have separated them at Oxford and done something to emphasize the differences between them. But the basic difference between the two, and one which Harry must instinctively have realized and resented, was that Henry Chaplin was in fact something of a man of the world by the time he reached Oxford, and had already attained some degree of maturity. His grand manner and passion for only the best of everything may have been in part a pose, but it was also founded on a genuine appreciation of quality. But Harry Hastings still had a long way to go before he attained maturity, if indeed he ever did.

Henry Chaplin left Oxford at the end of the winter term of 1860, largely as a result of a difference of opinion with Dean Liddell over the purpose of a university education. Henry Chaplin was no intellectual, and in keeping with the traditions of the upper classes of the period he looked with some suspicion on those who were. He therefore made little effort to study during his first two years at Oxford. This fact did not escape the notice of the Dean, who summoned Henry to his presence and informed the Squire of Blankney that Christ Church should be looked upon as a place of learning and should not be used simply as a hunting box. He asked Henry what he proposed to do about this.

Henry replied that he was willing to fall in with any plans that the Dean might have and invited suggestions.

'I suggest that you go in for an examination,' replied the Dean curtly. 'It is customary at this University.'

It was a novel idea, but Henry viewed it almost with interest. He was not clever, but he was determined, and so he set about this new enterprise with characteristic thoroughness. A search for a suitable tutor revealed an elderly and 'bottle-nosed man' who sufficiently aroused his interest to make him work comparatively hard; and in due course he passed 'Mods' with distinction—a feat which astonished everyone including the Dean, the bottle-nosed tutor and Henry himself.

The Dean was delighted as well as surprised. He sent Henry a short note of congratulation, in which he urged his pupil to press forward against the ultimate goal of an Honours Degree, which he deemed to be well within Henry's compass. Finally he concluded with the enthusiastic forecast that Henry would end his scholastic career as a credit not only to the College, but also to the University of Oxford itself.

His optimism was premature. Henry Chaplin, in the manner of a rugby three-quarter who has summoned all his energies to fling himself over the line, had exhausted his mental powers. He had, so to speak, shot his academic bolt.

Alas for the honour of Christ Church, and for that of the University of Oxford! His note in reply to the Dean was cordial but firm. Attractive though the goal of an Honours Degree might seem to some, he regretted that he had an alternative project in mind for the immediate future.

He concluded his note with a brief statement of fact. 'I am very sorry to inform you that I have arranged to go for a trip to the Rocky Mountains.'

Henry Chaplin had a great-uncle on his mother's side who was closely connected with the fur trade in Canada, and through him the trip was arranged. Sir Frederick Johnstone, as his closest friend, was invited to join the expedition, and accepted with enthusiasm, and the two of them set off for New York in the early spring of 1861, accompanied by an expert guide. Throughout his life, Henry Chaplin showed a flair for choosing the opportune moment, and this he now revealed by arriving at New York on 7 April 1861. Five days later Fort Sumter was attacked, and the American Civil War had begun.

Henry and Sir Frederick were at once caught up in the ensuing activity. They contrived to witness—from a distance—the attack made by Southern troops on the Federal Armoury at Harpers Ferry; and later they were introduced to General Grant, who presented Henry with a pony which he later brought back to England. But as they were anxious to visit the Rockies and probably considered that the Civil War would anyway shortly be over, they left America and took a train to Toronto. Both were tough and resolute young men, who were by no means averse to hardship, and their final assault upon the Rockies consisted of sixteen arduous days on horseback, but their objective was not achieved. News reached them that some Black Foot Indians were on the warpath before them, and they were reluctantly forced to turn back. However, Henry and his companion did stake out one claim on posterity in Canada. Their guide discovered two large salt lakes in the vicinity of Moosejaw, and named one of them Lake Chaplin, and the other Lake Johnstone.

The party returned to England late in the summer of 1861. Henry Chaplin's university days were now over, and he looked forward to taking up the duties of Squire of Blankney—the chief of which was to hunt six days a week throughout the season. 'The sport to him was more than a pastime—it was a scientific study of absorbing interest,' wrote his daughter in her biography of her father. Henry was soon supremely happy at Blankney, with his hounds and amongst his tenantry, who adored him. The majority of the local farmers were also keen hunting men, but it was his knowledge of country life, and particularly of the problems of agriculture, which made him respected as well as liked. He was well-to-do, without being rich, and had it not been for his addiction to good living and lavish entertainment, he could have managed very comfortably on his income.

His outlook as a Squire was the same as that of his uncle, from whom he had inherited Blankney. That is to say he was autocratic, and a die-hard Tory, and would not tolerate argument or contradiction amongst his tenants; but on the other hand, his generosity was proverbial, and he was quick to help anyone in trouble. He was sympathetic to his tenants' problems, and had already decided at the back of his mind that his duty to them must ultimately carry him into politics, where he could represent their interests in the way they should be represented.

In all this he carried on the traditions in which he had been brought up and which he never thought to question. The upper classes were born to rule, and had to be obeyed without question. The lower classes were born to be ruled. But the duties which a Squire owed to his tenants were a sacred trust. In a way, he was their father. It was his function to protect them from want and to help them in adversity.

But he had no intention of spending all his time at Blankney, and the many friends whom he had made at Oxford, and above all the Prince of Wales and Sir Frederick Johnstone, were not content that he should bury himself in the country throughout the year. Neither were the society hostesses of London. So charming and so eligible a bachelor could not be allowed to vegetate at his country seat during the Season, and so, when hunting ended in the spring of 1862, Henry Chaplin abandoned the life of a country Squire and came to London to live a life of fashion and leisure, and to entertain and be entertained by the highest in the land and notably by the heir to the throne.

The Prince had also gone down from Oxford at the end of 1860, and Harry Hastings had been left there to enter his second year, and to take a more leading part in the social life of the College now that his rival was no longer in command of it. Harry left Oxford in 1861 in the same way as he had left Eton—abruptly and for reasons unspecified—and he, also, returned to his country seat for a period before coming to London for the Season of 1862.

Henry Chaplin had spent 1861 in Canada, becoming a man. Harry Hastings spent the same year at Oxford and at Donington, remaining an immature youth. He had still very little experience of the world, no sense of responsibility and lacked judgment in everything, especially in the matter of choosing his friends. Already he was surrounded by spongers, sycophants and weak-willed young noblemen such as himself. He was popular in Castle Donington after a fashion, because he was so friendly and democratic in his manner, and because he entered into the sport of the district. He drank in the local inns, watched the bull-baiting at The Calais and was always to be found in the old barn off Featherbed Lane, in Ashby, when cock-fighting was in progress. The more respectable elements in Castle Donington and Ashby looked upon this behaviour with disapproval, and his tenants—although they had affection for him—were already beginning to wonder what the future might hold for all of them if this carefree life of dissipation were to continue unchecked. If Harry were ultimately to ruin himself by his excesses, then he would ruin many of his tenants with him, for the economy of the little community was largely dependent on the solvency of the Lord of the Manor.

The advent of Harry Hastings and Henry Chaplin for the Season of 1862 delighted London Society, and especially those matrons with daughters of a marriageable age. They at once started to weigh up the situation with all the care of a financier assessing the relative merits of two very different types of stock. Harry Hastings, with his numerous titles and his inheritances, seemed at first the more desirable, but he was clearly the more unstable of the two. Henry Chaplin had no title, but he was well-to-do and reliable. He was also a close friend of royalty. There was, of course, a risk over both—and risk was something which was becoming increasingly abhorrent to the cautious Victorian mind, whether it was engaged in acquiring shares or a son-in-law. There was something so comforting in being safe, and neither Harry Hastings nor Henry Chaplin, with their wild habits and extravagance, could be described as that. On the other hand, the prize in each case was a substantial one.

It was all very intriguing and very frustrating. Each matron studied her offspring in hope or exasperation and wished that Mary could have been blessed with a better figure or that Emily's spots might disappear.

One thing was certain. Both young men would be selective; and neither would fancy a girl who was in any way dowdy or puritanical. Indeed the future wife of either Harry Hastings or Henry Chaplin would have to be broad-minded, to say the least, for it was only too evident, as 1862 wore on, that both were determined to enjoy themselves to the full.

Victorian respectability was all very well, but a mother who was looking for the ideal partner for her daughter could well afford to overlook the habits of eligible young men of fashion. Moreover, respectability was a virtue that could easily be acquired in middle age. It did not really suit young men of breeding. The Victorian outlook was nothing if not practical—and far more broad-minded than later generations were to realize. One did not ask of a young man that he should be perfect—only that he should have an income of ten thousand a year.

And what of the two young men themselves? Each was

undoubtedly bent only on enjoying himself to the maximum and experiencing all the delights which London could offer. Henry Chaplin, with his mature outlook, was probably already beginning to consider marriage, because he was at heart a family man. Harry, on the other hand, was in no way concerned with his future responsibilities. He had come to London simply to enjoy himself. But enjoyment included keeping company with glamorous women, for a swell's reputation was in part assessed by the standard of feminine beauty with which he surrounded himself.

There is no evidence to indicate whether Lady Florence Paget was then known to either of them. Her début in Society was not made until a year later, and it seems probable that during this summer of 1862 she was still living in comparative retirement in the country. Each may well have encountered her. Harry Hastings knew her brothers and sometimes played country-house cricket with them. But the full impact of Florence's beauty on them, and on Society, had yet to be made. For the time being they were free to savour the flattering position of being much sought after in society, and they set about distributing their patronage accordingly. Two untroubled years still remained to them before the Hastings story was to reach its remarkable climax.

CHAPTER THREE

THE SALAD DAYS

To every thing there is a season, and a time to every purpose under the heaven:
A time to be born, and a time to die; a time to plant, and a time to pluck up that which is planted.

THERE is also a time to sow wild oats.

In mid-Victorian days a youth of quality settled down in London for a period to indulge in the pleasures of metropolitan life and to become 'a man of the world'.

To the Victorians, 'a man of the world' was one who had broken away irrevocably from his mother's apron strings, and who had gambled unwisely, drunk excessively and seduced freely. This, it was felt, was part of the process of becoming both manly and worldly. Whether the person in question ever learnt anything about life in the process was altogether another matter. The Victorians were not given to self-analysis, and the young men of fashion were certainly not given to clever talk, for brains as such were rather despised. Suffice it that a fellow could drink his quota like a gentleman, and boast of his sexual prowess with assurance. A woman's place was in the home, and a man's place, in youth at least, was in one of the brothels of the Haymarket. Only thus could true worldliness be achieved.

These were the salad days, when young men were green in judgment; and by the time the gay 'sixties were fully under way there were three young men in Mayfair who were determined to make the most of them.

Harry Hastings, Henry Chaplin and Albert Edward, Prince of Wales, were of much the same age. The Prince was the eldest, and he came of age in November of 1862. Henry Chaplin, who was next, reached his majority just before Christmas in the same year. Harry Hastings, the youngest of the three, became twenty-one on 22 July 1863.

By the autumn of 1863 each was fully launched on London society, a free agent able to do very much as he pleased and to enjoy himself very much as he wished. All three were determined to indulge themselves as much as possible. They moved in the same circles and went on the town together, although their tastes in dissipation varied. The ring-leader in the wilder episodes was Harry Hastings. Henry Chaplin took charge when the dissipation was more orthodox and was limited to the pleasures of wine, women and song; and Bertie followed in their wake, still trying to catch up with the lost opportunities of his youth.

The differences which had separated them at Oxford seem to have been quickly forgotten; at least by Henry Chaplin and the Prince, who may never have realized that any had existed. Henry Chaplin, when first he came into contact with Harry Hastings in this, their initial London season, may even have searched his memory for where they had met before, and then remembered the rather insignificant young freshman who had come up to Christ Church in Henry's last term. The Prince, as well, may have only remembered Harry vaguely. But Harry himself would have remembered both of them well, and especially 'Magnifico'. It is doubtful if his jealousy of Henry Chaplin had subsided, but the intervening year had done something to bolster Harry's ego. Now they met on equal footing—and indeed Harry even held a slight advantage, with his many titles and his great expectations. He could never outdo Henry Chaplin in dignity or self-assurance, but there were moments when Harry's carefree indifference to all forms of orthodoxy was able to make Henry Chaplin look rather dull and prosaic in comparison.

Their backgrounds differed in many respects. Bertie was already married and thus had a respectable as well as a disreputable side to his daily life. Henry Chaplin, already the typical country Squire and hunting man, spent much of his time either in the formal circles of London Society or in entertaining lavishly at Blankney. Harry Hastings, who disliked hunting and hated all aspects of formal life, was the rebel of the three, to whom all manifestations of Victorian orthodoxy were an anathema. His interests were in gambling and low life. Moreover it was fast becoming essential to his ego that he should be outstanding in whatever company he was in. This was not possible in London society, but in the 'night-houses' of Leicester Square and the Charing Cross Road, in the slums of the East End and in the opium dens of the docks, Harry—by virtue of his charm and wealth—was soon a king without a rival.

When in London, the young swells of the period usually put up at the Clarendon Hotel, Long's, Stevens' or Limmer's—all close to each other in or around Bond Street. It was Harry's custom, in his early days of dissipation, to make his headquarters at Limmer's, which was in Conduit Street. Later on, he settled down at 23 Park Lane, but during 1863 Limmer's became his spiritual home. This, in view of its sporting clientele, is not surprising. Gronow referred to it as 'a midnight Tattersall's', and described it as the dirtiest hotel in London. It was gloomy, grimy and unscrubbed, but was yet so popular during the height of the racing season that even the dingiest of its bedrooms were hard to come by. But its attractions, other than that of meeting everyone who was anyone in the racing world in its uncomfortable coffee-room, was the fact that it served excellent plain English food (the Clarendon was the only hotel in London where you could get anything approaching a Continental meal) and that the port was excellent. Its devotees were also much addicted to the hotel's famous gin punch.

No one in this disreputable hostel ever seemed to go to bed, meals and drinks were served throughout the night by sleepy waiters (although the cutlery was always of silver), and the management had no objection either to the hours or to the company which its patrons kept. St George's, Hanover Square, was just around the corner for those who wished to get married, whilst the Burlington Arcade was equally adjacent for those whose requirements were merely for sex. The neighbourhood abounded in well-appointed brothels, and the ladies of the town were usually out on their beat well before the first gas-lamps were lit. The chamber-maids in the hotel, though slatternly, were always willing to oblige clients who could not be bothered to go out, and who were anyway not too fussy in their requirements. In short, there was nowhere in London where it was easier to lay a bet or a woman than at Limmer's, and the two were sometimes even done simultaneously. It was a racing man's heaven.

Harry could scarcely have found a residence more suited to his tastes. As a jumping-off ground for a night's adventure it was ideal, and there was always the billiards room to offer a chance for reckless wagering if the weather made it impossible to go out.

Thus the year of 1863 was really a starting point for each of these three young men—Harry Hastings, Henry Chaplin and Albert Edward, Prince of Wales. By the late summer, all three had come of age and were largely committed to the life which they proposed to lead; and already they were beginning to give indications as to the paths which they were likely to follow in the years to come.

Henry Chaplin and Albert Edward, dissipation or no, seemed likely to be heading for a public career and ultimately a sense of responsibility; and Henry also seemed likely to be heading for the highly successful type of marriage which Bertie was now enjoying.

No one quite knew what Harry's ultimate destination would be. It seemed reasonably certain that he would end up by ruining his health, dissipating his wealth and going rapidly downhill, probably without even a temporary period of restraint, unless perhaps he married a woman who could control him. But there seemed no reason why Harry should marry. Gambling was his obsession, not women; and family life as such had no appeal for him. He was a Tory by family tradition, but had not the slightest interest in politics, and although he had accepted an honorary appointment as a cornet in Prince Albert's Own Leicestershire Yeomanry Cavalry, there was no warlike spirit in him.

Henry Chaplin, patriot though he was, had also no leanings towards a military career, and although Bertie would have liked to become a soldier, it was clear that parental consent would never be given to any warlike ambitions which he might have.

One path of Victorian glory alone remained open to them— a path which could lead to resounding victories and popular acclaim. This was the turf. The fields of battle were admittedly no more than those which Epsom, Ascot and Newmarket could provide, but the rewards of achievement were tantalizing. It is not surprising that Harry Hastings should have been the first to succumb to these temptations, or that his racing career should, in the end, have proved to be the most meteoric and sensational. Nor is it surprising that the Prince and Henry Chaplin should later have followed his example, and should also have dedicated themselves to winning the Blue Riband of racing. But which of these three young men was destined to achieve this supreme honour, it would have been hard then to forecast. In fact, two out of the three were ultimately to accomplish this life's ambition and thus attain immortality on the turf.

But in the summer of 1863 these ambitions were as yet scarcely born. The immediate aim of these three young men was self-indulgence. It was also happiness, but the two are not synonymous.

There was one incident in this summer which might have given each of the three young men food for thought had they been in a mind to digest it, for it was in this year that the Prince paid his first visit to Epsom to see the Derby.

He was accompanied by Henry Chaplin and Sir Frederick Johnstone, but not by Harry Hastings, who on these occasions preferred the company of his wilder friends. The Prince was in the public eye, and had therefore to be on his best behaviour. Such conformity never suited Harry Hastings, who liked the democratic atmosphere of the open Downs. The Derby, to him, offered a unique opportunity for betting, drinking and enjoying mixed company, for nowhere in the world was the company more mixed than on Epsom Downs on Derby Day. This was Harry's world, and the tumult of the Ring was soon destined to become the music of his life.

There was also another possible reason why he did not accompany the Prince. He may not have been asked. For although Harry was by now one of Bertie's regular drinking companions, he was not of his intimates. Moreover the rift caused by the Lady Flora episode still existed between the house of Hastings and the Crown. It was not referred to by the Queen, but she still frowned upon Bertie's association with Harry and discouraged any public demonstration of friendship between her son and the head of the Hastings family.

Sir Frederick Johnstone, already an established owner and a well-known figure on the turf, had a strongly fancied runner named The Gillie in the big race, and so the mood in the royal party was one of conviviality and expectancy. Sir Frederick was always extolling the delights of racing and seeking to persuade his two friends to take up ownership, and while both the Prince and Henry lent a ready enough ear to his suggestions and were impressed by his enthusiasm, they were not yet prepared to commit themselves fully to the turf.

Bertie was obviously enjoying himself, and the crowd were delighted to have him amongst them, and sharing this, their national festival. They cheered him wildly on his arrival, and when he entered the Grand Stand the betting-ring suspended business for a full two minutes whilst they joined in the popular acclaim—in itself a remarkable honour!

A few of those present had seen the Derby of 1840, when the young Queen had come to Epsom, and they were conscious of the fact that this royal patronage of racing had proved very short lived. But here was the Prince, smiling and happy and in the company of an enthusiastic young owner, and so it might well be that racing might again become the sport of kings.

It was well known that the Queen did not approve of racing. She hated gambling, and all the other weaknesses which she felt so strongly were undermining the aristocracy, who should have been setting an example to the nation. There had been all too many scandals involving betting, and she was becoming increasingly aware that gambling was again establishing itself as a national vice, as it had been in the Regency days. She was convinced that no good could ever come out of backing horses.

This royal attitude was held to be particularly ill-advised in 1863, when the gambling fraternity had for once something which they considered in the nature of a near-certainty. This was a colt named Lord Clifden, which was owned by Lord St Vincent, a descendant of the famous Admiral of Nelson's day. Lord St Vincent had become so convinced of his colt's superiority that he had not only backed it heavily himself, but had persuaded all his aristocratic friends to do the same. Indeed the peerage, as a whole, stood to win a huge sum on Lord Clifden, and the popular view was that the horse was unbeatable, especially as George Fordham, the greatest jockey of his day, had been engaged to ride him.

Only one thing marred the prevailing mood of gaiety. The weather was deplorable, and the rain came down in torrents.

To make matters worse, there was a considerable delay at the start. The starter, Mr McGeorge, had been signally unsuccessful in the previous year. A fussy and self-important little man, who had only just been appointed to the post, had caused such confusion in 1862 that the Stewards had been tempted to declare the race void, since half the field had been facing the wrong way when he had dropped his flag. Now, in 1863, he was determined to re-establish himself.

As a result he signalled no less than thirty-four false starts before he permitted the field to go on its way, with the majority of the runners so fretful and excited that they were in no state to do themselves justice.

Fortunately Lord Clifden was well away, and when he took the lead from Macaroni at Tattenham Corner, and entered the straight in front, with Fordham looking round for any signs of danger, the race appeared cut and dried.

The way to Hell, it has been said, is paved with good intentions. It is also peopled by jockeys who have looked round. This has spelt disaster in the past, and will do so again as long as there is racing on Epsom Downs.

Chaloner, the jockey on Macaroni, saw his opportunity, and drove his mount up to challenge. Fordham had to transfer his whip from one hand to another, and his colt faltered. Then, with the winning post but a few yards away, and Lord Clifden still in the lead, the colt trod on a piece of orange peel and momentarily faltered. The two runners passed the post locked together.

'Lord Clifden by a head' was the verdict of the onlookers, but the judge did not agree. Macaroni was awarded the race, and a dejected backer in the stand was heard to observe that the decision had beggared half the aristocracy of England.

What was the lesson? That a jockey should not look round? That Fordham was not the man for Epsom? That betting was a fool's pastime? Or that those who disposed of orange peel should be careful where they threw it?

But whatever the moral it was certainly lost on Harry Hastings, on Henry Chaplin and on Albert Edward, Prince of Wales. None of *them* had been beggared by the incident, and they drove back to London in the best of spirits.

But there was one person on whom the lesson of the 1863 Derby was *not* lost. George Fordham, the jockey on Lord Clifden, was bitterly distressed. He had arranged to dine on the night of the race with some friends at Carshalton and he rode over in the evening with an old friend of his, a steeplechase jockey by the name of Sait. An acquaintance of Sait passed them on the road, and called out that he had lost heavily on the Derby, but would have won had not Fordham pulled his mount outrageously and thrown the race away.

This was too much for the rider of Lord Clifden. He jumped from his hack, seized the accuser by the scruff of the neck and thrashed him violently with his whip. On arrival at Carshalton he was so overwrought that he refused anything to eat or drink, and would not even enter the dining-room. Instead he sat miserably on the stairs outside, and cried tears of frustration, for he who was known throughout England as the arch 'kidder' and the jockey who could always be relied upon to fool an opponent in a tight finish, had himself been fooled.

Back in Newmarket they were ringing the church bells to herald Macaroni's victory, but no bells were being rung in Carshalton. To George Fordham, cleverest and most sensitive of jockeys, it was the words of his critics that were now ringing in his ears. 'Fordham will never make an Epsom jockey. He has not the courage to come down the hill.'

They had been whispering that for some time now, and Fordham was beginning to fear that they might be right. He, too, had a life's ambition to win the Derby. It would be a cruel fate if he were to be robbed of achieving it by the fear which sometimes overcame him as the field swept round Tattenham Corner, and the jockeys struggled mercilessly amongst themselves for a good position.

Coming events cast their shadow before them. But there are few enough who have the wisdom to learn from this. Back in London, Harry Hastings, Henry Chaplin and the Prince of Wales were in no mood for foreboding, but it is possible that there was one observer of Lord Clifden's defeat who realized the dangers of gambling on horses. Lady Florence Paget had accompanied her father, Lord Anglesey, to the Derby and had seen him bet heavily on the horse whom Lord St Vincent had assured him could not be beaten. The second Marquis was himself an enthusiastic owner of racehorses, and although he had not had a runner in the big race, he had run his two-year-old colt, Rattler, on the first day of the meeting, and had seen him finish nowhere. The financial difficulties under which Florence had lived throughout her life had been largely brought about by her father's love of racing, and by his reckless gambling. Now he had lost heavily over Lord Clifden, as had so many of his friends, and once again the ever-recurrent problem of settling day had to be faced, when bookmakers had to be asked for time to pay, or recourse had to be made to moneylenders or other methods of raising money. Florence had been brought up as a child to love horses, but already, as a girl, she had learnt to distrust racehorses, and the distress which could follow in their wake.

No such inhibitions beset Harry Hastings. He was enjoying the summer immensely, and now that the Derby was over, he had Ascot to look forward to, and then the great occasion of his twenty-first birthday, with all its accompanying festivities at Donington Hall.

His rival, Henry Chaplin, had celebrated his coming-of-age

the previous winter, and Harry was determined to outdo him. Henry Chaplin, of course, was very popular with his tenantry and they had toasted him with warmth. He had inherited estates in three different counties, including those of Blankney, Tathwell, Metheringham, Temple Brewer and Little Claythorpe, together with half a dozen smaller ones, each in Lincolnshire, and amounting to some 25,000 acres in all. There were also minor estates in Nottingham and Yorkshire. This made Henry Chaplin a landed gentleman of some standing, but these properties could in no way compare in size and number with those to which Harry Hastings was to become master on his twenty-first birthday.

By the June of 1863, Harry Hastings' plans for this, the greatest occasion in his life, were already far advanced, and he was making preparations on a most lavish scale. He was determined that if ever a town was to be set alight by universal rejoicing, it would be Castle Donington during the week which marked his coming-of-age.

As for the good people of Castle Donington themselves, they were equally as anxious to make the occasion unique. The Prince's marriage to Princess Alexandra in the spring had given them an opportunity for a dress-rehearsal. On this occasion, they had built their triumphal arches across Market Street, hung out their gaily-coloured bunting, sung patriotic songs, drunk many patriotic toasts and staged a grand firework display on Castle Hill. The weather had been none too good, but this had not depressed them. They now looked forward with confidence to the great day itself, Wednesday, 22 July, when their young Marquis reached his majority, and ushered in what all devoutly hoped would prove to be the golden age of Donington Hall.

> Wednesday was the eventful day—that on which the Marquis really came of age: other gatherings therefore which had taken place at Ashby-de-la-Zouch, at Moira, at Church Gresley, and at a number of minor places, were but anticipatory of the great day at the Park. The weather, which had not been propitious on Tuesday, opened somewhat dull on the day following. The quantity of moisture in the atmosphere was considerable and, unable to retain itself in that form, it descended in shape of rain just as dinner was about to commence. . . .

Thus *The Leicester Journal*, in its issue of 24 July 1863,

referred to the weather in its official description of Harry's coming-of-age—a description which ran to six full-length columns that contained some 15,000 words in small print. Their rival, *The Loughborough Monitor*, had to cover the story in two parts, so enthusiastic was its reporter, and this latter journal devoted much space to the eulogistic poems which were composed in honour of the occasion by the local men of letters, who compiled lengthy panegyrics, and searched both the classic and romantic poets for quotations that were erudite, high-sounding and comparatively apt. Some, while bent on lauding the occasion, also took the opportunity to sound the necessary note of caution and admonition, so dear to Victorians, and while wishing Harry long years of happiness and prosperity, also felt it beholden to them to remind him of a man's ultimate destiny and the life beyond the grave.

From all this welter of journalistic exuberance, with speeches recorded in full and with suitable bracketed interpolations, such as 'cheers', 'great cheering' and even 'great and protracted cheering'; with addresses presented in vellum, and toasts drunk so often and to so many different people and causes, the main facts of Harry's coming-of-age emerge as follows:

Preparations for the great occasion began fully eighteen months before the day itself, and the Hall was—if not rebuilt —certainly substantially altered, enlarged and improved in order to accommodate Harry's many guests, and to bring it into line with the most modernized of ancestral homes.

It must also be remembered that the family had not been in residence at the Hall for several years, and to many local inhabitants it must have seemed that the great days of the first Marquis might have passed away for ever. Therefore the excitement of the inhabitants over Harry's twenty-first birthday was not only an expression of affection, but was also their way of demonstrating to Harry that they longed for the old and spacious days to return, when their Squire was the head of his family of tenants and the Hall was the centre of the county's social life.

Among the improvements were 'a new kitchen, of noble proportions, with adjacent offices, fitted with all the necessary apparatus for keeping up the usages and customs of old English hospitality in the Baronial style'; 'bells and speaking tubes, communicating with all parts of the mansion, from between thirty and forty of the principal apartments'; new and enlarged stabling; and the general restoration of both the interior and exterior of the mansion.

The comment made by *The Loughborough Monitor* that 'We are informed that all the accounts were discharged on or before the 18th of the present month' may or may not have had significance, in view of what was to come later, but there seems no reason to doubt that Harry, at this time, was not only a liberal spender but also a punctual settler. In accordance with tradition, all those who had been engaged on these alterations and additions were invited to attend the festivities on the Thursday, as were, of course, 'his lordship's tenantry, workmen, labourers, and "the jolly colliers" of Moira, together with two thousand Sunday School children, with their teachers'.

The celebrations went on throughout the entire week, beginning on Monday, 20 July, and reaching their climax on Harry's birthday on the Wednesday.

On the evening of his birthday a private dinner was held at the Hall and was followed by a fancy-dress ball. 'The dining-room was splendidly decorated for the occasion, and illuminated by means of chandeliers of infinite number and variety. The sideboard groaned under a display of massive gold and silver plate, and the dinner itself occupied the attention of seven London cooks, and was of the most *recherché* character.'

The fancy-dress ball was held in the library, which was lit by hundreds of wax candles, whilst 'mirrors glittered in every recess, and garlands of flowers festooned the walls'. Music was supplied by Nicholson's quadrille band, assisted by Messrs Coote and Tinney's, of London and against this picturesque background turbaned Turks, hooded monks and rollicking cavaliers supported on their arms exquisitely gowned Indian princesses, Spanish dancers and dainty shepherdesses. Lady Alice Hill went as 'La Folie', with coxcomb cap and bells; Lady Constance Hastings appeared as 'Undine'; Lady North as 'Christmas' in a white dress flecked with snow and with a robin redbreast picking crumbs from off her shoulder; and—by way of contrast—Lady Edith Hastings as 'Midsummer Night', in a costume of white and blue tulle, over silver tissue, and with a magnificent circle of diamond stars in her hair.

The central character was Harry himself, and he appeared as Charles II, in a dress composed of blue and scarlet velvet with silver lace, richly studded with brilliants and carrying a diamond-hilted sword. He was in his element, the centre of attraction and the recipient of endless expressions of goodwill. He was gay and charming, flushed and happy, but still wearing that boyish and rather wistful expression which the women found so irresistible in him.

The company numbered between 200 and 300, a superb supper was served at one o'clock, and dancing was then resumed and continued until the morning, and the last of the guests—some of whom had come from as far as 30 miles away—did not call for their carriages until after seven o'clock on the Thursday morning.

All this was followed by a tenants' and tradespeoples' ball, with Harry and his sisters in attendance and being warmly congratulated on all sides, and with their healths drunk at midnight to the accompaniment of prolonged and tumultuous cheering.

About all these festivities there must have been a genuine touch of merrie England; and a joyous and spontaneous eruption of warm-heartedness that was in no way contrived. Harry was no speech-maker, but he was called upon to reply to many toasts, and all this he did with a boyish charm and an infectious gaiety. Like his father, he was a good mixer; and like his father, he could talk to his poorest tenants in their own language.

Harry, indeed, was in his element. He was the centre of attraction and was being accepted on all sides as a jolly good fellow. This was an immense stimulant to him, and while the week of celebrations lasted, and the honest cheers of his tenants rang out across the parkland of Donington, startling the deer, he must have felt a considerable sense of elation and perhaps even one of purpose. But birthdays are soon over, and a mood of elation soon passes unless it is restimulated by other similar events. With the week ended, and the little community settling back into its rural calm, and with the call of London in his ears, Harry soon became bored by life at the Hall. There was the racing at Goodwood, the yachting at Cowes, and all the excitement of being at the centre of society.

His financial position, now that he had come into his full inheritance, was highly satisfactory. Throughout the era of the first Marquis, the estate had been crippled by the debts which his generosity had incurred. 'His ample fortune absolutely sank under the benevolence of his nature', to quote the phrase of a biographer, and money was still scarce in the time of the second Marquis. But capital had accumulated during Harry's minority, and now, at the age of twenty-one, he was worth something in the nature of a quarter of a million, with all assets included; and his income was in the region of £20,000 a year. On the debit side was the very heavy cost of upkeep of his many properties, none of which was run with any sense of economy. A little more organization and supervision would have made him a warm man, with income enough to have satisfied even the most extravagant tastes; but from the outset he chose to ignore all advice, and to take no interest at all in the business side of his affairs. Even so, he was rich by any standards, and his future looked pleasant indeed. The world was at his feet.

But Donington was not the world. There were wider fields to conquer and other spheres in which he could become famous. His vanity and his passion for gambling craved for satisfaction, and were insatiable. But now that he was wealthy, he knew that he held one of the aces in any gambler's hand, for he could afford to lose more than his opponent, and that is a formidable weapon in any game of chance. If a man's ambition is to break the bank, it is an immense advantage to him if he is richer than the bank, for no one dares to play 'double or quits' with a gambler who can afford to go on losing until he wins.

He had already registered his racing colours—scarlet and white hoop, with white cap—and had run a few moderate horses in the name of 'Mr Weysford'. His friendship with John Day, the famous trainer of Danebury, was ripening, and one of the best birthday presents which he had received had been the notification that he had been elected to membership of the Jockey Club. But at twenty-one he was still apprehensive of taking the plunge, which John Day kept urging on him, and entering upon ownership in a big way. In his heart, he knew that his decision to do so could not be long delayed. The turf was his destiny.

His thoughts turned to London and to Newmarket. London, for the time being at least, offered a fruitful field for dissipation, extravagance and the flouting of convention. But such a life could not in itself provide him with the scope that his vanity demanded, even though he was now a recognized leader in the Prince's set. To become famous, really famous, and to be known throughout the whole of England as a true swell; and to be recognized wherever he went and to be acclaimed as he had been acclaimed in Donington—this was an ambition that could not easily be satisfied. Money alone could not buy him universal recognition, and his vanity demanded that such recognition should not be simply the result of wild improvidence. There must be dangers to face, a battle to be fought and an enemy to conquer. And again his thoughts turned to the turf. Here was the ideal battle-ground; and here was the ideal enemy, the Ring, waiting disdainfully to take him on, and laughing already at his novice efforts at plunging on alleged 'good things'.

Well, he would show them that he was made of sterner stuff than they imagined. The Ring, they said, was indestructible. No one had ever got the better of it, not even Lord George Bentinck in his hey-day.

But Harry Hastings could do it—and he would. Furthermore, he would do it according to his code of life, with a casual smile of indifference. Others might laugh when they triumphed or yelp when they were beaten, but Harry himself would remain imperturbable, true to the traditions of Eton and the heroes of Whyte-Melville's novels.

Yet at this moment his plans were still unformed. Donington did not hold him for long. His house-party broke up, the temporary stables were dismantled and the triumphant arches and the flags were taken down in the main street of the little town. Harry returned to London and took up the threads of his old life. For the moment the turf could wait.

He was welcomed back by his cronies and took up residence once again at Limmer's. Although he spent a certain amount of time in the company of Henry Chaplin and the Prince of Wales, his intimate friends were Bobby Shafto and Freddy Granville, and his chief rival, so far as cock-fighting was concerned, was the young Duke of Hamilton, a character almost as wild and extravagant as Harry himself. Harry also contrived to surround himself with a curious collection of foreign Princes, Barons and Ambassadors, who looked upon him as their guide to the seamier side of London life. There was Count Kilmanseg, said to be the best whist player in Europe, the young Prince Hohenlohe, Baron Spaum, who was destined to become the Commander-in-Chief of the Austrian Navy, an amiable Russian aristocrat named Count Adelberg, and numerous young bucks from the fashionable regiments. Freddy Granville was perhaps Harry's closest friend—a typical English gentleman with his wavy blond hair, his frank and open countenance, his genial manner and the cherubic expression which so belied his moral outlook. Women adored him, as they adored Harry, blushed demurely when transfixed by his innocent blue eyes and frequently woke up—quite literally—to discover that he was an artist in the matter of feminine seduction.

Cock-fighting and visits to the dens of vice in the East End and the 'rookeries' off the Gray's Inn Road were the chief diversions of the Hastings set. Within a few weeks of returning to London from Donington, Harry was taken to court and fined £5 for fighting a 'main' of cocks in his private room on a Sunday, but these contests took place for the most part at Faultless's pit in Endell Street. Here Harry would match his favourite champion, The Sweep, against the best that the Duke of Hamilton could produce, and here he earned for himself the much-prized title of being 'a perfect Cocker'. To live up to this title was now becoming one of the most important things in Harry's life, for it suggested recklessness allied to sportsmanship, and bravado suitably cloaked by an air of casual indifference. In short, panache.

One of the most daring exploits in which 'the perfect Cocker' might indulge was an expedition to the lowest slums in London. Here there was real danger to be encountered, even if the visitor went in the company of a detective or enjoyed the protection of a hired pugilist. In the alleyways surrounding the London Docks, and especially along the notorious Ratcliff Highway (now St George's Street), even the police walked in pairs, and the lone traveller stood an even-money chance of being not only robbed but also violently assaulted. Drunken sailors of all nationalities staggered from inn to inn with knives in their belts or fought over the filthy prostitutes whom they encountered, and there were 'sing-song caves', dancing booths and opium dens, as well as brothels which offered opportunities for vice and perversion unrivalled even in Port Said.

The arrival of a party of swells on a sightseeing trip was bitterly resented, and nothing was more indicative of Harry Hastings' charm and friendliness than the manner in which he could enter an East End tavern and transform an atmosphere of baleful hostility into one of jovial good-fellowship. In this, more than anything else perhaps, he revealed himself as 'a perfect Cocker'.

Donald Shaw, a young subaltern who accompanied Harry Hastings on many of these expeditions and had the highest opinion of Harry's warm-heartedness and generosity, described a typical incident in his book, *London in the Sixties*, which he wrote many years later, when nearly all his old cronies were dead. Harry and his party, immaculate in evening dress, opera cloaks and hats, arrive at the most notorious tavern of all, The Jolly Sailors, in Ship Alley, by Well Close Square. They are warned at the door that they will be ill-advised to enter, but Harry and Bobby Shafto ignore the warning and the party of swells saunters in.

The scene that presented itself was not an encouraging one; perched on a rickety stool was a fiddler scraping with an energy only to be attained by incessant application to a mug of Hollands that stood at his elbow, and to which he appeared to resort frequently. Polkaing in every grotesque attitude were some twenty couples, the males attired for the most part in sea-boots and jerseys, their partners with dishevelled hair and bloated countenances, all more or less under the influence of gin and beer; here and there couples apparently too overcome to continue the giddy joy, were propped against the wall gurgling out blasphemy and snatches of ribald song, whilst in the alcoves or leaning over the trestle table were knots of men smoking, cursing, swilling strong drinks, and casting wicked eyes at the intruders. ' 'Aven't they a leg of mutton and currant dumplin's at 'ome wi'out comin' 'ere?' inquired a ferocious ruffian. 'What for brings 'em a-messing about 'ere, 'd like to know?'

'Blast me if I wudn't knife 'em; what say you, lads?' replied a stump-ended figure, stiffening himself.

'Bide a while, lads; let's make 'em show their colours. What cheer, there?' shouted a huge Scandinavian as a contingent, detaching itself from the main body, lurched towards the explorers.

'What cheer, my hearties?' sang back Hastings, and, with a diplomacy that might have done credit to a Richelieu, the entire party were fraternizing within a minute.

It has been already remarked that one of the curiosities of the Victorian period was that the highest and lowest in the land understood each other much better than they understood the newly-developing, smug and self-satisfied middle classes, for this was altogether a new type of Englishman.

On a public holiday such as the Derby at Epsom, carriage-folk and beggars rubbed shoulders on the Downs as a matter of course. There was an affinity between them because they understood each other. Certainly as regards the men, they shared a common interest in drinking, gambling and fornication; and in many respects they talked the same language.

On the face of it, it would be hard to imagine a more incongruous figure in the filthy interior of an East End drinking dive than the fragile, casual and dandified figure of Harry Hastings. Yet within minutes he would be talking to those present in their own language, and they would be toasting him with shouts of 'Good old 'Arry!' The affinity was complete.

His acceptance as a good fellow built up his ego. He paid for it, of course. The drinks were on him, and everyone was included in his hospitality. Even so, it is not so easy to buy the *genuine* friendliness of East End labourers—and they did *genuinely* like Harry Hastings. Sprawled across the bar, so elegant and refined, and talking in his aristocratic Oxford drawl, they could yet accept him as one of themselves. He laughed at their jokes, told filthier ones himself, drank with the best of them, and cheered as loudly as any man in the room when some drunken harlot tripped up over her dirty skirts and lay prostrate on the floor with her legs in the air and her loins laid bare.

Harry saw in all this a means of demonstrating his manliness. He was never so happy as when in some low dive or cellar, betting £500 or £1,000 on the number of sewer rats a terrier could kill in an hour and graciously accepting the Master of Ceremonies' request that 'the Markis will take the Chair'. Then with six cases of champagne ordered and consumed, and everyone a little drunk, the toast would be given again and again, 'The Markis—Gawd bless 'im.' And the whole company would unite to sing 'For He's a Jolly Good Fellow'.

Thus Harry spent his nights in his chosen heaven.

Of course the cock-pits of Endell Street, Drury Lane and other such venues offered him an opportunity for gambling, and he could match a bird of his for £1,000 against one of the young Duke of Hamilton's; but it is doubtful if this was his only satisfaction. It was not the sight of a dead bird in a pit, or of the Duke of Hamilton counting out a bundle of notes, that filled Harry with satisfaction. No—it was the sound of hoarse cheering, and the cry that went up as the company applauded his success. 'The Markis—Gawd bless 'im.'

Harry was always a renowned practical joker, and in common with so many other practical jokers he quickly became peevish and resentful if the joke went against him. This is only natural in those who are normally spoilt and fawned upon, for they are too accustomed to getting their own way in everything. An evening that started out gaily with Harry often ended in uproar and recrimination, when the practical joking went too far and someone got hurt.

A story that was often told of Harry at that time was of how he bought 200 sewer rats from a professional rat-catcher named Jimmy Shaw, of Windmill Street; and how he and Bobby Shafto then carried them through the streets in sacks and smuggled them late at night into Mott's dancing rooms in Foley Street, when the festivities were at their height.

The rooms were crowded with a number of young swells, including Lord Londesborough and his set, who were dancing with certain well-known harlots, and these young ladies were making a great show of their femininity and allure, ogling their companions and simpering prettily as they waltzed and pirouetted daintily round the room.

Harry crept stealthily into the cellars and turned the gas off at the mains, and when the rooms were plunged into darkness, Bobby Shafto released the rats, which ran squeaking in panic across the dance floor, viciously nipping at the ankles of anyone whom they found in their way. The dancing-rooms were crowded with couples, and the panic which ensued was so great that the police had to be summoned as it was feared that a riot had broken out. A number of the women fainted and had to be carried into the street, and several were badly bitten as well.

The evening in question is typical of Harry's activities at this time, for it was not yet midnight, and so Harry was eager for further diversions. While the police were trying to sort out the confusion at Mott's, Harry and Bobby Shafto hailed a hansom and drove down to Cremorne, where they were just in time to take part in a fight which had broken out there, due—as was so often the case in those days—to one young buck having brought down his cane on another's top hat and smashed it in. This was considered a very comical exploit and always guaranteed to cause much laughter and to start a brawl.

Once again the police arrived to try to restore order, and when things had quietened down Harry and Bobby Shafto drove back to a coffee room near Piccadilly Circus where they joined forces with two of their cronies, wild Scottish subalterns named John Stewart, of the 72nd Highlanders, and John McNair, of the 79th, renowned as the handsomest man in the Highland Brigade. It was now nearly dawn, so they settled down to a meal of eggs and bacon while they discussed what other practical jokes they might play. A drayman's cart chanced to pass by at this moment, so they seized upon it, rewarded the astonished drayman with a sovereign, and the promise to return it to him shortly, and then drove the cart to a pile of gravel which they had seen on a building site near Scotland Yard. They filled the cart with gravel, and then took it to the house in St John's Wood of a famous brothel-keeper, Kate Hamilton. (This was not her place of business, which was situated at 8 New Coventry Street, but was in fact the place where she lived in discreet respectability with an elderly lover.) They tipped the load of gravel on to her front steps, and then loudly rang the bell. When a sleepy servant finally opened the door, they pushed McNair inside, where he collapsed in a drunken heap, and then decided to call it a night.

Harry retired to Limmer's Hotel, and rose the next morning at mid-day to partake of his favourite breakfast—mackerel friend in gin, caviare on devilled toast and an *hors d'œuvre* named 'Fixed Bayonets', the whole washed down by a claret cup. It was neither a diet nor a way of life which was calculated to sustain health or promote longevity.

In all this, Harry was only trying to live up to the Regency tradition, when young bucks went about London committing unprovoked acts of violence and hooliganism; and to the legendary feats of the young Crockford set, and particularly to those of aristocrats such as Lord Waterford, who had been freely acknowledged as the greatest practical joker of his day.

The young Lord Waterford had been just the sort of rebel Harry admired. An old Etonian, who had been a champion oarsman and boxer while at school, he had also displayed an exceptional talent for practical joking. He once put aniseed on the hooves of a clergyman's horse and then 'hunted' him through London with a pack of bloodhounds, and on another occasion he caused the greatest commotion ever witnessed in the Haymarket (an area not unaccustomed to scenes of riot and abandon) by walking into the Turk's Head tavern and offering a free butt of sherry to any woman present who could prove to his satisfaction that she was a harlot. It was not long before the women were fighting each other, Lord Waterford was fighting their escorts and the police were fighting everyone indiscriminately. It was a scene not altogether lacking in piquancy.

Harry Hastings had neither the physique nor the inventiveness of Lord Waterford. He was trying to prove himself to be a real buck in society, but he was not doing it very well; and the fact that neither Henry Chaplin nor the Prince were ever very impressed by his practical jokes merely aggravated the inferiority complex that was growing within him. The resentment which he felt against Henry grew ever stronger.

There was also another way in which Henry Chaplin irritated Harry Hastings, and increased his sense of inferiority. Henry, as befitted a close friend of royalty, was most careful how he chose his friends. There are always those in any community who try to ingratiate themselves with their social superiors, and Henry Chaplin had a lofty disdain for all such upstarts and social climbers and carefully avoided them.

Harry was quite different. Although an aristocrat himself, he had no objection to the parvenus of society, and he was quite content to accept the friendship and hospitality of someone who was palpably not a gentleman. If the fellow were amiable and entertaining and a good host, then Harry was perfectly willing to dine with him, and accompany him to the races. It also amused him to observe the scandalized glances which were often thrown in his direction when he did so.

More and more, during these early days of dissipation in London, he found himself attracted to the comforts and good living which he encountered in one of the most opulently appointed houses in Mayfair—situated at No 2 Hill Street, Berkeley Square. This was the home of the money-lender, Henry Padwick, and a residence much patronized by the younger members of the aristocracy who found themselves financially embarrassed.

Harry Hastings had no need to borrow money, and he accepted Padwick's frequent invitations to Hill Street because he enjoyed the company he met there. This was not the sort of invitation which Henry Chaplin or the Prince would ever have accepted. Padwick, to them, was an upstart and a bounder, and they warned Harry that he should not be deceived by Padwick's amiability and extravagant hospitality. They looked down their noses when Harry Hastings referred to him.

Harry Hastings was annoyed by their disapproval. Henry Padwick, as far as Harry was concerned, was a delightful fellow, broad-minded and sympathetic.

It had been while he was still at Oxford that Harry had first encountered Henry Padwick, when he had been introduced to Harry by Charles Symonds, the owner of one of the town's most popular livery stables. The introductions may, or may not, have been contrived. It probably was, for Henry Padwick was always in search of wealthy young aristocrats to add to his collection of possible clients for the future. He was a good deal older than Harry Hastings and a clever and sophisticated man of the world. In his younger days he had been on the perimeter, as it were, of the famous 'Danebury Confederacy' which had flourished under the aegis of the celebrated ex-pugilist, John Gully, in the 1840s, and acting both as bookmakers and backers had so confused the racing fraternity that no one had ever quite known what the Confederacy were up to, other than the devious art of making a great deal of money out of racing. Padwick had been a crony of Gully's, and had been involved in some of his obscure transactions, but he had only taken up ownership of racehorses in 1849.

It was Henry Padwick's custom at all times to combine business with pleasure. He mixed freely with all the young bloods of the turf, flattered them by his friendship, and gave them much fatherly advice. He was tolerant of their indiscretions and most sympathetic to them over their losses. Then, when things became really bad, they strolled down Hill Street to visit him at No 2, and there drank his vintage port and poured out their troubles to him. A loan was always readily forthcoming, so long as the security was good and the young debtor's family could be relied upon to underwrite him in the event of any unforeseen catastrophe.

In these early days of the Hastings story, Henry Padwick is no more than a shadow cast across Harry's path. He is seen only occasionally, as he waits in the wings. Later he was to be branded as the villain of the piece, the *éminence grise* lurking behind Harry and manipulating his affairs, but since his activities are of such importance later on, one may spend a few moments examining him now.

Short and of stocky build, he was, in his middle fifties, a man of distinctive and indeed of imposing appearance. He was charming, courteous and a good listener, witty and amusing in conversation, an attentive host with a flair for giving his guest his full attention and implying that what was being discussed was of the greatest interest to him. There was about him almost a touch of the Disraeli charm—and charm is a quality which so many of the central characters in the Hastings story seem to share.

He had been born at Horsham, in Sussex, the son of a butcher, but he had been well educated and early in life had learnt to ape the manners and tastes of a country gentleman. As a young man, he had trained to become a lawyer (he would certainly have made a clever and persuasive advocate), but he deserted jurisprudence in favour of money-lending. In this, he was a product of his age. The idle aristocracy and gentry needed horse-racing as an outlet for their gambling instinct, bookmakers as a medium for indulging this instinct and finally money-lenders who would help them out of their difficulties when they lost more than they could afford. It was Crockford who raised the status of the bookmaker, and gave him affluence and a standing in society. Henry Padwick did the same with money-lending.

He learnt much from Crockford's methods. He, too, operated from the heart of Mayfair, in a house which was a byword for its lavishness and good taste. He, too, employed one of the best cooks in London, and he, too, kept one of the best cellars. He, too, did not therefore need to go touting for clients. They came to him and were hospitably received. Like Crockford, he had his private intelligence service which kept him fully informed of the exact financial status of all his clients. He was honest, as Crockford was honest, and reliable, for neither could afford to be anything else. He lacked Crockford's cunning, perhaps, but made up for it by being almost a gentleman, whilst 'Crocky' could never hide from anyone the fact that he came from the lowest slums of London.

Padwick, like Crockford, had a weakness for women, but whereas Crockford seduced at random simply to satisfy his carnal desires, and won for himself women of high-birth and refinement merely by a display of brutish sexual prowess, Henry Padwick was a far vainer man, whose ego needed feminine flattery and adoration. Padwick sometimes allowed a woman to make a fool of him, but Crockford rarely made this mistake.

Both were gamblers, both made immense fortunes out of gambling, and particularly out of horse-racing, yet neither had any judgment as far as racehorses were concerned. Each turned to ownership as a relaxation, and each failed altogether to apply to it the caution and cunning which they brought to their business transactions.

'Neither a lender nor a borrower be' was *not* a slogan which

Padwick observed, for in fact he was both. His policy was to borrow money and pay 2 per cent on it, and then to loan it out at rates which varied from 20 per cent to his intimates to 60 per cent to comparative strangers whom he could trust, and at anything up to 500 per cent to rogues, dupes or clients whose potential for repayment was in doubt. He had little difficulty in borrowing money himself, either from his rich associates in the Danebury Confederacy such as John Gully, or from the banks. Victorian bankers, when they loaned money to their clients, were accustomed to receive no more than 1 or $1\frac{1}{2}$ per cent, so that Padwick's 2 per cent was always acceptable, especially in view of the fact that he could always be relied upon.

But Henry Padwick did not deal only in currency. If one of his aristocratic clients found himself unable to settle in cash, then Henry Padwick would suggest, with seeming magnanimity and a disarming friendliness, that his client should make over to him instead a few of his racehorses, a hundred acres or so of his land or even some desirable country mansion. In this way he became the owner of Spye Park, which was one of the most delightful country estates in the South of England; and on the walls of his town house in Hill Street there hung more than one Old Master which he had acquired in settlement of a debt.

Harry found Henry Padwick a delightful companion for many reasons. Both were fascinated by the turf, and both shared the ambition to win the Derby. Harry admired Padwick because he was one of the most fearless plungers on the turf. He had won £80,000 on his filly, Virago, in 1854 (and lost it all in a matter of months on a stock exchange tip which a novice would have looked upon with suspicion), and he was always ready to join Harry Hastings in a game of cards or dice. When Henry Chaplin and the Prince were attending their balls and dinner parties, and mingling only with society's *crème de la crème*, Harry Hastings would often drop in at No 2 Hill Street to spend an evening with Henry Padwick and talk about racing.

It is quite possible that at this time Henry Padwick genuinely enjoyed the company of his young guest, and the discussion which they shared. He delighted in the company of young people, and, like Harry, he was a good mixer. If Harry brought with him some dissolute rake either from Belgravia or the gutter, Henry Padwick was at once able to make the visitor feel at home, for such is the power of charm. It would be absurd to suggest that Padwick was not motivated by self-interest, or that he was not already looking ahead to the time when Harry Hastings himself might be forced to visit Hill Street on business, and not for pleasure. But for the time being Padwick was more than content to remain as the genial host and the fatherly adviser to the novice owner.

In 1863 the shadow of things to come had not yet fallen across the life of Harry Hastings. Henry Chaplin might scorn Henry Padwick, and dismiss him as a dangerous scoundrel and no gentleman, but Harry was less fussy over the company which he kept. As the year progressed, it must have become increasingly obvious to Harry that he was growing further and further away from Henry Chaplin and the Prince of Wales. Henry was maturing rapidly, and with his growing sense of responsibility and his fairly extensive knowledge of the world outside Mayfair and the hunting country (there can have been very few members of Society at that time who had had actual experience of the American Civil War), he was rapidly losing interest in the schoolboy acts of dissipation which still delighted Harry Hastings and his set. Albert Edward was also losing his taste for low life, if indeed he had ever really enjoyed it. Not that he had settled down to a life of domestic bliss, but rather to that pleasant round of the country houses of England and the foreign capitals of Europe which was to be his delight for years to come. He was intrigued by the company of pretty women, of whom there were so many in Society or on the stage who were only too willing to accommodate him that he really had no need whatever to go a-whoring round Leicester Square with Harry Hastings, a pastime which had very soon lost its attraction in the first place.

Both Bertie and Henry Chaplin were great sportsmen. In October they went deer-stalking in Scotland, and throughout the winter they hunted and shot. Both were active-minded men who liked to be doing something, even if it was no more than attending the endless run of fashionable dinner parties, balls and opera parties of the London season. There were visits to Cowes in August, and much pleasurable time could be spent in their clubs. Together they led a full life.

Harry, busily engaged in his own peculiar activities in the East End, and becoming more and more absorbed in the more futile exploits of a gambler's life, must often have felt that he was no longer holding his own as a leader of the Prince's set.

His entertaining was as lavish as anyone else's, but it was inclined to be wild and unruly. Had he been dedicated to hunting, as was his father, he might have spent many happy months at Donington Hall, but the only part of hunting which really appealed to Harry was the drinking that went on after the chase had ended. He disliked the effort of getting up early enough in the morning to ride a horse and still more the effort required to remain seated on it over any distance of country.

Perhaps Harry began now to realize that he was in danger of becoming a playboy whose antics were beginning to pall. Bertie was married, and it was obvious that 'Magnifico' would be snapped up before long. He would then have a fashionable wedding, which would be attended by the Prince, and settle down to being the Squire of Blankney. Added to this, his strong sense of *noblesse oblige* would almost certainly lead him into work of public service. Henry Chaplin would live to a ripe old age and die, honoured and revered, with at least a column devoted to his obituary in *The Times*.

And what had Harry to look forward to at this time? More important still, how could he hope to retain his place as a leader of the fast set?

He could marry brilliantly, and bask for a time in the reflected glory of a beautiful wife. This was certainly a prospect which appealed to him. But it was the turf which remained as the perfect sphere for his self-expression. *Here* he could win the great races that would make his name safe with posterity. *Here* he could show his own special brand of courage and defiance by betting more heavily than any gambler had ever done before and winning or losing without any visible signs of emotion.

To lead in his Derby winner to the cheers of the crowd, while Bertie and Henry watched in envy and the bookmakers counted their losses ruefully—that would be the supreme moment. Then, in truth, would 'The Markis' be in the chair. And then, in truth, would Harry Hastings become 'a perfect Cocker'.

CHAPTER FOUR

THE CALL OF THE TURF

The honour of being 'the man who belongs to' the Duke, or the Earl, or little Lecturer, was no burden to him. He took quite naturally to the turf from the first, enfolded under the wing of Danebury. In 1862 not six people at Newmarket knew who the slim lad was on the grey cob; but the Ring soon saw that he was a veritable Hampshire ambassador when he put down the money so unflinchingly on a Danebury pot.

AGAIN and again, as one traces the events of the Hastings story, one returns to the obituary notice which 'The Druid' wrote after Harry's death. 'The Druid' understood men as he understood racing, and he wrote with heart and compassion. To him the story of the man 'who belonged to' the Duke and little Lecturer was one of infinite sadness.

The turf was always Harry Hastings' destiny. With his love of gambling and his desire for popularity and adulation, the only surprise was that his entry into racing was comparatively cautious and on a moderate scale. In due course he would be ready to do battle with the Ring in a way which was to astonish them, but in 1862, with his Oxford days only just behind him, he was content to watch and listen. The slim lad on the grey cob was happy enough to learn his trade under the all-embracing wing of Danebury.

It was while he was still an undergraduate at Christ Church that Harry had been introduced to the famous trainer, John Day of Danebury, by his guardian, Earl Howe. Howe was not a great racing man himself, but he was a close friend of the Duke of Beaufort, who was a keen turf enthusiast and a prominent member of the Jockey Club, the ruling body in racing. The Duke had horses in training with John Day at Danebury, and it was at Newmarket one afternoon that Earl Howe introduced Harry to John Day with the remark that if ever Harry fancied buying a few horses, he could not do better than to seek the guidance of Day.

Harry had extended his hand as the trainer touched his cap

with deference. It was a momentous meeting for each of them, and they must have gazed at each other appraisingly. Harry had been impressed both by Day's reputation and by his obvious shrewdness. Here was clearly a man who knew a great deal not only about the art of preparing a horse for a race, but also about the best way of backing it at the most advantageous odds. The Ring had a considerable respect for his astuteness.

The stories of the betting coups which had been engineered at Danebury had already by then become a part of turf history. Above all, the notorious 'Danebury Confederacy' which had been led by the ex-pugilist, John Gully, and his cronies, had taken a fortune out of the Ring. John Gully, who had risen from being an inmate of the Fleet Prison to become one of the wealthiest and most respected owners on the turf, died in the spring of 1863. The Mayor and Corporation of Pontefract escorted his coffin to the grave, and the racing world mourned the loss of 'a true sportsman and a sterling Englishman', unmindful for the moment of his more dubious enterprises.

On one thing all were agreed. The golden era of Danebury was ended. There would never be another Danebury owner who would bet so fearlessly or so successfully.

There was thus a great tradition for Harry Hastings to follow when he was himself taken under the wing of Danebury. He was assured of expert tuition in the art of backing horses, and he placed himself in the hands of those who had waged a long and successful campaign against the Ring.

There had been Days at Danebury for generations—all racing men, who had ridden, trained, gambled and schemed. A talented family. A shrewd and dedicated family. Small and wizened little men with racing in their blood. Cheerful, hardworking and—for the most part—honest, but martinets in their way.

As a family, they had never heard of Keate and his methods of enforcing discipline at Eton, but their attitude to discipline was the same. They believed that stable lads only understood the birch, and racehorses only understood the whip. You drove them both, as you drove yourself, to the limit of endurance, in the certainty that hard work had never killed man or beast. Because they themselves were tough and sturdy countrymen without any great gifts of imagination, they never realized that hard and relentless exercise can sour a high-spirited horse, and that discipline, when it is excessive, can produce a mood of sulky rebellion. Indeed, they probably never fully realized that no two men, and no two horses, are ever quite the same, and that what is effective treatment for one may be useless for another.

Grandfather Day, a John Bull of a man who trained for Lord Palmerston, had founded the family tradition for riding and training in the eighteenth century, and his two sons, John Barham and Sam Day, had carried on the tradition. Both had become jockeys, and both had learnt their trade the hard way, hacking a hundred miles to a meeting before they rode and earning a pittance for their trouble. Sam showed some restraint in the saddle, but John Barham scorned finesse. He was at his best when riding some brute of a horse that fought him all the way down to the start, and was soon taught who was the master and who the servant. Both brothers earned a reputation for being 'good rough riders'. Not for them was the quiet patience of the great Jem Robinson, nor the artistry of Fordham. They used whip and spur and never yielded an inch. But they were honest and resolute and always gave of their best; John Bull stock, as their father had been before them.

Sam Day won the Derby three times, starting with Gustavus in 1821 and finishing with Gully's Pyrrhus the First in 1846, when he was dragged back from retirement by brother John, who made him reduce his weight from eleven stone six pounds to under eight stone seven pounds in the space of two months in order to ride this Danebury 'pot'.

John Barham Day himself never won the Derby as a jockey, but he won the Oaks five times, and gained for himself the nickname of 'Honest John'. When he took up training he moved to Danebury, and there found patrons in plenty who were willing to put their horses in his care.

Chief among these had been Lord George Bentinck and John Gully. Lord George spent a great deal of money improving the gallops at Danebury in the eighteen-thirties, and John Barham Day repaid him by winning some fine races. But the pair had too much in common, being both self-willed and stubborn, and in the end Lord George removed the whole of his string from Danebury and sent them to be trained instead at Goodwood.

Old John Barham Day had had three sons, each of whom carried on the family tradition of training racehorses, and he had retired in favour of his eldest son, young John Day, by the time that Harry Hastings came on the scene. Young John, born in the year of Waterloo, was already middle-aged when he first met the young Marquis, and there was already much of old John about him. He had learnt a great deal from his father, but old John could not teach young John what he himself had never learnt—that some horses should be trained and ridden with gentleness and sympathy

When Harry Hastings was first introduced to John Day, he must have viewed the veteran trainer with awe. When John Day suggested that it behove a young peer of Harry's wealth and standing to own a string of racehorses, Harry readily agreed; and when John advised the purchase of certain animals and announced how they would be trained and for what races they would be entered, Harry concurred without remonstrance. Despite his upbringing, Harry was no expert on horseflesh. The only aspect of racing which really interested him was the betting, and he had sense enough to realize that he had a great deal to learn about this specialized field of operations.

Thus it was that in 1862 not six people at Newmarket recognized the slim lad on the grey cob. The role of kindly mentor suited John Day well. That of humble pupil also suited Harry Hastings—for a time.

As they walked together towards the parade ring in these early days, with arms linked and the youngster hanging on every word which the old man had to say, they must have looked almost like father and son, had it not been for John's outward concession to the required deference which befitted their very different social grades. The pretence that Harry was the master and John Day the servant was always maintained. Meantime Harry was told no more than it was necessary for him to know, either about his own horses or other people's.

The change that gradually came over Harry Hastings after his coming of age in 1863 must have given John Day much food for thought. Outwardly their relationship remained the same. Harry was no longer quite so slim, and he no longer rode the grey cob, but he still took his trainer's arm with that same charming and characteristic gesture, and he still laughed and talked as gaily as before. But the appearance of master and servant was no longer a pretence. Harry's manner, although never dictatorial, was now becoming authoritative and assured. Moreover the size of his bets began to stagger his trainer—a man who had seen heavy wagering in plenty in the days of John Gully and the 'Confederacy'.

Harry's manner of betting, John Day could only condemn, for Harry's conceit made him revel in the newly found deference of the Ring, and he loved to see his runner made favourite. This led him into the fundamental error of accepting under the odds, an error which Gully and his cronies would never have committed.

But Harry had learnt quickly, despite his outward appearance of indifference, and the time was not far off when a leader of the Ring was to say to him, 'Heaven has been very kind to you, my lord, for you look a fool but you aren't one.'

Thus it became gradually apparent both to John Day and the Ring that Harry Hastings had a natural flair for assessing form. And although his vanity caused him to trade at under the odds, it also made him reject the advice of other people. In this he showed wisdom, for in racing the backer should always go by what he sees rather than by what he hears, and this Harry Hastings proceeded to do.

Harry, of course, heard a great deal. There were any number of touts and racing acquaintances eager to whisper secrets in his ear, but for the most part he was content to back his own judgment. The popular belief, which lingered on long after he was dead, that Harry Hastings ruined himself by his ignorance of racing cannot be supported by the facts. Indeed it might almost be said of him that the only occasions in his life on which he showed a mature judgment were when he was assessing a handicap. He had an exceptional facility for weighing up what is known in racing parlance as 'collateral form'.

The Ring itself must have watched this growing shrewdness and authority with the same interest as did John Day. This slim lad who had set out to do battle with them so casually and whom they had at first looked upon almost with pity in his youthful attempts to live up to the great Danebury tradition, was not perhaps such a pale shadow of John Gully as they had imagined him to be. And he was not quite such a fool as he looked.

Thus the battle was joined. And although there were none in the Ring who had any doubts about its final outcome, there were yet those amongst its leaders who—by 1864—were beginning to realize that some of the engagements in this battle were likely to be bitter, and that the losses—on *both* sides—might well be heavy before this particular struggle between ruthless professionalism and carefree amateurism was finally to be decided in favour of the former.

Harry Hastings became an owner officially in 1863; and he was elected a member of the Jockey Club on his twenty-first birthday in July of the same year. His colours were registered as 'scarlet and white hoop, white cap',[1] and these were destined for a few short years to be as well known as any on the turf.

His ownership had really started in the previous year, however, when he raced under the name of 'Mr Weysford' and his colours were 'scarlet, grey spots'. It was in July 1862 that he attended a meeting at Southampton, and on John Day's advice bought a filly called Consternation out of a selling plate for ninety-five guineas.

She ran her first race for him in the Pavilion Plate at the Brighton meeting in August, when she was ridden by J. Grimshaw, started without a quotation in the betting and finished down the field.

Consternation ran on eleven other occasions for 'Mr Weysford' in 1862, and won twice for him—at Dover in a small race over hurdles and in a match at Warwick in September. In this latter race the filly was ridden by George Fordham. It was the beginning of what was destined to be a notable association. The filly started at 5 to 2 *on*, and her owner backed her substantially, for there was no better jockey in England at riding in a match than the arch 'kidder', George Fordham. However, Fordham did not ride for 'Mr Weysford' again that season, or indeed for many months to come.

During the following winter, Harry Hastings laid his plans for a far more ambitious campaign in 1863, the year which would see his coming-of-age. The pseudonym of 'Mr Weysford' was abandoned, and after long discussions with John Day it was decided to make an early start to the new season, the method generally to be adopted being that of buying a promising youngster either direct from an owner or out of a selling race after it had proved itself by winning a race. Already Harry Hastings was beginning to show a preference for fillies, a portent of things to come, for a filly was destined to play the decisive part in his career as an owner.

The organization of racing in England at this period was very different from what it is today. The season began very early, at Lincoln, usually around the end of February, and continued till its completion, usually at Liverpool or Shrewsbury, towards the end of November. A few races were run over hurdles at the beginning and end of the season, and an average meeting would often include several matches between two horses during the afternoon's card.

[1] His second colours were scarlet and white hoop, scarlet cap.

The majority of the famous meetings of today were already in existence, as were the majority of the great races of the turf, whether classic races or handicaps. The principal courses were at Newmarket, Epsom, Ascot, Goodwood, York and Doncaster, as they still are today, but there were also a number of smaller meetings which have long since disappeared from the racing calendar. Places such as Reading, Weymouth, Chelmsford, Oxford, Reigate, Worthing, Walsall and Abergavenny had each their one-day meeting, which attracted a largely local entry of runners. Harry Hastings, as befitted the Squire of Donington Park, used to favour his local meeting of Derby; Henry Chaplin loved to take the members of his house parties over to his local meeting at Lincoln.

Although the season lasted longer than today, the opportunities of winning races were far less. Racing did not take place on nearly every day of the week, as it does at the height of the season today, and the problems of travel were considerable, even though the railways were already operating fairly extensively throughout Britain. But there were still many owners then alive who could remember the old days before the advent of steam, when horses had often to be hacked over long distances in order to reach Epsom or Doncaster. (It had been Lord George Bentinck who had astonished the racing world of his day with his revolutionary idea of a 'horse box' on wheels, by which he had transported his colt Elis to Doncaster by road before winning the St Leger of 1836. This had caused consternation among the bookmakers who—having been informed by their spies that Elis was still in his stable at Goodwood a few days before the race—had assumed that it could not possibly reach the course in time and had laid against the colt accordingly.)

The comparative shortage of races in the calendar, coupled with the problems of travel, led to the common practice of running a horse in more than one race at a meeting and even of running it twice in the same afternoon, for it was generally felt that once a horse had been transported to a meeting it might as well be fully employed there.

There were two schools of thought in this matter. The diehards like Lord Glasgow were of the opinion that an animal that could not stand up to hard training and racing was not worthy of being called a racehorse; and that a racehorse was anyway expendable. If you broke the heart of one, there was always another to take its place.

The more humane and understanding trainers, such as John Kent, held quite a different view. They were firmly of the opinion that the ruination of a horse was caused more often by overtraining and over-racing than by anything else.

Harry Hastings was never a true lover of horses, and he subscribed to the former view, as did his trainer, John Day. They raced their horses hard and often.

During the season of 1863, Harry Hastings embarked on a much more ambitious programme on the turf than in the previous year. From the outset he raced his horses under his own name, and although he achieved no outstanding success during the season, he won a number of minor races with a string consisting of some half dozen or so horses, most of them two-year-olds.

His finest runner of the 1863 season was a two-year-old bay colt called Garotter, who ran unplaced at Northampton in March but won his second race, a maiden plate run at the first spring meeting at Newmarket, in April. Garotter ran eighteen times during the year and won three races.

A two-year-old chestnut colt named Redcap ran on eight occasions without winning a race, and was one of Harry Hastings' few unlucky buys. Redcap ran twice on the same day at Stockbridge in June, twice on the same day at Nottingham in July, and on consecutive days at Harry's home meeting of Derby in September.

His other horses were raced equally hard, but enjoyed more success. Tippler, a two-year-old bay colt, ran ten times after being bought at Ascot in June and won six races. He was required to run twice over a mile at Brighton on the same afternoon. Attraction, a two-year-old bay filly, was bought after winning at the Lewes meeting in August and won for her new owner on the following day. She ran eight times for him in all and won four races.

Old Fuller, a two-year-old chestnut colt, ran four times but did not win. Trumps, a three-year-old colt, bought out of a selling race at Brighton, ran three times for his new owner and won once. Odine, a three-year-old bay filly, bought in August, ran five races thereafter and won once. East Sheen, a five-year-old bay mare, and an unnamed two-year-old filly by Fandango were each bought late in the season, and each ran once for Harry Hastings without winning.

This was a reasonably successful start for a novice, and by the time the 1863 season had reached its conclusion in the gloom and fog of Liverpool in mid-November, Harry had become an experienced owner and backer. He had not won a big race, but he had seen his colours carried successfully both at Newmarket, the headquarters of the turf, and at Ascot, the fashionable centre of metropolitan racing. Already the man in the street knew his name and looked up to him as a patron of racing, and already the punters on racecourses throughout England were becoming accustomed to seeing the Hastings colours and to cheering home 'the scarlet and white'.

Ownership gave to Harry Hastings the popularity and notoriety for which he craved. Now, when he walked into some low dive, he was hailed as one who shared the common man's pastime of racing. The turf united the sportsmen of England into one vast club, all of whom talked the same language and discussed the same problems. In the taverns they shouted for Harry and toasted his name. What did it matter that he was an aristocrat and one of the richest men in the land? He was also a sportsman and one of them. So the toast was always the same: 'The Markis—Gawd bless 'im!'

For Harry Hastings, the year of 1864 was the year of destiny. The whole course of his short life was to be shaped by the events of the first seven months, but he can have had little premonition of this when the year began.

Flat racing started early in those days, and the Lincoln Spring Meeting of 1864 opened on Tuesday, 23 February, with 'The Trial Stakes of five sov. each, with twenty-five added' run over a distance of a mile. There were nine runners, including the Marquis of Hastings' chestnut colt, Redcap, which started at 100 to 15 and finished nowhere.

It was an inauspicious beginning, but in retrospect it can be seen that the chief players in the Hastings drama were already assembling in the wings, and that the curtain on this drama, which was to contain every ingredient of passion, folly, romance and misfortune, was about to rise.

One of the principal players took his place on the stage in a manner that was as dramatic as it was characteristic. With a month of the season already passed, Harry Hastings had seen his colours carried on several occasions, but without a winner. Besides Redcap, which had lost at Lincoln, Quadrille, East Sheen, the filly, Roulette, and Tippler had each failed to gain even a place.

On the second day of the Northampton and Pytchley Hunt Meeting at the end of March, Count F. de Lagrange's filly,

Brioche, was made odds-on favourite in a field of five, which included Harry Hastings' filly, Lady Egidia. There seemed little danger to Brioche but, although she won, it was only by a short head that she held off a tremendous challenge in the last few yards by Lady Egidia, on whom George Fordham rode a brilliant race.

It was the first time that year that Fordham had ridden for Harry. He had not taken part at the earlier meetings, but he and Harry were already well acquainted, and Fordham had ridden once previously for Harry when he had won in a match for him on Consternation at Warwick in 1862. John Day knew what was needed in jockeyship, and it had been he who had advised Harry to engage a rider whom he knew to be a master of his craft.

Fordham had been born at Cambridge in 1837, and was just reaching his prime when the Hastings era began. He had ridden his first winner at Brighton at the age of thirteen, when his weight was only three stone, eight pounds. He was a simple and kindly man, devoted to children, fond of harmless practical joking and scrupulously honest, who in private life belied his racing nickname of 'The Demon'.

As a jockey he could scarcely have been more different from Old John Day in his racing days. Old John had been 'a rough jockey'. Fordham was an artist in the saddle. Old John had believed in the use of whip; but George had no stomach for thrashing a mount beyond its natural capabilities. For this reason he used to discourage his owners from betting heavily on two-years-olds in their first race, no matter how useful they might seem to be, because, if he was riding them, he could not bear to break their spirits in a punishing finish. As he confided to Baron Rothschild, 'when I get down to the post on these two-year-olds, and I feel their little hearts beating under my legs, I think, why not let them have an easy race, win if they can, but don't frighten them the first time out'.

This was not the spirit that inspired Old John, and it was not the policy which his son now instilled into Harry Hastings. That is why George Fordham never fitted completely into the pattern of the Hastings drama. Harry was not basically inhumane, but he had no real love for horses. The frightened beating of their little hearts was never a matter which gave him any concern.

Historians of the turf are generally agreed that the two finest jockeys of the Victorian era were George Fordham and

Fred Archer. Their careers overlapped, but Fordham was much the older man. Both of them were fine horsemen and expert jockeys.

The distinction between a horseman and a jockey is not always appreciated by the layman. Horsemanship is the understanding of the horse and the ability to master him and control him. Jockeyship is something quite different. It includes horsemanship, but it is also the art of race riding, and involves tactics, subterfuge, the ability to make lightning decisions, coolness, balance and—above all, perhaps—the judgment of pace.

In all these things both Fordham and Archer were supreme. Neither were great stylists, and indeed both looked ungainly in the saddle. Fordham, in particular, had an ugly seat, which was made to look worse by his careless appearance as he went down to the start and by his curious habit of shrugging his shoulders. But he had good hands, and horses always ran kindly for him and finished well balanced and without changing their legs. In a tight finish Archer would be half-way up his mount's neck as they passed the post, but Fordham would still be sitting well back, relaxed and unflurried.

Archer was great at the start; Fordham at the finish. He was the best judge of pace in his day and would never hit his mount except in the last few strides. Above all, he was the supreme 'kidder', for he would suddenly come with a rush when it appeared that his mount was tiring and had nothing left. This meant that he was invaluable in a handicap race for, when he won by a neck or a head, it was impossible for the handicapper to tell how much he had in hand.

He had many other tricks when riding a finish, which included emitting strange noises to encourage his mount. Archer used to complain that he could never fathom Fordham's trickery. 'With his clucking and fiddling you never know what the old chap is up to.'

But there was one quality in which Archer was later to prove himself superior. He had more courage. Fordham, quiet, gentle and unassuming, lacked the ruthless determination which drove Archer on in the face of danger. That was why Archer was a great Epsom jockey and Fordham was not. In the Derby, with so much at stake and with jockeys riding with a recklessness and aggression that they would not normally adopt, George Fordham would sometimes flinch at a moment of crisis when Archer would drive fearlessly forward. At

Tattenham Corner, when the field was bunched and a good position was essential; when tiring horses were beginning to falter and become unbalanced; and when the whips were out and the jostling was at its height, Archer would be in his element, but Fordham would not. He was haunted by the sickening fear of a fall and of being kicked to death beneath the flying hooves.

As a tiny apprentice he had once been thrown from the saddle when riding a difficult filly in a stable yard. His foot had caught in the iron, and the filly had bolted round the yard, lashing out viciously and trying to dislodge him. He was badly shaken, and the memory of the incident remained with him throughout his racing career.

Archer worshipped money. It was his god. They called him 'The Tinman' after the couplet which some wag had written about him: 'He rides to win, he rides for the tin.'

Money was of no great importance to Fordham. A simple man, who loved simple pleasures, he must often have been bewildered by the habits of the Hastings set, with all their ostentation and gambling. Nor could he have understood Harry's love of flattery, for to George the attention of sycophants was distasteful. He was shy and hated the limelight, but he shared one of Harry's weaknesses, and that was for drink. This forced him to abandon racing for a time, and it was partly due to Harry's encouragement that he became an addict. He was never a man who found it easy to say 'no', and he could be led into many bad habits except one; his integrity on the turf was impregnable. His owners knew that they could trust him implicitly and that, no matter what the inducement, Fordham could never be bought.

Hastings, John Day and George Fordham made a strange trio. The vain and impulsive owner, the shrewd and calculating trainer and the kind and gentle jockey with the artistry of genius—it was an unlikely combination, and it is not surprising that it was not wholly successful. But there were moments when it made the Ring tremble.

CHAPTER FIVE

THE POCKET VENUS

It was during the season of 1863, when their friendship—and their rivalry—had become established, that Harry Hastings and Henry Chaplin became fully aware of Lady Florence Paget. They may, it is true, have encountered her before, but it was her advent in Society during this season of 1863 which arrested their attention. She created a sensation on her début, and both—as befitted men of the world—were quickly alive to it.

She was heralded as a great beauty. Some even spoke of her as one of the outstanding beauties of the mid-Victorian era. Beauty, of course, is largely a matter of fashion and contemporary taste, and what is hailed as supreme loveliness in one age may not be considered outstanding in another. One era may extol the taller woman with the fuller figure; another may favour a figure that is slender and petite. The contemporary cult may favour bosoms, or maybe thighs. To some, the wasp-like waist may be the very essence of femininity.

Certain factors remain constant, however. Good colouring, lovely eyes and hair, a smooth skin and well-proportioned features—each contributes to an overall effect of beauty. Gaiety and charm enhance it.

Lady Florence was outstanding in nearly all these attributes. The few photographs existing of her probably do not do her justice, for the colouring and the texture of her skin can only be surmised. But there seems no reason to doubt that she was exceptionally lovely, and that to this beauty was added a warm and friendly nature, a happy disposition and a natural charm of manner.

Henry Chaplin's younger sister, the Countess of Radnor, who subsequently had no grounds for showing any affection towards Lady Florence, described her as the most beautiful woman she had ever seen, the only flaw in her appearance being an unevenness in her teeth. 'She was not very dependable, but was most fascinating, and I was very much taken with her.'

The Victorians, of course, tended to favour small women. It was an era when men loved to demonstrate their manliness, their authority and their importance; and so their ideal wife was dainty, demure and submissive. The pride of London's *demi-monde* at the time was the celebrated 'Skittles', who, while being certainly neither demure nor submissive, was yet a tiny little creature, with a fragile, slender figure. She, too, was famous for her high spirits, her gaiety, and the warmth of her personality; and she, too, took London by storm, though her background—and her morals—were very different from those of Lady Florence Paget.

They may have met. If they did, they would almost certainly have enjoyed each other's company. They both had courage and defiance, and both were ready to flout convention. The Prince of Wales, in his time, was fascinated by each of them.

It is not surprising that the society papers of 1863 and 1864 contained many eulogistic comments on Henry Paget's lovely daughter, and referred to her with admiration.

'Among the belles of our English aristocracy,' said a writer in *The Queen* magazine, 'few of late years created such a sensation on her début as Lady Florence Paget, the youngest daughter of the Marquess of Anglesey. Gifted with the hereditary beauty of her family to a rare extent, her petite figure and dove-like eyes caused her at once to become the rage of the park, the ball-room, the opera and the croquet lawn.'

Thus described, she makes an enchanting picture of English girlhood; but the writer has a more pointed observation to make. 'Deprived of a mother's care at an early age, her education was hardly so advanced as might have been anticipated from her sphere in life, and she seemed to have made Diana Vernon her model.' This was an instructive comment. It told *The Queen* readers a great deal if they were acquainted with Scott.

Diana Vernon is a character in *Rob Roy*, being the niece of Sir Hildebrand Osbaldistone's wife. She is something of a tomboy and something of a Paget. She is unorthodox and self-willed. *The Dictionary of the Characters in the Waverley Novels* describes her as follows:

> The heath-bell of Cheviot, and the blossom of the border. She confided to Frank Osbaldistone that for three things she thought herself 'much to be pitied'. 'I am a girl, and not a

young fellow, and would be shut up in a madhouse if I did half the things I have a mind to do.... I belong to an oppressed sect and antiquated religion.... I am by nature, as you may easily observe, of a frank and unreserved disposition—a plain, true-hearted girl....'

Probably the adjective 'plain' is the only term with which one need quarrel in the above description. The main impression left by Florence is of a girl who was self-willed and unconventional, but also loyal and resolute.

One tries to imagine a girl such as Diana Vernon being brought suddenly to London and thrown into the whirl of fashionable life, with its strict codes and many false values. The result would certainly have been explosive and might well have proved catastrophic.

During the season of 1863, both Harry Hastings and Henry Chaplin must have met Lady Florence fairly frequently; and it is possible that by the end of the season each was fascinated by her and possibly half in love with her. *The Queen* magazine, in its issue of 13 June 1863, describes a grand fancy dress ball which was held at Willis's Rooms in aid of the Royal Caledonian Society and of the Royal Scottish Hospital. The highlight of this ball was a Quadrille arranged by the Duchess of Roxburgh and the Countess of Seafield, in which those taking part represented the four seasons of the year. The four ladies representing spring were dressed in green, and they included Lady Florence Paget. Amongst the four men dancing 'Winter' was Henry Chaplin.

It is not surprising to find that Harry Hastings' name was absent from most of these social functions. The solemnity of a fashionable ball in aid of charity was not his idea of entertainment; nor was he an enthusiastic devotee of the Quadrille. He left such orthodox functions to Henry Chaplin, preferring to spend his evenings carousing in the East End.

However, his rivalry with Henry Chaplin was now being sharpened by their mutual admiration for 'The Pocket Venus'. Both were prominent in society at this time, and both had won the reputation of being men of the world. Moreover Lady Florence Paget, as the most beautiful woman in London, constituted a prize such as the most highly bred young aristocrat might pursue with tenacity. It was not simply that she was desirable and beautiful and that she was also excellent company. The great attraction, for any young buck, was that once he entered a ball-room with so exquisite a partner on his arm he became the focus of all eyes and the envy of all male hearts.

It has already been remarked that, although Harry Hastings was a member of the Prince of Wales' set, he was never an intimate of the Prince, as was Henry Chaplin. For example, when in July of 1863 the Prince gave an entertainment at Marlborough House to a few of his close personal friends, it was noticeable that the guests included both Henry Chaplin and Lady Florence Paget, but not Harry Hastings. Bertie, with his eye for a beautiful woman, must have looked upon Lady Florence with undisguised admiration, and he no doubt congratulated Henry Chaplin privately on his good fortune at being chosen so frequently as her escort.

A few days previously—on Saturday, 20 June—Lady Florence had been presented to the Queen at St James's Palace. She had been generally admired, as on all other occasions, and the Queen herself had remarked on her grace and carriage. She had been dressed in a manteau of white imperial glacé, brocaded with white flowers in terry velvet, and trimmed with bouillons of tulle. Her petticoat had been of white glacé silk, with skirt bouillonnée to the waist, and a tulle veil corsage to match, trimmed with châtelaines of white Lebanon flowers. Her head-dress had been a wreath of Lebanon flowers, with diamond ornaments in the centre and diamond stars. Her necklace had been composed of pearls and diamonds. She had looked magnificent—and had been fully conscious of the stir which she had caused.

But if Henry Chaplin and Harry Hastings both pursued Lady Florence with some eagerness, it is not surprising that Henry Chaplin at first claimed most of her attention.

In the first place, his reputation was much more savoury than that of Harry Hastings, and in the second, his tastes were far more in keeping with those of a young girl. There is no indication that Lady Florence was either prim or sedate in her outlook to social life, but the sort of entertainments which Harry enjoyed could really only be shared by his male friends or by ladies of the town. Moreover Harry Hastings tended to shun the more orthodox entertainments of London society. A rebel against conformity, he openly derided the genteel pleasures of the ballroom and the croquet lawn.

But although Harry Hastings was apt to lose marks in the social graces he yet enjoyed several notable advantages. As a rebel, he was bound to appeal to that streak of Paget unorthodoxy which was as strong in Florence as in any of them. Moreover he held one immense asset over Henry Chaplin in Society, for Harry Hastings was already being listed by many matrons as dangerous, and young girls were being warned against him. Now there is nothing more attractive to an innocent young girl (especially if she be something of a rebel) than a young man with a bad reputation. A woman's curiosity, and her love of playing with fire, make any such man intriguing. While girls are young and in search of excitement, they are attracted by charming rogues; it is not until they begin to think seriously of marriage that they tend to consider the more solid virtues of a worthy and reliable suitor.

Harry Hastings knew all this, and was clever enough to play upon his reputation. At times he would appear in the role of the dare-devil rebel and the opponent of orthodoxy; but at other times he was certainly not above adopting the mask of being misunderstood. In either part, he was attractive to warm-hearted innocence. Moreover, Harry had the ability to *look* pathetic. Not surprisingly, because in many ways he *was* pathetic. He was essentially the type that has for ever been able to arouse the mother instinct in women—and that is the most compelling instinct of all.

Thus the contest for Lady Florence's attentions, and ultimately for her hand, gradually developed between these two young men during the latter part of 1863. Those who were prepared to bet on the outcome (and it was an age that was much given to such wagers) were for the most part happy to place their money on Henry Chaplin, for he seemed the obvious choice on form. But some of the shrewder backers favoured Harry Hastings. It was not a question of his wealth or titles. It was his hidden assets as a suitor; and his unexpected abilities to attract a woman. Moreover a Paget was unlikely to adopt the safe and obvious course. Harry, they therefore maintained, was clearly a very live candidate for this most desirable prize.

The three of them met frequently; not only on social occasions, but also at each other's homes. Harry Hastings and Henry Chaplin were now neighbours, for Henry had taken a house at 70 Park Lane, and Harry, not to be outdone, had left the friendly atmosphere of Limmer's Hotel and had occupied 23 Park Lane, which was not far from Piccadilly. Florence, when in London, either lived with her father at 70 Portland Place or at the St George's Hotel in Albemarle Street. It would not have been possible for Florence to have visited Harry in the old days, for he could not have entertained her at Limmer's. A Park Lane residence was something very different. In this respect, at least, Harry Hastings had made a gesture towards conformity and respectability.

But formal entertaining under his own roof (as opposed to wild parties at Donington Hall) did not appeal to Harry Hastings, and it was 'Magnifico' who staged the brilliant dinners at which the company were drawn from the highest in the land, and the food and wine were of the very best quality. Henry Chaplin was a charming and elegant host, and he flattered Florence by his delightful manners and his obvious admiration of her.

It was therefore Henry Chaplin who, from the outset, made all the running. It was obvious that he was already thinking of settling down, and was therefore in search of a wife of beauty, poise and breeding who could become the mistress of Blankney Hall and a hostess worthy of entertaining the heir to the throne. And since 'Magnifico' liked only the best in life, and Lady Florence, with her looks and title, clearly represented the best, there was no necessity for him to look elsewhere. She was the very epitome of all that he valued.

It would therefore seem that Lady Florence Paget was in an ideal position for a young woman. She was the toast of London Society and had its two most eligible bachelors at her feet. She had only to make up her mind which of the two was the more desirable, and then to contract a highly successful marriage.

However, it was not quite as simple as that, for Harry Hastings was far too unreliable to be counted upon, while Henry Chaplin was invested by Nature with a streak of caution. Harry Hastings was too unstable to fall head over heels in love. Henry Chaplin was too matter-of-fact and too rational to do so. Young though she was, Florence probably realized that she might quite easily end up without either of them.

As the year of 1863 drew to its close, Henry Chaplin became more and more attentive to her. They were constantly in each other's company, and yet he still held back. He was still very young, and the leisured life of a London bachelor, without cares or responsibilities, was very attractive to him. Marriage, he probably felt, could wait for just a little longer.

The Mayfair gossips, however, were busily at work, and Henry Chaplin soon found out that he was already being married off by rumour. Society hostesses made arch references to Florence and himself, and even Bertie was in the habit of assuming that Henry would not be remaining single for very long.

Henry Chaplin's reaction was characteristic of him. Indeed he followed what was almost a standard pattern for wealthy young Victorian bachelors who were suffering from doubts. He denied the rumours, packed his bags and retired to the Far East in search of big game, accompanied by his Oxford friend and confidant, Sir Frederick Johnstone. This was a repetition of their withdrawal from Christ Church, when they had gone buffalo-hunting together in Canada. As men of the world, they believed that they were best able to ponder on life while squinting down the barrel of a rifle.

Their big game expedition took them to India, and here they spent the winter. Henry returned in May of 1864, possibly with his mind still not made up; but he at once sought out Lady Florence and they again became inseparable. The memory of her beauty may have dimmed whilst he was so far away, but the effect of it upon him was once more quite overwhelming. She was now in the prime of her early womanhood, and looking lovelier than ever.

One thing, however, soon became clear to Henry. Harry Hastings had not been wasting his time while his rival was at the other end of the world. Henry Chaplin realized that Harry and Florence were now much more intimate in their manner than they had been before he left, and Harry's attitude to her had now become quite proprietorial. She had been seen frequently in his company, and Henry was warned by his friends that it would be unwise to remain undecided for very much longer if he was seriously thinking of asking Lady Florence to become his wife.

But Henry Chaplin still hesitated. He immediately recommenced the association which his sudden departure for India had so abruptly ended, and once again he became Florence's regular escort at the many fashionable balls, parties and social gatherings which they attended. But still he hesitated.

Nevertheless Harry Hastings' nose was soon put out of joint. He did not like balls; and he hated Quadrilles. Moreover he could not match Henry Chaplin's stories of life in the mysterious Orient and of the hazards and privations of safari. A Paget was bound to be attracted by anyone who had endured danger, and Henry spoke enthusiastically of his adventures.

Amongst the betting fraternity, the odds on Henry Chaplin carrying off the prize began to shorten. Harry, it was generally felt, was once again losing ground.

Meanwhile Harry himself had other interests to occupy his attention. The peak of the racing season was approaching, and while he had nothing in his string that was good enough to compete in the classic races, he was already enjoying several encouraging successes as an owner. Derby week arrived, and Harry threw himself with his customary abandon into all that this implied.

The programme on such an occasion never varied. On the night before the Derby, Harry and his cronies—Freddy Granville, Bobby Shafto and the rest—would travel down to Epsom to enjoy the fun of the fair and to assist in putting up the many booths on the Downs. On Derby Day itself, before the great race was run, the party would partake of a luncheon of such vast proportions that even that most accommodating of vessels, the Victorian stomach, was taxed to its fullest capacity; and finally, in the evening, the whole gang would drive out to Cremorne, where the festivities would go on all night and often so far into the morning that it was necessary to drive down to Epsom again without the benefit of sleep. At the weekend the entire company would be entertained at Donington Hall by their most generous host, where they would—if anything—drink and eat even more than they had done on Derby Day itself. Amidst such excitements, and in such hilarious company, no young man could spare the time to mope and sigh for his lost love. Harry, in short, would be enjoying himself far too much to be troubled by thoughts of the entrancing Lady Florence; and this was a fact of which the young lady herself would be fully aware. Harry, she also realized, would not be wanting, amidst all these revels, of charming young companions who would be only too willing to offer him solace, especially when he adopted his air of a little boy lost.

The Derby itself was won on this occasion by William I'Anson's Blair Athol, a colt who had never seen a racecourse before, but whom the Yorkshiremen in the crowd had backed to a man. The Londoners had not shared in their enthusiasm, but amongst the members of society it had been known for some time that the officers of two of Her Majesty's crack cavalry regiments had pooled their resources to win a fortune over 'the bald-faced chestnut', whose trainer had sworn was invincible, and Harry Hastings had been infected with some of their optimism. He had a good wager on the winner and surveyed the finish of the race with a half-suppressed smile of satisfaction.

Henry Chaplin, accompanied by Lady Florence, had watched the race from the royal box, in company with the Prince and Sir Frederick Johnstone. Like the majority of backers, he had supported the favourite, Lord Glasgow's General Peel. His Lordship was never one to mince words, and he had told the royal party that his bay colt was unbeatable. But Henry Chaplin's interest in racing was still only a mild one, and his bets were moderate. His attention was largely focused on the beautiful girl at his side, on whom Bertie also cast an admiring glance from time to time. In the betting over the Paget stakes, Henry was now generally thought to be a certainty.

Perhaps wind of this reached Harry Hastings. Or it may have been that Henry Chaplin was by now beginning to look complacent, and to treat Florence as his special property. Inevitably, when she went racing, Florence preferred to go with Henry, because this meant that she enjoyed the distinction of watching from the royal box. Moreover Harry was always so busy betting that he paid her scant attention, while Henry Chaplin ignored the betting, and even the racing, and devoted all his attention to her. Harry, however, had still one trump card up his sleeve after Epsom was over, and now he played it.

He had already flattered Florence immensely by naming one of his two-year-olds after her. Now he informed her that it was his intention to allow the filly to make her racing début on the first afternoon of the Ascot meeting, which was, as always, one of the highlights of the London season and which took place a fortnight after the Derby meeting.

Florence was naturally delighted and excited. When Harry Hastings asked her if she would accompany him to the meeting, and go with him into the paddock to inspect the other Lady Florence, she at once accepted.

Henry Chaplin had assumed that she would be going with *him* to Ascot. Both he and Sir Frederick Johnstone would be members of the royal party and would be entertained by the Prince in the royal box, and he had never imagined that she would find Harry's company more desirable. He was more than a little put out.

The first day of the Ascot meeting was on 7 June. The weather was fine and the sun shone down on the enclosures with their brilliant flowers and on the cream of Society which paraded before the stands and in the paddock. When the time for the third race on the card approached, Harry Hastings entered the paddock with Lady Florence on his arm. They made a stirring picture, she so radiant and excited and he retaining with difficulty his customary air of casual nonchalance. It was a picture completed by the filly herself. The little chestnut by Newminster looked superb in her summer coat, and danced and pirouetted on her toes as she circled the ring. There was a large field, and she was not fancied to win; but in looks it was clear that she could more than hold her own with any of them. The two Lady Florences were the centre of attraction, and few could have said which looked the more beautiful.

In the royal box, Henry Chaplin must have listened to the racing chatter with only passing interest. For some time now Sir Frederick Johnstone, already himself an established owner, had been trying to convince the Prince and Henry Chaplin of the advantages of owning a racehorse and seeing one's colours carried on an occasion such as this, but Bertie was still reluctant to launch out on a project of which his mother would certainly disapprove, and Henry was more interested in the horse as a hunter than as a racer. Now his eyes frequently strayed to where Harry Hastings and Florence were strolling together on the green lawns. The little chestnut filly did not win her race, and indeed was never seen with a chance, but there was no denying the pleasure which she had so obviously given to her namesake. Florence's eyes were sparkling. Racing was a strong stimulant to her, as it was to Harry. They were both very happy.

Ascot ended in a blaze of sunshine, and the motley crowd dispersed. The swells and the acrobats, the carriage folk, the touts and the tipsters returned to their several ways of life and to their homes—to their love-making, their ambitions and their regrets.

Henry Chaplin returned to his rooms in Park Lane. Here he found it impossible to obliterate Florence from his thoughts. Any hesitancy which had previously existed in his mind was now rapidly disappearing in the face of this renewed competition from Harry Hastings.

He was in a position only too familiar with young lovers, for although the girl in whose company he had spent so much time appeared always to be both open-hearted in her affections and uncomplicated in her character, she yet remained mysterious and unpredictable. He could not say for certain what exactly she was thinking and what were the promptings of her heart. He knew that she had the warmest affection for him and that she both respected and admired him. But was she in love with him? And just what exactly was her attitude to Harry Hastings?

These were questions which could be answered in only one way. The time for uncertainty was past. He must settle the matter, once and for all, by asking her to marry him.

Proposals are sometimes premeditated and sometimes made on the spur of the moment; but time and place play an important part. There seems little doubt that Henry Chaplin had decided to ask Florence to be his wife soon after her return from Ascot, and an admirable opportunity was soon to present itself.

The next major event in the London season was to be the dinner and ball which the Marquess and Marchioness of Abercorn were giving at Chesterfield House in honour of the Prince and Princess of Wales. It was to be held on the evening of Monday, 20 June, and everyone who was anyone in London Society had already been invited.

Lady Florence had accepted, and was to be escorted by her father. Harry Hastings had accepted, and so had Henry Chaplin. It was clearly going to be a brilliant occasion. In view of the setting, the music and the atmosphere, it could also prove to be a very romantic one.

Chesterfield House, on the night of 20 June, was elaborately decorated. No expense had been spared for the reception of the Prince and his Princess. Rare tropical flowers had been imported to lend an exotic air to the main hall and ballroom, the band of the Coldstream Guards were in attendance, and the gardens in the rear of the house were illuminated by coloured lights. Dinner was held shortly after the arrival of the royal couple at 8.15, and dancing to Coote and Tinney's Band began at eleven o'clock. There was the inevitable Quadrille.

When Lady Florence arrived on the arm of her father, she looked radiant and serene. When Henry Chaplin arrived, immaculate and elegant as ever, he looked nervous and distrait. When Harry Hastings arrived, he wore his customary air of indifference and boredom, which suggested that he found such orthodox entertainments of little interest to him.

It has so far been possible to gauge with some degree of accuracy the emotions felt by each of these two young men. It is not so easy to assess what was going on in the mind of Florence herself.

Even a young and inexperienced girl is seldom in any doubt as to the moment when a man is preparing himself to propose marriage to her, and as Florence danced to the sentimental strains of Coote and Tinney's Band, she must have known what was going on in Henry Chaplin's mind. She must also have weighed up the situation for the last time.

It was not an easy situation for a young girl to face, especially for a young girl who was without a mother's guidance and without very much experience of the world. Had she been a little more prosaic in her outlook, a little less romantic and altogether less of a Paget, she might well have found the problem easy enough to solve. She must have realized that she could prevaricate no longer. It was now necessary for her to commit herself, one way or the other. It was the tragedy of these three young people that they had to make their decisions early, at a time when each would have been far happier sitting for a little while longer on the fence.

Harry Hastings was a stimulating and an amusing companion, and his lack of convention intrigued her. She shared his interest in the turf and admired his determination to break the Ring. The courage with which he was setting about this task appealed strongly to the Paget in her.

She was also worried about him. He was drinking too much, gambling too much and burning the candle at both ends. His friends were for the most part unworthy of him and seemed bent on his destruction. His charm and his courage were indestructible, but each day he looked a little more forlorn. Battling with the Ring and winning or losing with panache, he was in his way a hero; but off-guard, in moments when she studied him covertly, he was still a little-boy-lost. He aroused the mother instinct, which was strong within her, and also the reforming instinct, which inspires so many women in their relationship to the male. Harry was beginning to go downhill fast, and she may well have decided that only the love of a woman who understood him could save him from his ultimate goal of self-destruction.

Yet Harry was undeniably a rake, and she had already experienced what that could mean in a family by the examples set by her father and her uncle. The danger with anyone set on self-destruction was always that he might drag down those associated with him. Harry was selfish and unpredictable, and there was no very concrete evidence that he was really in love with her or was seriously considering getting married. In many ways, he was a quite impossible person. Judged even by the lowest standards, he would probably make a deplorable husband.

Henry Chaplin could hardly be more different. Judged by even the highest standards, he would make an excellent husband—and an ideal father. He was manly, generous and kind. He had wealth, charm and good looks—and a fine country seat. He was a close friend of the Prince of Wales. Florence's father had the greatest admiration for Henry Chaplin and had told her that she could not find a better husband. Her brothers had told her the same.

Henry was above all things a *man*. He was healthy, masterful and mature. The woman in her admired this male domination; but the Paget in her made her resentful of it. With her beauty, and her powers of persuasion, she believed that she could probably make Harry do anything she wanted. She was not so sure about Henry Chaplin.

In his way, Henry may have puzzled her. There had been his curious behaviour when rumours of their forthcoming engagement had been circulated in London the previous autumn. He had then hastily retired to India. That had piqued her vanity. A man becomes twice as desirable in a woman's eyes once she thinks that she may have lost him. She had not lost Henry Chaplin, but the fact remained that she could not be quite certain of him.

He must have looked magnificent as he stood before her, so healthy and strong. She knew that he would protect her all his life, that he would adore her and would lavish gifts upon her. She would become the mistress of Blankney Hall and an intimate friend of the Prince of Wales. She would have no further worries in her life if she accepted him. But if she married Harry, she probably would not know a moment's peace. Life with Henry Chaplin would be well-ordered and serene. Life with Harry Hastings would be hell.

The woman in her must have warned her that there was only one possible answer to her problem; and the Paget in her was for the moment quelled.

So when Henry Chaplin finally achieved his moment of

courage and asked her to marry him, she did not hesitate in her reply. Her answer was 'Yes'. His boyish delight, his eagerness and his humbleness must have touched her deeply. She realized that she had made him supremely happy.

This realization was strengthened by the events of the next two weeks. His pride in her was only equalled by his pride in the home which was soon to become her own. She was at once taken to Blankney to decide upon any alterations which she might care to make. She was proudly introduced to his staff as their future mistress, and it was obvious that they were as happy as their beloved master in his boyish enthusiasm. The house, the gardens, the stables and the kennels were each paraded before her eyes, and any alteration that she suggested was at once acted upon.

He took her shopping in Bond Street, and the jewels he bought her were so magnificent that they were placed for a time on display in the jeweller's window. Her trousseau, the fashion papers assured the world, 'engaged the attention of the first *modistes*'. Wedding presents were showered upon them. The staff at Blankney subscribed together enough money to present them with a silver teapot, sugar basin and cream jug. The Marquess of Anglesey was still in straitened circumstances and there was no question of a substantial dowry, but the matter was of supreme indifference to Henry Chaplin. All his worldly goods were at Florence's disposal.

The news was announced in *The Queen* and in *The Morning Post*, with suitable editorial comment, and copied by *The Times*, who were not to be left out of things; and London Society discussed it avidly. Those who had backed Harry Hastings in these matrimonial stakes assumed they had lost their money.

Congratulations poured in from every side. One of the first was from the Prince, who wrote to Henry as 'an old Oxford friend' and an admirer of each of them. They were two very charming and popular young people, and the news of the engagement was genuinely applauded.

The young couple decided upon a relatively short engagement. A date early in August was tentatively decided upon, for the marriage would then come at the end of the season and shortly after the Goodwood Meeting. Invitations were widely sent out and at once accepted.

The two lovers were constantly to be seen in each other's company, at balls, dinners and in the Park. Henry was the proud owner of a smart 'cab', and he would collect his fiancée in the afternoon and take her along 'The Ladies' Mile' from Apsley House to Kensington, with a little 'tiger' standing up behind and looking as proud as his master. And the single horse would be high-stepping in front, itself as proud as either of them. Not even 'Skittles' herself aroused more attention in the Park, and all eyes turned to watch Henry Chaplin and his Pocket Venus as they drove by. All the world loves a lover. There can have been few who did not wish them well.

One, of course, was Harry Hastings. He had been beaten on the post, and for once his languid calm almost deserted him. However, he still contrived to see her on occasion and to deliver notes to her hotel. He had been at pains to prove his sportsmanship (and perhaps his indifference) by being one of the first to congratulate both her and Henry Chaplin; and Henry, in his turn, had been one of the first to commiserate with Harry that he should have proved the loser in the contest for Lady Florence's hand.

This was not magnanimity nor patronage on his part, for Henry Chaplin was delighted with his own good fortune and not a little surprised by it. He knew that Lady Florence had been strongly attracted to Harry, and that she had always found him good company. Because of this, he went out of his way to see that Harry should still enjoy her company, and invited him to join them when they visited the theatre or the opera. Henry Chaplin was himself a man of stubborn integrity, who followed the English gentleman's rigid code of honour. It never entered his head that others might not be so high-principled.

It is not surprising that Harry Hastings, having lost the exquisite Florence to his rival, should have turned to the turf for consolation, and at first he met with some success. The ball at Chesterfield House had taken place on Monday, 20 June. On the Wednesday, Harry Hastings travelled down to the Bibury Club Meeting, in Hampshire, to see his two-year-old colt, The Duke, make his début on the turf. The Duke was a colt of immense potentiality, whom John Day was already speaking of as the possible Derby winner of the following season, and Harry experienced much consolation in watching his handsome bay by Stockwell parading before the race. He then proceeded to back him so heavily that the colt was soon favourite in a large field. The issue was never in doubt, and The Duke won most handsomely. Harry Hastings returned to

Park Lane with an air of defiance and implied to his friends that he would sooner be in possession of a future Derby winner than a future wife. For a few days he treated Florence, when he met her, with a casual indifference; and when he talked to her, it was only of The Duke and his Derby prospects.

From then on he determined to forget Florence and to devote himself exclusively to racing. He was already beginning to bask in the reflected glory of owning the Derby favourite for the following year, but at Newmarket a fortnight later his optimism received a shock. In the July Stakes The Duke was opposed by a very good colt of Mr Merry's called Liddington. After a desperate struggle, Liddington beat The Duke by a head.

Harry lost £1,000, but not his confidence. He announced that the result was a fluke and challenged Mr Merry to a second encounter, a challenge which was readily accepted. The two colts raced against each other again two days later, and the result was the same—except that Liddington now won more easily. Harry lost £2,000 and returned to Park Lane to lick his wounds. The Duke was no longer being referred to as the probable Derby winner of 1865.

Harry returned to his old haunts in the East End, disgruntled and disappointed. Such emotions invariably accentuated his outward pose of carefree nonchalance, and now he laughed at any suggestions that his losses in the fields of racing and romance had caused him the slightest worry. But he was beginning to look tired and ill. He still continued to see Florence, although usually in the company of Henry Chaplin. With them he was careful to preserve his air of indifference, but Florence was not deceived; and she began to worry about him. She never worried about Henry Chaplin because he had no urgent need of her.

A week after The Duke's second defeat by Liddington, Henry Chaplin, now as excited as a schoolboy, escorted his fiancée down to Blankney to show her the kennels and stables, which had recently been enlarged, and to inspect some further improvements which had been carried out at her request. His loyal staff welcomed their Squire and his future wife with warmth and noted his obvious happiness and satisfaction.

They returned to London that night, for they were both looking forward to a special occasion on the following evening. This was their visit to the Opera House at Covent Garden, where Henry Chaplin had booked a box for a performance of

Faust. It was the night of Friday, 15 July, and the occasion marked Mlle Adelina Patti's last appearance of the season. Henry, with characteristic generosity, had suggested to Florence that Harry Hastings should join them, and she had at once concurred. Opera-going, she knew, was not very much to Harry's taste, but she agreed with Henry that a quiet evening spent in gracious surroundings might make a pleasant change for him.

They sat together in the box, on either side of Florence, while Mlle Patti sang to a packed and appreciative house. During the performance, there were many in the stalls who looked up at the three figures in the box. Henry Chaplin was obviously enjoying himself. Lady Florence was silent and pre-occupied with her thoughts. Harry Hastings sat moody and expressionless.

The events of the next day, Saturday, 16 July 1864, have been variously described, nearly always inaccurately, and have been variously interpreted, usually without any real understanding of the motives which inspired them. One point, at least, was afterwards agreed upon. These events constituted one of the most remarkable scandals of the Victorian era. The actions of the central characters appeared, at the time, to be inexplicable. And when they *were* explained, it was through the eyes of those who saw these events as some sort of inverted morality play of the period, in which sex, sin and selfishness momentarily triumphed over honour and integrity, while retribution waited in the wings.

There have been so many different accounts of what happened that it is difficult to find a way through the labyrinth of legendary stories, incomplete anecdotes in biographies of the period, and gossip which is still being handed down by those whose forbears were in some way connected with these events.

It is to be assumed that what did happen must have been the result of a plan made suddenly in strictest secrecy and carried out quickly and in equal secrecy. None of the parties intimately concerned with the events of 16 July ever showed any subsequent desire to discuss what happened, or to indicate what plans had in fact been previously made. One can only give credence to those reports which furnish facts and details that can be checked as accurate, and for the same reason one must discount reports which can be proved to be inaccurate in part and therefore probably in the whole.

The first main point of doubt concerns where Lady Florence

spent the Friday night. It must either have been at the St George's Hotel in Albemarle Street or at her father's house at 70 Portland Place. *The Queen*, in its subsequent report, stated emphatically that it was at the hotel. *The Morning Post*, a trifle smugly, then printed a comment to the effect that they had been asked to correct a statement made by a contemporary which had said that she had stayed at the hotel; and that she had, in fact, stayed with her father.

This is probably correct, for Henry Chaplin's daughter, the Marchioness of Londonderry, in her biography of her father, states that on the Saturday morning Florence dressed up in her wedding dress, which had only that morning been delivered, and then showed herself to the Marquess. This is also probably true, but if it is, it seems to make nonsense of what happened next, for Lady Florence then announced that it was necessary for her to do some more shopping in connection with her trousseau. She either used her father's brougham (according to *The Queen*) or used a carriage which she had previously hired. *The Queen*, which maintained that she was at the St George's Hotel, said that she instructed the hall porter before she left to tell Mr Chaplin, if he should call, that she would not be returning to the hotel before two o'clock.

In either case she travelled alone, which was unusual for a young lady of her class. However, her destination is generally agreed upon by all who recounted her actions that morning. She went to the fashionable store of Messrs Marshall and Snelgrove in Oxford Street, arriving there shortly after ten o'clock.

Opinions vary as to where she stopped her carriage, and by which door she entered. It was either the main door in Oxford Street or the side entrance in Vere Street. If it was by the main entrance, then she would have found herself passing through the departments of haberdashery, hosiery and linens into the main hall of drapery and silks: if by the Vere Street entrance she would have gone through smaller and more intimate departments devoted to the sale of costumes for mourning, and would thence have passed into the large hall which was devoted exclusively to all aspects of mourning—a subject of much importance in the Victorian way of life.

Lady Florence was bent on keeping a secret assignation, so one favours her entrance by the side, or Vere Street, entrance as being more discreet, for she would have found herself in a department which would have been unlikely to be crowded.

Once inside, she was met by one of four people. The Marchioness of Londonderry, in her biography of her father, said it was Harry Hastings himself who was waiting for her. *The Queen* said that it was Harry's sister, Lady Edith Maud Hastings. Donald Shaw, in *London in the Sixties*, said that it was Harry's closest friend, Freddy Granville, who was there; and *The Morning Post* declared that it was Freddy's wife who was waiting. (The Granvilles had only recently been married.)

Whichever of the four it was, all accounts are agreed upon what happened next. After a short and hurried consultation, Lady Florence left by either the main or the Vere Street entrance and entered a cab.

She was driven down Bond Street into Hanover Square, to St George's Church, and there she married Harry. By mid-day she was the Marchioness of Hastings.

This is fact. The Marriage Register of the church, dated 16 July, records the marriage of Henry Weysford Charles Plantagenet, bachelor, rank Marquis of Hastings, residence 23 Park Lane, to Florence Cecilia Paget, spinster, residence 70 Portland Place. The officiating minister was the Rev John Knipe, MA, the curate of Wellesborne, Warwickshire, a minister who had been specially brought in for the occasion and had no connection with St Georges. The witnesses were Frederick Granville, Edith Maud Abney Hastings, Viscount Marsham and Frederick John Blake.

There were no members of the Paget family present, and in the absence of her father the bride was given away by Captain Frederick Granville. The best man was Mr. Blake.

Others present at the ceremony were a Miss Congreve, a Mr Wombwell and a Mr Wilkinson.

When the ceremony was complete, the bridal party went to the Granvilles' lodgings in St James's Place, where the reception, such as it was, took place. Here the bride sat down and wrote a long letter to Henry Chaplin, which was at once dispatched to him in his rooms in Park Lane.

The bride and bridegroom then set off for King's Cross Station, where a special train had been ordered for them (not, in itself, such an unusual or costly method of travel in those days, when special trains were often used). This train took them to Loughborough, where Harry's travelling carriage, with its four horses and coachmen, was waiting to meet them, his staff having been notified of his arrival by telegraph.

Before describing the further events of this remarkable day, it is of interest to consider some of the other stories that were circulated at the time, and which some people still maintain to be true.

The chief one, which is believed by many people even today, is that Lady Florence actually took Henry Chaplin with her when she drove to Marshall and Snelgrove, and that she left him outside while she entered the shop. Assistants serving in the shop later declared that they had seen him enter in search of her, and that he had grown increasingly alarmed and distraught; and that he had finally called for the manager and demanded that the premises should be searched.

This seems improbable for two reasons. In the first place, it is inconceivable to think that Lady Florence would have committed so heartless an act. She may have been thoughtless, but she was never cruel. And, in the second place, the story does not ring true because Henry, at that time, can have had no suspicion of what was about to happen, and if he had accompanied Lady Florence on a shopping expedition and she had disappeared into the shop, he would surely have assumed that he must have missed her and simply gone home without ever demanding to see the manager. Moreover such an action on her part would suggest that she was motivated by a sudden wild impulse when she chanced to meet Harry Hastings inside, but all the evidence proves that there was definite premeditation in the elopement, and that arrangements, both at the church and elsewhere, had already been made, albeit somewhat hurriedly.

Another version of this story, even more improbable than the first, was that she actually took Henry Chaplin into the shop with her, and that for a few minutes they stood together while she examined some beautiful lingerie for her trousseau which was laid out on the counter in front of them. Then she excused herself and disappeared.

A further story, widely circulated, was that the incident never took place in Marshall and Snelgrove's at all, but a mile away at Swan and Edgar's in Piccadilly. Here she is said to have left her brougham at the Piccadilly entrance and to have escaped by the side door into Regent Street. One suspects that this story may have emanated from Swan and Edgar themselves, for it must have been galling to find a rival store receiving so much gratuitous publicity. They certainly never denied this version of the story.

It is interesting to speculate on which of the four people

referred to—Harry's sister, Lady Edith Maud Hastings, his friend, Freddy Granville, Mrs Granville or Harry himself—was waiting for her once she did enter the shop. Probably it was Mrs Granville. The Granvilles themselves had only been married a fortnight before, and in rather romantic circumstances, and were probably still in a matrimonially conspiratorial mood. It might have been Lady Edith, but one contemporary account of the wedding stated that she was only informed of the wedding by her brother at the last moment and only just managed to reach the church in time for the ceremony. It was surely *not* Harry, who would have been reluctant to show himself at this juncture and was anyway no doubt waiting at the church.

Which door she entered and left by must be purely guesswork. One tends to favour her entrance by the Vere Street door. This would have brought her directly into the section of the store which was devoted to mourning apparel. Such departments, one suspects, would have had only a few customers, no doubt deeply engrossed in their own mournful affairs and therefore unlikely to pay much attention to any surreptitious meeting or hurried and whispered conversation. Lady Florence was bent on keeping a secret assignation of great importance, and it would have been easy for her to recognize the person who was waiting for her the moment she entered the side door from Vere Street. Once they had met, they could then walk quickly together through the shop and out of the busy main entrance, still unnoticed. However, advocates of the lingerie school of supposition, who declared that she actually stopped to buy some additional piece of decoration for her wedding dress, will no doubt favour her entry by the main, Oxford Street, door, as she would then have been faced immediately with departments selling haberdashery, hosiery and ribbons!

One report of the affair which is intriguing is the statement that her unfortunate coachman waited for more than six hours outside the shop before finally deciding to go home.

The degree of premeditation in the whole affair is underlined by the ordering of a special train from King's Cross. This cannot have been done without some warning having been first given to the station staff. But the suggestion that Lady Edith Hastings was only told at the last minute, and only just reached the church in time, does imply that it may only have been decided upon very hastily. No member of the Paget family was present at the ceremony, which is not surprising, for both Lady Florence's father and her brothers would certainly have advised her strongly against such precipitate action and might even have tried to take steps to prevent the elopement.

But once the marriage had taken place, one would have expected some formal notification to have been given to the family, unless the whole marriage was almost an impromptu affair. In fact, no one except Henry Chaplin seems to have been told by the bride, and the rest of her family were left to find out for themselves. The Marquess of Anglesey, when he was told, refused to believe the news. Lady Florence's brother, Lord Uxbridge, and her brother-in-law, Lord Winchelsea, were taking part in a pigeon-shooting match at Hornsey on the day in question when they happened to overhear a remark about the elopement having taken place. They, too, at first refused to believe it could have happened.

It is probable that the bridal couple travelled to Loughborough on the same day as their wedding, but it may have been the next day. The staff at the Hall, and the inhabitants of Castle Donington, were certainly taken by surprise. They had been expecting Harry's arrival during the course of the week because it was his birthday on the following Friday, when he would be twenty-two. He always spent his birthday at the Hall, amidst his devoted and enthusiastic tenantry, and they had been busily engaged on their usual task of erecting triumphal arches in the little town to welcome him.

News of his wedding must have astonished them. Indeed *The Loughborough Monitor*, always an informative source concerning Harry's activities, stated that when the Marquis and Marchioness arrived in their carriage, with their coachmen and servants wearing wedding favours, the good citizens of Castle Donington took it all to be a joke, and part of the birthday gaieties.

Another report, this time in *The Leicester Journal*, under the heading of 'The Recent Elopement and Marriage in High Life', stated that they left their train at Peterborough Station, where they were met by friends, who were astonished to see Lady Florence, but it then went on to state that 'To show the marriage could not have been an impromptu affair, as some people imagine, the fact of the happy couple being received at the station by his tenantry, who had erected no less than nine triumphal arches trimmed with flowers, at once discloses.'

It is more probable that the tenantry had no inkling of the

marriage and were taken completely by surprise. However, one can accept the statement in *The Loughborough Monitor* that once the news had been circulated and accepted on the Saturday evening, the happy couple 'were welcomed by merry peals from the church bells which continued ringing during the evening, and our newly-formed brass band had the honour of assisting in the welcome, by performing during dinner at the Hall. Early on Monday morning the town assumed a holiday aspect, many of the houses in the Borough Street displaying flags and floral devices.'

No doubt Castle Donington was by then accustomed to Harry's wild escapades and sudden, unexpected actions and merely accepted the marriage as a further example of their Squire's unpredictability. He had married a woman of title and of great beauty, and they toasted his good fortune with enthusiasm.

There is no mention of a honeymoon, or any excursion abroad. Perhaps Harry's racing interests at this time discouraged any desire to leave England. The Goodwood Meeting began on 26 July, and he had two of his horses, Tippler and Trumps, entered in the big handicap, The Stewards Cup, which was on the first day.

However, *The Loughborough Chronicle*, in its account of all these remarkable events, added a further comment of its own which was, in its implications, even more remarkable than any of them. 'The Marquis of Hastings,' it wrote, 'intends to dispose of his racing stud, with the exception of The Duke, which is entered for next year's Derby and is second favourite. This sale will take place at Brighton races.'

There must have been some grounds for such a statement. Perhaps Harry, in the first flush of marriage and under the already reforming influence of his young bride, may have publicly renounced his former life of dissipation and promised her that he would give up both racing and betting.

If she *was* determined to save him, both morally and physically, by preventing the over-indulgence which was ruining his health and the over-spending which was ruining his finances, she would have tackled these problems from the outset when he was under her influence and amenable to her suggestions.

If she *did* extract from Harry a promise to give up racing, it was a considerable achievement; but it cannot have been long before she realized the emptiness of all such promises. The

Brighton Meeting, which followed immediately after Goodwood, came and went without any sale. Redcap ran in the Brighton Stakes and won at 7 to 1. The implication was probably not lost on Harry. His luck was in and the turf was eager to retain him within its ample bosom.

And what of Henry Chaplin all this time, left almost at the altar without his bride? He was a proud young man, who valued his position in Society and the heartbreak and humiliation must have been extremely painful to him. It is not uncharitable to say that the latter may have been greater than the former. He was in love with Lady Florence, and he was in love with her beauty, and the loss he suffered must have left him momentarily beaten down and overwhelmed. But not fully heart-broken. The evidence of his previous hesitation, and of the time which it had taken him finally to make up his mind, does not suggest a wild and uncontrollable adoration. He was deeply hurt and greatly depressed; but not quite heart-broken.

His humiliation, however, must have been overwhelming. Suddenly, and without any previous warning, he was made the centre of a scandal that shook Society. The fact that he was the injured party, and that he had been shamefully treated by his fiancée and by one of his close friends, was no consolation to his pride. He was left with the need for cancelling all his wedding arrangements, returning all the presents and notifying everyone that his marriage would not take place. He was a proud man, and he found himself the object of pity. He was a self-important man, and he found himself an object of ridicule. The world looked upon him as a cuckold—a man who has put his trust in a woman who was in reality the property of someone else.

There is no evidence to suggest that Lady Florence had ever been Harry Hastings' mistress, but the gossips of any community can always be relied upon to conjure up fire from smoke. It was soon being suggested that she *had* been his mistress; and that she had never really intended to become Henry Chaplin's wife.

It has always been the custom, in yellow journalism, to arouse malicious gossip by suggesting that an issue is one of rich versus poor, or of class distinction. Lady Florence was promptly branded on both counts. She had given herself to the richer man, and the man with a title. She was therefore considered to be worthless and despicable.

More than 100 years have now passed since Lady Florence

came to the decision which made her forsake one man and turn to another. In this time, her action has frequently been referred to in newspaper articles and in biographies. And during this time no one seems to have made any serious attempt to analyse her decision, or indeed to do anything but to condemn her for it. It is so simple to brand her action as that of a fickle and selfish young woman, without heart or principle. But this must be unlikely because none of the evidence available ever suggests that she was such a woman. This was not 'Skittles', selling herself to the highest bidder. This woman was a Paget, whose menfolk were heroes and whose women were angels.

Lady Florence may not have been an angel, but she was certainly not a trollop. Her motives may have been misguided, but that is not to say they were ignoble.

The most informative piece of evidence is the note which she wrote in haste at the Granvilles' lodgings in St James's Place before she hurried away with her husband to catch the special train which was to take them North to Castle Donington.

This is what Henry Chaplin read in what must have been a mood of utterly bewildered incomprehension when it was delivered to him on the afternoon of 16 July, the night after he had taken his fiancée to the Opera and but forty-eight hours after she had spent the day with him going over their future home at Blankney Hall.

July, 1864, Saturday.

HENRY—To you whom I have injured more deeply than any one, I hardly know how to address myself. Believe me, the task is most painful and one I shrink from. Would to God I had moral courage to open my heart to you sooner, but I could not bring myself to do so. However, now the truth must be told. Nothing in the world can ever excuse my conduct. I have treated you too infamously, but I sincerely trust the knowledge of my unworthiness will help you to bear the bitter blow I am about to inflict on you. I know I ought never to have accepted you at all, and I also know I never could have made you happy. You must have seen ever since the beginning of our engagement how very little I *really* returned all your devotion to me. I assure you I have struggled hard against the feeling, but all to no purpose. There is not a man in the world I have greater regard and respect for than yourself, but I do not *love* you in the way a woman ought to love her husband, and I am perfectly certain if I had married you, I should have rendered not only *my* life miserable, but your own also.

And now we are eternally separated, for by the time you receive this I shall be the wife of Lord Hastings. I dare not ask for your forgiveness. I feel I have injured you far too deeply for that. All I can do now is to implore you to go and forget me. You said one night here, a woman who ran away was not worth thinking or caring about, so I pray that the blow may fall less severely on you than it might have done. May God bless you, and may you soon find someone far more worthy of becoming your wife than I should ever have been—Yrs.

FLORENCE

Two points emerge clearly from this letter. Lady Florence had been trying to tell Henry Chaplin for some time that she could not marry him; and secondly she had been trying to tell him that she was not in love with him.

'There is not a man in the world I have a greater regard and respect for than yourself, but I do not *love* you in the way a woman ought to love her husband. . . .'

This is possibly the essence of the whole sad affair. A warm, vital and probably a passionate young woman found to her dismay that she was not physically attracted to the man whom she had agreed to marry. He was so suitable in every other way that she tried to convince herself that such a feeling could in the course of their marriage be overcome; and he was so kind and so sympathetic to her that she had not the heart to tell him something so intimate—and so wounding.

Henry may well have been insensitive and unobservant of her moods. The fact that he did not attract her physically may not have registered with him, or he may have mistaken her reluctance for maidenly modesty. On the other hand, he may have been slow in showing any emotion or passion himself, so that she began to suspect that he was not really experiencing any. Possibly this was because he did not, in fact, experience any. He may well have belonged to that Victorian school of thought which considered passion to be something that one shared with one's mistress, whilst it was affection which one shared with one's wife. One did not subject a gentlewoman to the lustful enthusiasm which motivated one in profane love. Genteel women were not passionate, and Florence was so evidently genteel (and the word had a far higher meaning then than it has today). Henry Chaplin was a perfectly normal, virile and gentlemanly young Englishman of his period, which is to say that he probably knew nothing about women at all.

These are all suppositions, but they are ones that fit the facts. They may appear to be a defence of Florence, but she is a woman who has always been in need of defenders, for her own generation condemned her without pity.

It must also be remembered that she had always been under strong pressure from her father, her brothers and her friends to accept Henry Chaplin. Indeed everyone had been so busy telling them both that it was an ideal match that they had come to believe it themselves, almost without question. An ideal match, in the eyes of the world, was usually an arranged match, and much of what happened had been arranged. If Florence had demurred in any way or hinted to her relations and friends that she was suffering from a certain physical reluctance, she would undoubtedly have been told not to be foolish. She would have been assured that most young girls who had been properly brought up might be expected to view the physical side of marriage with apprehension, and even abhorrence. But she should not let this worry her. Everything would be all right on the night.

All this offers a possible explanation for why she ultimately came to the conclusion that she could not go through with her marriage to Henry Chaplin. But why did she suddenly decide to run away with Harry Hastings?

Whatever may be said of her conduct, the weight of evidence about her character does not for one moment suggest that Lady Florence was ever either calculating or materialistic in her attitude to life and certainly not to marriage. She was never a young woman who would marry for money or a title. It is true that she had known the embarrassment of comparative poverty, with a father who was frequently in debt and hounded by his creditors, but there is no suggestion that she was wildly extravagant. Therefore Henry Chaplin's more than liberal endowment, and his great generosity, would have provided her with everything she needed. He had no title, it is true, but he was a close friend of the Prince of Wales. Moreover Florence was the daughter of a marquess—she was not some cheap upstart or snob, eager to better herself in the social sphere.

Was she a romantic? No doubt she was. But the popular view that she forsook a dull and worthy young man, the stuffy son of a country parson, in favour of a dashing young gallant, simply does not hold water.

But why did she suddenly decide to run away with Harry Hastings? The answer, surely, is that Harry Hastings needed her and Henry Chaplin did not. In the eyes of the world, Harry had everything and Henry had nearly everything, but this would not deceive a sensitive woman. It was Henry Chaplin who had everything, because he had health, self-confidence and security. He was the product of a happy home and was without complexes or inhibitions.

But Harry Hastings—the rake, the gambler, the little-boy-lost—was in desperate need of both pity and understanding. He was going downhill fast, and only a woman's love could save him. A woman does not love a man for his virtues but for his weaknesses, and Harry was weak, foolish and urgently in need of reformation. A woman who married Harry might achieve something. She might save a soul. A woman who married Henry Chaplin would not be required to save him. He was perfectly capable of looking after himself.

It is suggested that these are the factors which motivated Florence when she suddenly decided to elope. Of course, she behaved foolishly and irresponsibly. Faced with a situation which was untenable, she did nothing about it until it was too late. Then she acted precipitously and betrayed a man who had never shown her anything but kindness. For this she cannot be excused. She failed to live up to the Paget tradition of courage and honour.

But she was not yet twenty-two. It is scarcely an age of sober judgment and considered action.

The one person who came out really badly from this whole affair was Harry Hastings. Throughout he behaved like a cad. He continued to share Henry's hospitality and friendship at a time when he was scheming to steal his future wife; and he showed no compunction at any time. When he found that his own weaknesses, his gambling and his ill-health each combined to arouse Florence's sympathy and affection, he played these cards to their fullest effect, for he knew well enough the power he held over her when he looked pathetic. His behaviour was unforgivable, and yet he had constantly been forgiven for it, especially by women.

One thing is certain. The stimulus to his ego must have been immense. Here was dashing Harry Hastings, the irresistible Don Juan, running off with another man's betrothed right under his nose—and she the most beautiful woman in Society! At Donington, where they cheered him with gusto, and on his visits to the haunts of vice and dissipation which he had no intention of giving up, he was the hero of a sparkling enterprise. He probably did not suffer a moment of remorse.

In the taverns where they toasted his success in the nuptial bed with many a leer and wink, he replied with his usual *bonhomie* and charm before standing a round of drinks. And the toast remained the same:

'The Markis—Gawd bless him!'

There is really nothing to be said in mitigation of Harry's conduct.

The wicked flourish like a green bay tree, and Harry was soon enjoying not only the delights of marriage, but also the more concrete ones of success on the turf. Of the two, the second was to him the more important. Harry was too selfish and probably too indolent to make a successful lover, even on his honeymoon. He continued to drink far more than was good for him, and to gamble wildly. Florence did her best to restrain him, but it must have come as a shock to her quite early in her marriage to discover that her proposed transformation of a foolish young rake, who was ruining his health, into a respectable young man of whom she could be proud was going to prove far more difficult than she had ever foreseen.

The worst thing that could have happened to Harry at this period was that he should have started winning. It is hard to imagine, admittedly, but if mounting debts at this period had really frightened him, and a few salutary defeats on the turf had really convinced him that his mission in life was not, after all, to prove himself the scourge of the Ring, then it is possible that Harry might have reformed. But this was not to be. The racing events of 1864 were beginning to prove to him, to his own satisfaction, that he had a flair for betting and for ownership. And above all, the supreme prize, the Blue Riband of the turf, was already being dangled tantalizingly before his eyes.

He had bought The Duke on John Day's advice. A bay colt by Stockwell out of Bay Celia, The Duke was a flashy and high-tempered animal, very much after Harry Hastings' heart, for although Harry scorned displays of ostentation and exuberance in himself, he enjoyed seeing his horses 'put on a show'. And the Duke, no matter what his mannerisms, was clearly something out of the ordinary. On his first appearance, at the Bibury Meeting in June, he had won most convincingly, and although Liddington had beaten him twice at Newmarket, John Day still maintained that the colt was a potential Derby winner. Some five weeks after the elopement, Harry Hastings escorted his bride to the York races to witness The Duke's reappearance on the turf in the ninth North of England Biennial Stakes. The Duke won, and restored himself to popular favour. George Fordham rode him and spoke warmly of his ability on his return to the weighing room. George, too, had his eye on the Derby of 1865. Danebury was altogether well satisfied.

Harry Hastings was now riding the crest of the wave. He owned the most beautiful woman in England as his wife, and the favourite for the Derby. In the eyes of his cronies he was, indeed, a perfect Cocker.

As the weeks went by, and the autumn drew on, he spent more and more time at Danebury, endlessly discussing the future of his Derby candidate. Florence was at liberty to accompany him, but she did not often avail herself of the opportunity. She soon began to realize that The Duke figured as importantly in his life as she did herself. It was not a very flattering situation for a young bride after only a few months of marriage.

In his many secret trials, The Duke went from strength to strength, and Danebury's hopes grew daily stronger. John Day gave it as his opinion that if he went on as he was doing, then he must represent a good thing for the Epsom classic; and so Harry Hastings started backing him accordingly. Whenever a reasonable price was offered against his horse, he at once accepted it—and often accepted an unreasonable one as well. Long before the 1864 season was ended, he was heavily committed. Florence tried to reason with him, and to discourage his optimism. It was useless. Harry Hastings had already decided that he was destined to go down in turf history as one of the very few owners to have won the Blue Riband at the first time of asking.

But there were other more immediate triumphs to be savoured. By late summer he had really 'arrived'. His colours were now known to every punter on the course, and the bookmakers, who not so long before had looked upon him as a novice whom they could easily fleece, now began to watch him with a wary eye. His assessment of form, they soon realized, could on occasions prove as accurate as their own.

His second full season as an owner, and as a member of the Jockey Club, was finally crowned by a truly sensational tilt at the Ring, when he decided to stage a major betting coup over the Cambridgeshire, a popular handicap which was run at Newmarket at the end of October.

At the Newmarket Meeting which had been held a fortnight before this race, Harry had been impressed by the running of a three-year-old brown gelding named Ackworth, which had finished third in the Cesarewitch Stakes, another popular autumn handicap and a long-distance race which called for exceptional courage and resolution on the part of both horse and rider.

Ackworth was owned by a Mr Hill, for whom he had run twice previously during the season, but without winning. Harry approached this gentleman with his usual air of indifference, and asked him carelessly if Ackworth was for sale. Mr Hill, who was fully alive to the potentialities of his brown gelding, replied with an equal show of indifference that he might consider selling—at a price. He suggested 2,000 guineas.

It was an immense sum to ask for a handicapper—and a gelding at that—but Harry Hastings paid it without troubling to bargain. Ackworth was transferred to the care of John Day at Danebury, and despite his hard race in the Cesarewitch, was put into training for the Cambridgeshire.

Harry Hastings told Florence that his new purchase was bound to win the race and that he proposed to make a fortune over him. Florence was alarmed. It was already clear to her that all Harry's avowals after their marriage that he was going to give up racing had meant nothing at all. Now he was planning to bet on a far bigger scale than he had ever done before. Previous bets which he had made with the Ring had amounted to no more than preliminary skirmishes. Now, on Tuesday, 25 October, the first major battle was to be fought; and Harry assured her that she need have no worry about the outcome. Ackworth would win the Cambridgeshire, and would credit his owner with a fortune in bets. And the Ring would be shaken to its foundations. It was no use attempting to reason with him; and perhaps, in these early days of her marriage, she was still impressed by his courage and fired by his enthusiasm. She agreed to accompany him to Newmarket and to watch the race.

No less than thirty-eight runners went down to the post, and the betting covered a wide range. Such a large field offered a strong market—that is to say, the Ring were prepared to lay long odds to substantial amounts because of the huge volume of money which was pouring in—and despite Harry Hastings' obvious confidence in Ackworth, the layers were eager to oblige him. They introduced Ackworth into the betting at 25 to 1, but the size of Harry's bets soon astonished them. The price was shortened to 20 to 1, and then to 15 to 1, which was the final offer available as the runners came under the starter's orders. By this time Harry Hastings stood to win some £70,000 if Ackworth triumphed. He had been racing in earnest for scarcely a year, and until recently had been looked upon by racing men as the veriest novice at the sport. And he was now committed to one of the biggest gambles of the season.

Tom Cannon, a promising young jockey not yet out of his teens, had ridden Ackworth in the Cesarewitch, and Harry had wisely decided that there should be no change of rider for the Cambridgeshire, especially as John Day had a high opinion of him. Trainer and owner dispatched horse and jockey from the paddock with a final word of encouragement. Tom Cannon touched the peak of his cap with his whip, and the scarlet with white hoop was given a cheer as Ackworth cantered down the Rowley Mile to the start.

Harry Hastings rejoined his young wife and escorted her to a place in the stands. He was cool, smiling and unruffled. This, he told her quietly, was to be one of the great moments of his racing career.

There was the invariable cry of 'They're off!' followed by a few seconds of silence as countless anxious eyes tried to assess the start and to sort out the early leaders. For a time the huge field thundered down the course like a cavalry charge, but as the winning post grew near, it was seen that two runners had forged ahead of the remainder and had the race between them. One carried the scarlet and white hoop of Ackworth; the other the dark blue of Baron Rothschild, whose filly, Tomato, was putting in a tremendous finish.

Harry remained motionless and seemingly without emotion as the two horses raced past the post, locked together and matching stride for stride. And once again silence fell upon the course as the crowd waited for the judge to give his verdict.

After a few moments it came. Ackworth had won by a head.

Harry Hastings walked slowly through the excited throng to

lead in his winner. Outside, on the course, his faithful followers were cheering him wildly. He gave a nod of recognition and accepted the congratulations which were poured upon him with a slight smile. He still looked little more than a boy, and his cheeks were flushed even though he was trying to hide all evidence of his elation.

Back in the Ring, the layers were counting up their losses. Harry had hit them hard, but the motto amongst bookmakers is that there is always another day. So the young buck had won a fortune from them! Never mind—it would all come back to them in the end!

Nevertheless the purchase of Ackworth had suggested shrewdness and judgment; and victory by so short a margin had further suggested that Harry was lucky. The Ring has as much respect for luck as the backer. It is a factor in racing that can never be discounted.

Florence was left bewildered and breathless. Ackworth's victory and the size of Harry's winnings naturally delighted her. But she was woman enough to know that such a success could only act as a spur. Harry had won the first round in his fight to beggar the Ring, and now he would be planning finer victories and greater financial gains. And he was only twenty-two, and she was the same. It was very young to take on the cleverest and most merciless of professionals at their own game and not a hope of defeating them. Perhaps, in her heart of hearts, she wished that Acworth might have lost. From now on there would never be any hope of persuading Harry to give up betting. From this time on, she realized only too well, Harry was married to the turf as much as he was to her. Children, home life and a settled existence were of no importance now that the most dazzling prizes of all seemed in his grasp. His ultimate destiny lay at Epsom. If they cheered him at Newmarket after the Cambridgeshire, how much louder would be the cheers after the Derby. She would never be able to restrain him now that those cheers were already beginning to sound in his ears.

CHAPTER SIX

THE BIRTH OF RIVALRY—1865

It was said of Henry Chaplin in the year which followed the elopement of Lady Florence that he began 'to buy horses as though he were drunk and to back them as though he were mad'. This behaviour on the part of a young man whose previous interests in the horse had been largely concerned with hunting, and who had shown no great predilection for the turf, was taken as a sign that he had become obsessed with the desire to revenge himself upon the Marquis of Hastings, and had chosen the racecourse for the prosecution of their rivalry.

At the time it must have seemed a reasonable assumption. Harry had two ambitions in life. One was to break the betting Ring. The other was to win the Derby. He would therefore bitterly resent any other young man who set out with the same intentions. And he would particularly resent that young man if he were someone over whom he had already triumphed.

Victorian Society accepted the situation with relish, and sat back to watch the development of the feud. It gave an added piquancy to the running of the great races of the turf.

What few people realized was that Henry Chaplin had no interest in revenge. His character was a denial of anything petty or spiteful. He was a big man in every way, both physically and mentally, and he never stooped to petty acts. The loss of his future wife came as a terrible blow to him, and it almost broke his spirit. Yet he bore no malice. He was never obsessed with revenge. For a time, perhaps, he determined to forsake women. But if he echoed in his heart the mood of Swinburne and vowed to himself that he would never again be friends with roses, his outward demeanour remained proud and defiant. No one was allowed to pity him.

True to his way of life, his first reaction had been to escape to some remote place where he could hunt—and think. He retired to the Reay Forest, in Scotland, which he had rented for the deer-stalking, and there he licked his wounds in solitude.

It was here that he received a number of letters of sympathy from his close friends and above all from the old confidant of his boyhood days, Lord Henry Bentinck. This eccentric bachelor had no illusions about what had happened. He considered that Henry had had a merciful escape and said so. 'When that event occurred which will have annoyed you so much, he wrote, 'but which all your *true friends* ... look upon as a blessed deliverance.'

And again, a month later. 'If you will only open your eyes to the whole truth, and nothing but the truth, then the wound will become callous at once. Otherwise, neither Scotland nor exercise, nor three score years either, will heal such a sore.'

The truth, to Lord Henry Bentinck, was that Chaplin had been deceived by someone who was wholly unworthy of him and he was well rid of her.

These counsels at first failed to bring to Henry the peace of mind which was necessary to him. So he left Scotland and once again summoned his trusted friend from his Oxford days, Sir Frederick Johnstone, to come to his side, and together they left for yet another hunting expedition to India.

His aim in this was twofold. Firstly, to forget. Secondly, to give the scandal time to die down.

He returned in the early spring of 1865, refreshed and no longer disillusioned. He had forgiven Lady Florence, and he had even forgiven Harry Hastings. But there was one thing which the new Marchioness did not comprehend at first and perhaps never quite comprehended throughout her life. Henry's love for her was dead. He continued to admire her, and he soon began to pity her for the disillusionment which she quickly suffered with Harry. But love was dead. She never again had the power to hurt him.

The reason for his sudden and violent interest in racing was no more than an urgent need for excitement and stimulation. He was a restless young man, as his frequent travels abroad revealed, and now he sought some distraction that would wholly occupy his mind. As a happily married man living at Blankney, he might never have taken to the turf at all. But as an escaped bachelor, so to speak, he took to it with abandon. For a time he did, in truth, start buying horses as though he were drunk and backing them as though he were mad.

The rivalry which developed between Harry Hastings and himself was therefore not of his making. It was Harry who saw in it a move against himself and an attempt to steal his thunder. And so when Henry Chaplin started buying horses as though he were drunk, Harry began to do the same. The money which both laid out at the beginning of the racing season of 1865 staggered the racing world. They started bidding in thousands where other men had been accustomed to bidding in hundreds.

Sir Frederick Johnstone had often spoken enthusiastically to Henry of the pleasure of owning racehorses. He had been an owner himself almost from his Oxford days, and had already made several attempts to win one or another of the classic races. While they were on their Indian trip in the winter of 1864-5, he must have frequently suggested to Henry that the turf was as good a way of forgetting one's sorrows as any. He would have pointed out that Henry was acknowledged to be as fine a judge of a horse as any hunting man in Lincolnshire, and that he would therefore have a great advantage over owners such as Harry Hastings himself, who had to rely at the start of his racing career on the advice given him by his trainer.

Henry Chaplin never did anything by halves. He liked the best in everything, and so when he decided to take up racing, he did so in a big way. He determined to buy the best horses available, and to send them to one of the best trainers.

It was a period of many brilliant and successful trainers. There were men such as John Day; John Kent, whom Lord George Bentinck had nearly killed with over-work; John Osborne, of Ashgill; Matthew Dawson; John Porter, of Kingsclere, and several others—all shrewd and skilful, knowing all the tricks, as indeed they had to, watchful, autocratic and tight-fisted, although happy enough to put their money down when they knew that they had something on which to bet. Men of integrity for the most part, but suspicious of everyone; dictators in their own little world, and ready enough to dismiss a stable-lad on the instant if they caught him writing too many letters or displaying a new watch. They made their living by training for the wealthy gentry and the aristocracy, and telling their masters just as much as it was necessary for them to know.

When Henry began to discuss the breeding of racehorses with his friends, he was impressed by the unanimity with which they advised the 'Queen Mary' blood. Their idols were the immortal mare, Blink Bonny, who had won the Derby of 1857, and her equally illustrious son, Blair Athol, who had won the race in 1864. Blink Bonny was by Melbourne out of Queen Mary, and her name had become a legend among racing men in Yorkshire, as indeed it is to this day. In turf history she can justly be spoken of in the same breath as Pretty Polly and Sceptre.

Blair Athol, in his day, was destined to build up almost as fine a reputation; and the story is still told of how he had been brought into the auction ring on the death of his owner, and the auctioneer, Edmund Tattersall, revered as the best judge of horseflesh in the country, had turned quietly to address the crowd who surrounded the ring and asked them to bid for 'the best horse in the world'.

Both Blink Bonny and Blair Athol had been owned, bred and trained by William I'Anson senior, a Scot from Gullane, who had crossed the border in 1849 to start breeding horses at Malton, in Yorkshire. Henry Chaplin met I'Anson at Newmarket one afternoon, early in the season, and asked him if he had any promising three-year-old colts for sale with Queen Mary blood in them which were engaged in the Derby. I'Anson replied that he had two, and added that despite what was being said and written about the Marquis of Hastings' obvious chance of winning the great race with The Duke, he was convinced that either of his two, for all that they were virtually untried, had the beating of The Duke at Epsom. He invited Henry Chaplin to come up to Malton and to judge them for himself.

To suggest that he had *two* colts in his yard which were better than the existing Derby favourite was a bold claim indeed; but Henry Chaplin knew that the trainer was not given to unwise optimism, and that what he said might well be true. Henry Chaplin was not interested simply in buying a horse that was better than The Duke. What he wanted was to buy a Derby winner. And here he was, in his very first season as an owner, being offered the choice of two colts whom a shrewd and experienced trainer was convinced had remarkable potential, even though they had yet to see a racecourse. Moreover the rumours which always abound in racing, particularly those concerning 'dark' horses, had already been in circulation for some time. Certainly the villagers of Malton were convinced that the Derby winner of 1865 was being trained in their midst. As is customary with rustic Yorkshiremen, their reaction was not to boast of these hopes, but rather to become secretive and silent.

Before he set out for Malton, Henry Chaplin was warned that the colts would certainly prove to be good, but they would also prove with equal certainty to be very expensive, for

I'Anson was a hard man of business.

This was no understatement. The two, named Breadalbane and Broomielaw, were paraded for Henry's inspection. He recognized at once that both were exceptional, but of the two he preferred Breadalbane. His dam was Blink Bonny herself, and there was more than a touch of the mother about the colt.

Henry asked the price, and was told that the colts were on offer at 6,000 guineas each. It was a staggering figure for those days, and Henry Chaplin was suitably staggered. However, Breadalbane fascinated him, and he agreed to buy him.

On the way back to the station in I'Anson's pony and trap, the trainer emphasized that *both* were colts of quite exceptional promise, and were untried. He was confident that one or other would win the Derby. The problem was which one? It would be most unfortunate if Henry Chaplin had chosen the wrong one.

The bait was proffered and accepted. Henry Chaplin agreed that it would be madness not to take them both and offered £11,500 for the pair—an offer which was accepted. It was agreed that the two colts should remain at Malton to be trained for the Derby by the old man's son, William I'Anson junior.

The news of the price which Henry Chaplin had paid for two untried three-year-olds astonished the racing world. He was certainly starting to buy horses as though he were drunk. Many declared that he had been cheated, but there were others who did not share this opinion. The magic of Blink Bonny's name could not be ignored. It could well be that one of the two *would* win the Derby. Moreover Henry Chaplin was known to be a good judge of a horse. If he had bought a future Derby winner, the price would not be excessive.

The person who reacted most strongly to the news was Harry Hastings. He was angered and indignant. He himself, for all his wild ways, had started his racing career with caution, and had bought moderate horses at moderate prices. He had already completed two full racing seasons, enjoying only modest success, and his biggest triumph until then had been to win the Cambridgeshire with Ackworth. Yet here was his rival, Henry Chaplin, starting out with far bigger ideas, paying far higher prices and seeking for success in far more important races. Everyone on the turf was now talking about Henry Chaplin, and applauding his courage and his enterprise. Indeed so much was being talked about Breadalbane and

Broomielaw that the chances of The Duke were momentarily being overlooked.

The situation to Harry Hastings was insufferable.

It has already been emphasized that the rivalry between Hastings and Chaplin was not of Chaplin's making. Chaplin was neither jealous nor revengeful. Harry Hastings, with his strongly-developed feminine streak, was both. One of the things which had angered him most was the fact that Henry Chaplin did not seem to resent the elopement as much as he should have done. It was almost as if he were saying to Harry, 'Take her, my boy, with my blessing—you need her more than I.' Moreover the attitude of Society to the elopement had not been quite what Harry, in his immaturity, had expected. The lower classes had shouted out, 'The Markis—Gawd bless 'im', and had reckoned him a daring and reckless fellow to have stolen the most beautiful woman in London from under another's nose. But Society was refusing to see anything either daring or reckless about it. He was frequently being cold-shouldered, and it was Henry Chaplin who was being made the hero, because of the gentlemanly way in which he had treated the whole affair.

Worst of all was the fact that his marriage to Florence was not proving to be a success. She was trying to reform him, and he did not want to be reformed. She was asking for children, and he did not want children. Responsibility was being thrust upon him, and he did not like responsibility. He wanted merely to go on drinking, gambling and racing. Above all, he wanted to achieve his life's ambition by winning the Derby.

The thought that Henry Chaplin was now in pursuit of the same objective, and looked as if he might well achieve it within the next few months, and at the expense of The Duke, was almost more than he could bear.

But a greater misfortune was about to befall Harry. The Duke, whom he so confidently expected to defeat whatever champion Chaplin might throw into the arena, was suddenly struck down in the spring with influenza, and this left the field clear for his enemy. Harry Hastings, besides having lost a small fortune in ante-post bets, now had nothing of any consequence at Danebury with which he could oppose Henry Chaplin in the classic races. He looked round in desperation for something which he could buy to rectify the situation.

He found what he believed to be the answer at the Craven Meeting which was held at Newmarket in April. The Biennial

Stakes for three-year-olds was won most convincingly by a 'Mr Henry's' bay colt, Kangaroo, from a large field which included Harry's own entry, Pantaloon. The identity of 'Mr Henry' was known to all. It was Harry's racing associate and kindly adviser, the money-lender, Henry Padwick.

So Harry Hastings walked down Hill Street to No 2, and there discussed his problems with Henry Padwick over a glass of the money-lender's vintage port. Henry Padwick proved a sympathetic and understanding confidant. He was well aware of Harry's acute rivalry with Henry Chaplin, for whom he had anyway no great love. Henry Chaplin did not approve of Padwick and had made little effort to conceal the fact; and so Padwick was more than willing to commiserate with Harry over The Duke's unfortunate illness and the fact that Harry had now no real opponent to match against Henry Chaplin's pair at Epsom.

Would Henry Padwick consider selling his own Derby prospect, Kangaroo, in order to solve the problem? Harry propounded his offer with his customary air of nonchalant indifference, and Henry Padwick considered it with *his* customary air of amiable co-operation. Yes—he was ready to consider the sale of Kangaroo, even though he might well, as a result, be forfeiting the opportunity to attain his life's ambition. For Kangaroo, he assured his young guest, was a very live Derby proposition. The colt's trainer, John Kent, had repeatedly assured Padwick that Kangaroo was a great horse in the making and was likely to prove more than a match for such as Breadalbane and Broomielaw. He was, in short, the probable Derby winner, and his sale would therefore be a great sacrifice and could only be made at a price.

And what might that price be? Again the question was propounded with seeming indifference and considered with kindly sympathy. Henry Padwick gazed ruminatively at his young friend over the rim of his glass and then gave his answer. His price for Kangaroo was 12,000 guineas.

Harry retained his air of nonchalance with difficulty, for he knew that if he accepted the offer, he would be paying the highest price ever given for a three-year-old during the long history of racing. In a way, the figure intrigued him. To accept such an offer would bring him instant notoriety. He would be the talk of the turf. Even veteran owners whose prodigality had become a by-word had never paid so huge a sum as this. And if Kangaroo *did* win the Derby, the colt would still prove cheap at the price. It was not simply a matter of hard cash. There would be the immense satisfaction of beating Henry Chaplin after all. This was the bait held out to him by his genial host, and this was the bait which he found impossible to resist. The vintage port was finished, and host and guest shook hands. When Harry Hastings stepped out into Hill Street and strolled across Berkeley Square, he was the new owner of Kangaroo, and Henry Padwick was the richer by 12,000 guineas.

The racing world hummed with excitement. The rivalry between Harry Hastings and Henry Chaplin was clearly to be fought out at Epsom, regardless of cost. Harry had already lost heavily in the winter bets which he had struck over The Duke. Now he was chasing his losses by buying Kangaroo. Henry Chaplin had paid £11,500 for *two* horses. Now Harry Hastings had paid 12,000 guineas for one!

Meanwhile Henry Chaplin, having registered his racing colours as 'all rose',[1] and having mentioned to his aristocratic racing friends that his immediate ambition was to become a member of the Jockey Club, devoted himself to pleasant speculation as to how Breadalbane and Broomielaw should be trained, and what races should be chosen for their respective débuts.

William I'Anson senior had bred them both. Each was sired by the illustrious Stockwell, and each had the blood of the peerless Blink Bonny in his veins. Each had been reared by a foster mother, or what was known in the curious terminology of the period as 'a Belgravian mother'. The foaling of Breadalbane had killed Blink Bonny, and Malton had mourned her passing as though the bereavement had been a personal one in every home. Her offspring took on a new attraction.

Henry Chaplin always favoured Breadalbane. His 'Belgravian mother' had been a cart horse, and the suckling of him by this sturdy mare seemed to have endowed the little fellow with added courage.

Broomielaw was a fine and handsome colt, but one cursed by Nature with that bitterness of soul with which she sometimes invests her best-bred products. It may have been a hereditary toothache, or some internal complaint that was never diagnosed. Whatever the cause, poor Broomielaw was destined to go through life hating the world and being himself hated by those who rode him.

[1] His second colours were rose, white cap.

From the outset of their careers the most sensational stories were circulated in Malton about their prowess. Long before either had ever seen a racecourse, both were being whispered as unbeatable. Malton was convinced that one or other must win the Derby for Henry Chaplin.

Neither raced in the early spring of 1865, and the first time Henry Chaplin's colours were carried on a racecourse was when Breadalbane went down to the start for the first of the classic races,[1] the Two Thousand Guineas, at Newmarket on 2 May.

Harry Hastings had taken up the challenge with his two classic contenders—Kangaroo, who was ridden by Fordham, and Pantaloon, ridden by Cannon.

Henry Chaplin's choice of jockey for Breadalbane was a youngster named Harry Custance, who was the same age as himself and held to be lucky by backers, who had seen him win the Derby at his very first attempt, on Thormanby in 1860, and very nearly win it on his second attempt in 1861, when he had finished second, thereby establishing himself as 'an Epsom Jockey', which the great Fordham was not. Also in the field was Liddington, who, as a two-year-old, had twice defeated The Duke; and also a real oddity of racing, a big-boned, ugly French horse named Gladiateur, owned by Count Frederick de Lagrange, the son of one of Napoleon's generals.

Harry Hastings and Henry Chaplin passed each other in the paddock, but only exchanged a nod of recognition. This was

---

[1] There are five races which, by tradition, are known as the classic races of the turf and are open to three-year-olds only. All runners carry the same weight, except that the colts make a sex allowance to the fillies. These five races are: *The Two Thousand Guineas* (for colts and fillies), established in 1809, and *The One Thousand Guineas* (for fillies only), established in 1814. Each is run over a mile at Newmarket in the Spring. *The Derby* (for colts and fillies), established in 1780 and named after the twelfth Earl of Derby. *The Oaks* (for fillies only), established in 1779. Each is run over a mile and a half at Epsom in early June, or late May. *The St Leger* (for colts and fillies), established in 1776 and named after Lieut.-Gen. Anthony St Leger. Run over a distance of one mile six furlongs and 132 yards at Doncaster at the beginning of September. Thus a colt can only achieve 'The Triple Crown' of *Two Thousand Guineas*, *Derby* and *St Leger*, but a filly can in theory win all five races. This has never been done, but Formosa (1868) and Sceptre (1902) each won four. 'The Triple Crown' has been won on fourteen occasions, the last colt to do so being Bahram in 1935. The first French horse to win the Derby was Gladiateur in 1865. The first American horse was Iroquois in 1881.

the first time that they had crossed swords, and first blood was important to each of them, but above all to Harry. If one lost and the other won, there would be the prize of a classic race to be acclaimed as a battle honour; and each young owner was smarting under the suggestion that he had paid an absurd price in an attempt to win this honour. In the betting in the Ring, Breadalbane was second favourite at 4 to 1, Kangaroo was 6 to 1 and Gladiateur at 7 to 1.

Henry Padwick was also to be seen in the paddock, amiable and suave as ever, and assuring all about him that Kangaroo had been cheap at the price and would win in a canter.

But neither Harry Hastings nor Henry Chaplin derived much benefit from the Two Thousand Guineas of 1865. Breadalbane ran a poor fifth, but neither Kangaroo nor Pantaloon made any showing in the race at all.

The winner was the 'Frenchman', Gladiateur.

This threw the whole Derby situation into some confusion. Few at Newmarket that afternoon accepted Breadalbane's running as representative. It was felt, especially at Malton, that he must have had a bad day. Kangaroo had looked dispirited in the paddock and was thought to be ungenuine—but still possibly formidable. Pantaloon had never been considered of much account, and so the race for the Derby seemed wide open.

Gladiateur's victory was looked upon as something of a fluke. The colt was known to be a martyr to lameness, and his jockey, Harry Grimshaw, was said to be so blind that he could scarcely see the winning post. Besides, the idea of a 'Frenchman' winning the Derby was unthinkable.

Harry Hastings retired to Danebury to discuss the Derby problem with John Day. He was disturbed by Kangaroo's poor showing in the Two Thousand and by the comments made behind his back that Padwick had made a fool of him and sold him an animal that was useless. His trainer assured him that he need have no worries. When he had received Kangaroo from Henry Padwick's trainer, John Kent (a rival for whom he had no great respect), the colt had clearly been under-trained. He would go to work on him during the ensuing four weeks before the Derby and send him to the post, fully trained for the first time in his career and as fit as a fiddle. All Kangaroo needed was plenty of sweating and some good, hard gallops.

Henry Chaplin retired to Malton and held similar talks with his trainer, William I'Anson junior. Here also the news was

Harry Hastings:
'The perfect Cocker'

Henry Chaplin:
'Magnifico'

Florence Paget: 'The Pocket Venus'

'The rage of the park, the ball-room, the opera and the croquet lawn'

Harry Hastings

Above left: The Prince of Wales as an Oxford undergraduate, 1859
Above right: Henry Chaplin

Below: The Bullingdon Cricket Club, 1859. The Prince of Wales centre and Henry Chaplin on his right

Florence Paget: 'Deprived of a mother's care at an early age, her education was hardly so advanced as might have been anticipated from her sphere in life. . . .'

Donington Park, Leicestershire. The seat of the Marquis of Hastings

Blankney Hall, Lincolnshire. The home of Henry Chaplin (demolished in 1961)

Hermit, with J. Daley: 'He destroyed a Marquis, avenged a Commoner, and attained turf immortality'

reassuring. Breadalbane, he was told, had not done himself justice at Newmarket. He would be a different horse at Epsom. Meanwhile Broomielaw was to make his racing début at Chester on 11 May in The Dee Stakes over the full Derby distance of a mile and a half. There was nothing to fear in this race. The opposition would not get near him. As for his temper, he was merely inclined to be a little irritable. Possibly this was due to the tooth trouble which ran in the family, for both Blink Bonny and Blair Athol had suffered from toothache. William I'Anson junior confidently predicted that on 11 May Henry Chaplin would see his colours carried to victory for the first time—but certainly not for the last.

This optimistic forecast proved substantially correct. Broomielaw appeared in the paddock looking fit but baleful, and eyed Custance malevolently as he climbed into the saddle. Henry Chaplin laid several substantial wagers in the Ring, which forced the colt to become odds-on, and then retired into the stand to watch the race. Harry Hastings stood some distance away, looking unusually subdued. The confidence behind Broomielaw was unmistakable.

In the race itself, Broomielaw did all that was expected of him. At half-way he responded to Custance's urging in a characteristic manner by swerving towards another runner, Breffni, and seizing hold of the jockey, Whiteley, by the leg, and he was only persuaded to leave go with difficulty. Finding himself then on his own, he ran on resolutely towards the winning post, which he passed some two lengths clear of his nearest rival. He was then pulled up after a struggle, but he only consented to enter the paddock after he had kicked down all the railings leading to it and had scattered the onlookers standing by.

Custance weighed in looking white and shaken. One thing had already become very clear to him. Broomielaw appeared to harbour a hatred for all mankind, but especially for Harry Custance.

The Derby problem was not greatly clarified by this performance. Broomielaw clearly had the ability to win, but possibly not the inclination. The stable's chief hope had still to be Breadalbane.

Meanwhile at Danebury there was bad news about The Duke, whom John Day considered would not be fit to race again until the autumn—possibly in time for the last of the classic races, the St Leger. Harry would therefore have to rely upon Kangaroo. But Kangaroo was not showing any marked improvement. Intensive training did not seem to suit him; and his trainer's promise to Harry that the colt would be 'a stone better on the day' seemed unlikely to materialize.

As the weeks of May went by, however, the news from Malton became ever more optimistic. Stories of sensational gallops in which Breadalbane had taken part were rife amongst the local Yorkshiremen, and local money was poured on to the colt by those who could ill afford to lose it. The more secrecy that was observed, the more the rumours grew. Henry Chaplin was advised by his trainer that he should keep himself hidden whenever he came to witness a trial, and the Squire of Blankney found himself approaching Malton like some archcriminal, arriving secretly by night and avoiding all main roads and the railway station.

The touts were not deceived. Their intelligence service would have done credit to any army headquarters in the field, and so bent old women hobbled painfully on crutches across the skyline as the Derby runners were exercised, while venerable clergymen, intent apparently on viewing only the beauties of nature, paused for a few seconds to watch the horses. Elsewhere bushes stirred unaccountably in the breathless summer air.

The sporting press echoed the mood of optimism, and since verse was an accepted method of tipping winners in those days, one prophet forecast the result in the following couplet:

The ribbon blue of '65, Squire Chaplin bears away,
　And Aldcroft and Breadalbane are the heroes of the day!

The reference to Aldcroft indicated that Custance was being claimed to ride Count Batthyany's King Charming, and so would not be available to ride Breadalbane—a sore disappointment to the stable, but something of a relief to Harry Custance.

However, Aldcroft, it was felt, would make a worthy substitute.

The son of a Manchester omnibus proprietor, Custance was a jockey of great dash, and—in his way—something of a buck. He had ridden Ellington to victory in the Derby of 1856, but he was equally famous in north-country circles as being the man who had introduced peg-top trousers into Middleham. This was held to denote class.

Meanwhile the news from Newmarket, where Gladiateur

was going through his final preparation, was equally optimistic; and although Grimshaw's eyesight was getting no better, the colt's lameness was getting no worse. It was whispered that he had run an amazing trial against his owner's filly, Fille de l'Air, who had won the Oaks in the previous year, and so Newmarket favoured his chances. The rest of England, patriotic to a man, would have none of him.

Derby Day, 31 May 1865.

A day of blazing sunshine and blue skies, which attracted an immense crowd to the course. But Epsom, on this occasion had an unusual experience. London racegoers on Derby Day were accustomed to hear the unfamiliar sound of broad Yorkshire accents, or even the lilt of a Welshman or two, but on this occasion they heard French. Many a cockney had never encountered the language before and viewed all who spoke it with dark suspicion. Rumours of a possible 'French invasion' had been current before the race and now here were foreigners by the score—and, what was worse, the horse which they had come to back was being made favourite.

The betting, in fact, concerned only two horses. Gladiateur was a clear favourite at 5 to 2. Breadalbane was second favourite at 7 to 2. Nothing else was being seriously backed to win the race. Broomielaw was on offer at 50 to 1 with few takers. Kangaroo could be backed at 100 to 1, but even Harry Hastings booked only a small bet at this price, for Kangaroo had appeared on the course looking listless and worn. All his old vigour had left him.

The Prince of Wales arrived on the course with Henry Chaplin, and made no secret of the fact that he was expecting to see his friend win. They were cheered as they were seen to enter the royal box and again when they walked down to the paddock. Both were immensely popular. A number of Henry's supporters had arrived wearing rose ties, in honour of his colours, and these supporters cheered lustily when, first, Breadalbane and then Broomielaw were led into the paddock. Breadalbane was soon to have his trainer, William I'Anson junior, at his head. This was taken as an indication of the importance which he attached to his charge. But Breadalbane looked to be dull in his coat and listless in his mood. Broomielaw, by way of contrast, was sweating and irritable. He lashed out occasionally, but did not appear to have sufficient energy in the heat to give his usual demonstration of ill temper.

Harry Hastings and Henry Chaplin met in the paddock,

and—as at Newmarket—contented themselves with a nod of recognition and a few stock phrases of good luck. Each was conscious of the fact that they were being closely watched by the large and fashionable crowd which surrounded the parade ring. Their rivalry was adding a pleasant flavour to the occasion.

Harry had brought his Marchioness, but Florence had remained in their box, excusing herself on account of the heat. She also was looking tired and worried, and it was noted that she had already lost much of her former gaiety and sparkle. She seemed at pains to avoid her old friends; and it was noted that Harry himself paid no great attention to her. Instead he gazed down upon the busy throng, listening to the clamour of the Ring which was the music of his life.

Kangaroo he had no great expectation of; Breadalbane he hoped most avidly would lose. Already he was manifesting that illogical antagonism to all Henry Chaplin's horses which was to become an obsession with him in the months and years to come. His resentment of Henry Chaplin and all he stood for—generosity, magnanimity and good sportsmanship—was growing increasingly greater. But outwardly he remained the same Harry Hastings—smiling, unruffled and debonair, seemingly oblivious of the issues at stake, and exchanging casual banter with his cronies, who crowded, as always, around him and laughed sycophantically at his every sally.

Out on the Downs, rumours were tossed back and forth among the crowd; and suspicion of the French contingent steadily deepened. It was common knowledge that the 'froggies' were convinced that some fearful British plot was being hatched to rob them of the race, and that if Gladiateur himself was not nobbled, then poor Harry Grimshaw certainly would be. It had been said of the French that they had brought over a contingent of 600 brawny prizefighters who would surround Gladiateur on the way to the start and act as his bodyguard, but when the runners did finally appear, the crush about them as they slowly wended their way up the hill was so great that no one could be certain whether his neighbour was an honest backer, a master nobbler or a foreign pugilist, and in the ensuing excitement it was only the pickpockets who really came into their own.

Harry Grimshaw, on Gladiateur, looked nervously about him through short-sighted eyes and gave every indication of being apprehensive, while excited Gallic shouts of 'Vive la

France' were as quickly drowned by honest British shouts of derision. In all, it was a scene such as Epsom Downs had never witnessed before.

Bad starting was a feature of racing at the time, and the usual trouble occurred on this occasion. There were several false starts, and one of the runners, with the unfortunate name of Joker, became so restive that he lashed out, fell and injured his jockey, E. Sharp. When the flag did finally fall, and the field was away, both Gladiateur and Breadalbane were badly off, and it was Broomielaw, showing the whites of his eyes, who was first round Tattenham Corner. Here Gladiateur was lying tenth, and Breadalbane was still in the ruck. But Broomielaw's bolt was quickly shot once the field entered the straight, despite the shouted encouragement of his supporters. Soon afterwards Grimshaw, peering short-sightedly over his mount's ears at the fast-approaching winning post, took up the running without effort and won comfortably by two lengths.

For a moment there was a stunned silence on the course. A Frenchman had won the Derby! It was unthinkable. The very foundations of the British Empire seemed to shake.

In a fashionable West End club, a week before, an elderly member had drawn Gladiateur in the club sweep and had rejected the ticket as an insult. Now, as the news filtered back to Mayfair by messenger, a nervous consultation was held in the smoking room to decide who should break the news to him.

It was the knell of doom. If a French horse could win the Derby, then anything might win it. An Irish horse, perhaps, or even an American one, though the stoutest of Englishmen boggled at the thought, and prayed that it might not be in their lifetime, happily unaware that even this final humiliation was not then so far away.[1]

> *Cockadoodledo, Jean!*
>   *Ha! mon Bull chéri.*
> *Ciel! Je ne moque pas mais*
>   *Des Anglais sans esprit.*
> *Vanquished on your proper ground,*
>   *N'est ce pas, mon chou?*
> *Cockadoodledo, Jean,*
>   *Cockadoodledo.*

The lines appeared in *Bell's Life* and were not considered to

[1] Iroquois, in 1881, was the first American horse to win the Derby.

be altogether in good taste. There were some things which one did not make fun of. Defeat in the Derby by a Frenchman was one of them.

The crowds melted from the Downs, and the inquests which are the aftermath of any great race were duly held in the public houses and training centres all over England.

Harry made no complaint about the running of Kangaroo. He was already resigned to the situation, although he did not understand it. Henry Chaplin was left in a less tolerant mood. His two runners had performed deplorably, and he wanted to know why. In this he was supported by Sir Frederick Johnstone, who had already appointed himself Henry's racing adviser and guide. Together they journeyed to Malton to have the matter out with the I'Ansons, father and son. It was said that there they quarrelled violently, although Henry Chaplin's continued friendship with the younger I'Anson in the years to come does not support this. The I'Ansons probably resented Sir Frederick Johnstone's interference and his advice, which was freely given. They also knew the vagaries of the Queen Mary stock, who were never easy to train and could not always be relied upon to give of their best, but they found this point difficult to prove.

Whatever the mood of the discussion, the outcome was a parting of the ways. Henry Chaplin decided to move his string from Malton, which was anyway a long way from both London and Lincolnshire, and to send them temporarily to William Goater at Findon, in Sussex, while he looked round for a young and enterprising expert who could manage his racehorses and supervise their training. In this connection, the name of the brilliant young Captain Machell was already in his mind.

As for the jockeys who rode in the Derby, he had no fault to find with them. It has always been a common practice amongst ill-informed racehorse owners to blame the jockey when anything goes wrong. Henry Chaplin was not ill-informed, and his loyalty to his jockeys was never influenced by what happened in the running. He chose riders whom he could trust, and then he trusted them. In this case, he blamed neither Aldcroft on Breadalbane nor Mann on Broomielaw. He accepted that they had done their best.

He may have been unjust to the I'Ansons, whose faith in Breadalbane and Broomielaw had been as great as his own.

The answer to the whole question was one which affected

Kangaroo as well. It was the *policy* of the trainer, not his integrity, which was in each case to blame. Breadalbane had been hurried unwisely in his preparation. Kangaroo had been grossly overworked.

Whatever Henry Padwick may have done to Harry Hastings in the years which were to follow, the condemnation of him which is to be found in almost every history of the turf—that he sold an inexperienced young owner a worthless horse for a fantastic price—cannot be supported by the facts. John Kent, who trained Kangaroo for Padwick when he won three races in succession before Harry Hastings bought the colt, wrote in his memoirs that Kangaroo was a powerful and muscular horse who might seem, to the uninitiated, to be only half-trained. When Harry sent the horse to John Day, the trainer announced his intention of sweating Kangaroo in several long, hard gallops as a means of bringing him on a stone at least in time for the Two Thousand Guineas. Kent, who was a wiser and more humane trainer than Day, warned him that the horse was already fully fit and could not be made any better, but John Day did not believe him.

But it was always Day's failing that he over-worked his horses, and often broke their spirits. This he almost certainly did with Kangaroo, and Padwick has been vilified by sporting writers ever since. Padwick may have been a money-lender and a hard man of business; and he was certainly not above asking an absurd price for an animal if he thought that he could get it. But he sold Kangaroo to Harry in good faith, believing him to be a good and genuine colt, as indeed he probably was.

It must be said to Harry Hastings' credit that he did not join in the popular outcry against Padwick. Harry was a professional in one thing; he was a professional gambler, and he took the rough with the smooth, as all professional backers must do.

Harry Hastings' critics have always condemned him for paying absurd prices for his horses. This is not so. He paid an absurd price for Kangaroo (though it might not have been such an absurd one had the colt kept his form and won the Derby, as he well might), but he did not make the same mistake again. Many of the good horses which Harry bought during his racing career were inexpensive. Unlike Henry Chaplin, he was never a prodigal spender, but only a prodigal backer. Again and again, when Harry's name is mentioned in the histories of the turf, it is in connection with his foolish extravagance over Kangaroo, yet this is probably the only horse for which Harry ever gave an excessive price. Two of the best horses he owned were The Duke and The Earl, for whom he paid 500 guineas and 450 guineas respectively, and each was cheap at the price. He paid 2,000 guineas for Ackworth but, in view of what Ackworth won him over his Cambridgeshire gamble, Ackworth was cheap at the price as well.

Harry's mistakes in racing were that he took under the odds and that he placed too much confidence in the traditional training methods of John Day. Unlike Henry Chaplin, Harry neither understood horses nor loved them, and so when John Day worked horses too hard, Harry did not complain. This was ultimately one of the main causes of his failure, and in this respect there may well have been a certain poetic justice in his downfall.

The events of Derby Day, 1865, therefore brought little satisfaction to either of the rivals, who were left to brood upon their losses and to consider their respective policies for the future. And it was now, largely by chance, that Henry Chaplin gave Harry Hastings a further cause for anger and resentment. In place of the I'Ansons, he chose as his future trainer a simple but wholly dependable Newmarket 'character' named Old Bloss, who resided at Bedford Cottage; and in view of the old fellow's obvious limitations, Henry Chaplin decided to place him under the surveillance of an astute and experienced racing manager. This post he offered to a close friend of Harry's, the brilliant young Captain Machell.

The pair were kindred spirits. They drank together, gambled together over cards or dice and discussed racing endlessly. Machell had all the qualities which Harry Hastings most admired. As a gambler he had courage, and as a backer he had brains. Newmarket was the centre of his world, and he weaved himself into the very texture of its racing life. He was an excellent judge of a horse and knew far more than Harry did about methods of training. The chief difference between them was that Harry had inherited wealth, whereas Machell was forced to live by his wits. They were more than able to support him.

The Victorian turf produced few more remarkable men than James Octavus Machell. He was a member of an old Westmorland family, the Machells of Crackenthorpe, and was born at Beverley Rectory in 1838, his father being the Reverend

Robert Machell, the priest of the parish. He was educated at Rossall, and at the age of eighteen he joined the 14th Foot, later the West Yorkshire Regiment, as a subaltern. He was a capable officer, a splendid athlete of remarkable physique, and a man of outstanding courage. When, in 1862, he was promoted to Captain and exchanged into the 59th Regiment, his army career seemed assured. Amongst the many legends current about him in the army at the time was that while at the Curragh he had repeatedly performed the seemingly impossible feat of making a stationary jump from the floor to the mantelpiece in Morrison's Hotel in Dublin. It is hardly necessary to add that bets were always laid on this event, and that he always won. He also won a bet of £1,000 when he beat the local champions in a walking race, and with this as capital he bought several racehorses.

All went well with him until the day when his Commanding Officer refused his application for a few days' leave in order to attend Doncaster Races. Machell was so indignant that he promptly resigned his commission and turned to the turf. He had little money and no prospects; but he did have his racehorses. One of these was a brown colt named Bacchus.

This was in 1863, at time when he and Harry Hastings were first becoming acquainted. Having resigned his commission, Machell was determined to make the turf his career and to take up training, but he had no capital to do so. He therefore decided to stake his whole future on a single gamble. If this came off, he would become an owner-trainer at Newmarket. If it failed, Newmarket would never see him again.

In the spring of 1864 he entered Bacchus for one of the big Newmarket handicaps in which he knew there would be a large field and heavy betting. The race was the Prince of Wales's Stakes, to be run over the Rowley Mile, and with money borrowed from friends he was able to trade at long odds over Bacchus and backed himself to win £10,000.

The mount was entrusted to a lightweight jockey named Tomlinson, and as Bacchus cantered down to the post, Machell was aware that his whole future on the turf was dependent on the combined efforts of jockey and horse.

Bacchus was slowly away, was interfered with in the running and finally swerved under pressure near the finish. He won by a neck, and the owner of the second horse promptly lodged an objection on the grounds of crossing.

Machell stood poker-faced and unruffled while the Stewards

considered their verdict. In due course they decided to overrule the objection, and Bacchus was allowed to keep the race. Captain Machell's career at Newmarket had begun.

Harry Hastings had watched the race and saluted the winning owner after it was over. It was a gamble after his own heart.

Captain Machell at once took Beaufort House and its stables, just outside Newmarket, and set up as a trainer, backed by two wealthy owners, Lord Lonsdale and Lord Calthorpe. Neither of these two patrons, nor Machell himself, had any real doubts about the outcome of this enterprise. Machell was shrewd to the point of being cunning, an expert judge of horses—and lucky. It is an invincible combination on the turf.

Because of his shrewdness, Machell began from then on to pay particular attention to the wealthy and reckless young aristocrats of the turf, as he realized that it was with such owners that he could be most successful. Harry Hastings was exactly the type of owner for whom he would have liked to have trained, because Harry and he understood each other so well, shared the same interests and talked the same language. From time to time he may well have put out a few tentative suggestions to Harry that he might train a few of Harry's horses, but Harry was wedded to Danebury. The magic of John Day's name was undeniable, and although Harry greatly admired Machell and found him a most convivial companion, he may well have been reluctant to entrust his destiny on the turf to someone who was only a few years older than himself.

It therefore came as a considerable blow to Harry when Henry Chaplin, showing far more enterprise and initiative, offered Machell the post of his racing manager at Newmarket —an offer which Machell immediately accepted. No doubt Harry preserved his usual air of indifference over the whole affair and warmly congratulated Machell on his good fortune, but it can only have served to anger him and deepen his jealousy and resentment towards Henry Chaplin. From then on, Harry and Machell continued outwardly as good friends, but each knew inwardly that they were now on opposite sides. Machell's allegiance was to Henry Chaplin, and his purpose was to win the Derby for his new patron. This could only be done at the expense of his old confederate in many a wild escapade, and racing secrets could no longer be shared between them. Machell had joined the enemy, and from now on no quarter could be asked or given.

Henry Chaplin soon realized the wisdom of his decision. The whole conduct of his racing affairs was now on a far sounder and more business-like footing than previously. Old Bloss was a simple countryman who both loved and understood horses. He treated them like children and even slept with them in their boxes if he thought that they were lonely or frightened. He knew little about betting or the Ring, but he knew a great deal about the training of a racehorse. And he could be trusted implicitly.

Captain Machell, on the other hand, knew everything about betting and the Ring. Moreover he appealed to Henry Chaplin because he was young, personable and well-bred—a gentleman who could be accepted as a social equal. In this he was very different from the generally accepted type of Victorian trainer such as John Day, a dour and suspicious countryman and certainly no gentleman. Henry Chaplin respected his new racing manager's judgment, and admired him as a man. As a result, Machell was soon accepted as a member of the Chaplin set, which meant that he also became acquainted with royalty. Being a shrewd and intelligent young man, he altered his way of life accordingly; and the Hastings set saw less and less of him. It was certain from then on that Captain Machell would enjoy a long and successful career on the turf. He had everything in his favour.

Thus by the late summer of 1865 the rivalry between Harry Hastings and Henry Chaplin had been marked by no notable triumphs on either side. Each had spent a great deal of money to little purpose, and neither had enjoyed any success whatever in the classic races. There was, however, one further classic race to be resolved. Harry had always maintained that The Duke would have beaten Gladiateur and won the Derby had his colt not caught influenza in the spring. Henry Chaplin, despite his disappointment over Breadalbane's performance in the Derby, still believed that the son of Blink Bonny might yet prove himself a champion. And a great many people throughout England still believed that the combination of the French cripple, Gladiateur, and his half-blind jockey, Harry Grimshaw, could scarcely be expected to go on winning classic races.

These matters could be settled, once and for all, in the final classic race of the season, the St Leger Stakes, to be run in mid-September over a mile and three-quarters at Doncaster. On the day of the race, Gladiateur was made favourite at 13 to 8 *on,* The Duke was backed down to second favourite by Harry and Breadalbane was unconsidered at 25 to 1. Broomielaw, now growing daily more unmanageable, was not required by his owner to perform. He had already chased several people off Newmarket Heath, charged a cow and bitten off a stable-boy's thumb. The only person who could do anything with him was his gentle and kind-hearted trainer, Old Bloss.

Turf historians have varied in their estimate of Gladiateur, some believing him to have been a great racehorse, others maintaining that he was no more than a good horse in a poor year. Whatever the truth, he had no difficulty in winning the St Leger and thus achieving 'The Triple Crown' of the three classic races. He won by three lengths, and the race was without incident, save for the objection lodged against him by a Mr Graham, the owner of the second, who declared that the winner was in reality a four-year-old and should therefore forfeit the race. On his failing to produce any concrete grounds for this remarkable assertion, the Stewards over-ruled what they no doubt considered an ill-advised attempt to gain the prize by trickery, and the stakes were paid over to Count Lagrange.

The Duke did not distinguish himself and only finished fourth. This seemed to dispose, once and for all, of Harry's boast that the colt would have won the Derby had he been fit. But he was clearly a very good horse, and Harry still had reason to have high hopes for him in the future.

Henry Chaplin was not unduly depressed by Breadalbane's further failure. The colt had won him two good races and was destined to win him two more before the end of the season. It had really been too much to hope that he might win the Derby in his first year as an owner.

Broomielaw, it was true, had proved a disappointment, and the 1,000 to 800 fearlessly laid with more than one operator in the Ring at York had been lost to the bookmakers when Custance could only finish second in the Great Yorkshire Stakes in August. But this had at least shown that Henry Chaplin, when he believed he was on a good thing, was almost as fearless a backer as Harry Hastings himself. He had ceased to buy horses as though he were drunk, but despite Captain Machell he was still backing them on occasions as though he were mad. He, too, was determined to break the Ring.

On 27 September 1865 Henry Chaplin was elected a member of the Jockey Club, an honour which gave him much satisfaction, for it added greatly to his self-importance and prestige. The Jockey Club was the ruling body of racing, and its members represented the cream of racing society. Its headquarters were at Newmarket, and as much a part of it, Frank Siltzer has said in his history of the town, as Wall Street is a part of New York or the Cathedral a part of Canterbury—an informative comment, for the arrangements of the Club certainly had a somewhat cathedral-like atmosphere, while the decisions taken by its committee could greatly influence the finances of the turf. He might have added, as a further comparison, the Law Courts in relations to London, for the function of the Jockey Club was both law-making and disciplinary. Its powers over the turf were all-embracing and its decisions subject to no appeal. The Stewards of the Jockey Club, in their own sphere of racing, had greater powers than the Judges of the High Court. To be elected a member of the Jockey Club was a signal honour. To be black-balled from it, or deprived of membership, was the ultimate disgrace for a man of quality.

It is one of the ironies of life that few men realize when they are face to face with Destiny. The supreme moment, when failure or success are balanced in the scales, is often unrecognized at the time.

It is doubtful if either Harry Hastings or Henry Chaplin, when they came to look back on the racing season of 1865 as it gradually drew to its end, could have chosen its highlight with any certainty. Henry Chaplin would probably have considered that his greatest moment came when his colours were first carried to victory on the turf on 11 May. Harry might have chosen one or other of his luckier gambles. Yet in fact the supreme moment in both their lives came on a pleasant Saturday afternoon in June, when neither was conscious of any sense of urgency or climax.

The best-known breeder of the day was a Mr Blenkiron, whose Middle Park Stud was the largest breeding centre in Europe and had produced many racehorses of the highest quality. It was his custom to hold a yearling sale after the last day of the Ascot Meeting, and so, on Saturday, 17 June 1865, a fashionable crowd of wealthy patrons of the turf assembled at Eltham, in Surrey, to watch the yearlings paraded before Mr Blenkiron and to bid on any they particularly fancied. 'There, in the sunshine near the graves of Kingston and

Defenceless, and in the trim garden with its white walls and their drooping laburnums, were assembled the *Magnates* of the turf.' So wrote the Marchioness of Londonderry in her biography of the life of her father, Henry Chaplin.

Henry Chaplin had driven down to Eltham in company with his racing manager, Captain Machell, and a party that included Lord Maidstone, Lord Grey and the uncrowned ruler of the turf and its autocratic dictator, Admiral Rous. Harry Hastings was also present, in his most casual mood, laughing and talking with his cronies and seemingly scarcely conscious of the yearlings who were parading before his eyes. Close by was the bearded Glasgow ironmaster, Mr James Merry, a rough diamond with a rough tongue, but already one of the most famous owners on the English turf, who had won the Derby of 1861 with Thormanby and collected some £40,000 in bets as a result.

These were but a few of the wealthy and well-informed racing men who had given up a Saturday afternoon on their country estates to engage in the fascinating pastime of trying to assess a yearling's hopes for the future as it walked, leggy, nervous and fretful, round Mr Blenkiron's little ring against the background of the trim white walls and the drooping laburnums.

The yearlings came and went, some whom the experts considered to be of exceptional breeding and conformation being knocked down for as much as a thousand or two, others fetching no more than a few hundreds. Harry was bidding freely and with his customary indifference as to price. He realized that much of what was happening amounted really to one vast gamble, for no one could say with any certainty how these youngsters might turn out, and so he bid often on impulse and out of intuition. Purchases made at yearling sales, as he knew well, were largely a matter of luck.

'Lot 27, gentlemen,' intoned Mr Blenkiron. 'A chestnut colt by Newminster out of Seclusion. . . .'

The colt, a dark chestnut, a little on the small side, but neat and well made, entered the ring unconcernedly and circled it with placid detachment.

'I don't have to remind you, gentlemen,' continued Mr Blenkiron, 'that Newminster is the sire of Sir Joseph Hawley's recent Derby winner, Musjid, and that Seclusion is descended from Bay Middleton. Here is an exceptionally well-bred colt. . . .'

Well-bred, perhaps, but not exceptionally. But a good-looker, none the less, with obvious potential. The bidding was languid at first and never reached any degree of urgency. Harry Hastings stood on one side of the ring, studying his catalogue and indicating his intention with the barest movement of his hand.

Henry Chaplin and Captain Machell stood on the other side, deep in consultation and also indicating their interest by a momentary signal to the auctioneer. The bidding rose by fifties until Henry Chaplin stood in at 900 guineas. The auctioneer turned to Harry Hastings, who nodded back.

'At 950 guineas . . .' said Mr. Blenkiron, raising his hammer.

Henry Chaplin turned to Captain Machell and whispered a few words. Captain Machell nodded towards the auctioneer.

'One thousand guineas,' said Mr Blenkiron, turning back towards Harry Hastings. Harry paused, pursed his lips, then shrugged and looked away.

There being no further bid, the little chestnut colt was knocked down to Captain Machell, bidding on behalf of Henry Chaplin, for 1,000 guineas.

The next yearling, another chestnut colt, was led into the ring and Mr Blenkiron addressed his listeners once again.

'Lot 28, gentlemen—a chestnut colt by Dundee out of Shot. You will recall,' and here he looked in the direction of Mr Merry, 'that Dundee finished second in the Derby of 1861. A most gallant performance. . . .'

There was no one present that afternoon who needed to be reminded of *that*, and least of all Mr Merry, who had seen his horse, Dundee, break down on both forelegs as he neared the post at Epsom and yet still struggle on with the utmost resolution to finish second. Mr Blenkiron had not exaggerated. The long saga of the Derby Stakes had contained no finer example of indomitable courage.

Lot 28, the chestnut colt by Dundee, was knocked down to Mr Merry for 1,000 guineas, and the two yearlings went their separate ways, one to old Bloss at Newmarket, the other to Mathew Dawson at Russley. They were destined to meet again.

On the way back in the coach, Henry Chaplin and Captain Machell fell to discussing a name for the yearling which Henry had just bought. The breeding, by Newminster out of Seclusion, suggested a certain monastic solitude. In the end they christened the little fellow Hermit.

CHAPTER SEVEN

EBB AND FLOW—1866

By 1866, Harry Hastings was beginning to deteriorate rapidly both physically and morally. His habits were becoming more dissolute, he was gambling far more heavily, and he was no longer a handsome young man, but already a pallid and often haggard-looking rake. He was in his twenty-fourth year and already he was beginning to look careworn and old.

Already, by 1866, Florence was beginning also to realize that her task in reforming him, and saving him from a mode of life which must ultimately ruin him financially and destroy him bodily, was doomed to failure. Harry did not wish to be reformed. And his affection for Florence was certainly not sufficient to make him take control of himself. He was dedicating himself to becoming his own executioner.

He had not married Florence out of love or passion, and neither therefore existed to keep them together in any sort of happiness, or even contentment. She did not like his friends, who were dissolute and weak like himself, and she was unable to live his sort of life, drinking until all hours of the night and then retiring at dawn to sleep through the day until it was time for another debauch. She was not a child, and she had seen drunkenness and dissipation before, but not on the scale to which he had become accustomed. Finally his reckless gambling appalled her. He was wealthy, but even his wealth had limits. She went racing with him occasionally to the more important and fashionable meetings and especially to Newmarket, Epsom and Ascot.

But it was not only his gambling on horses that alarmed her. On the racecourse he was shrewd, and although he often accepted under the odds and his vanity demanded that any horse of his which he fancied had to start favourite, he yet had an undeniable skill at assessing form. It was in the evenings, when racing was over for the day, that his wildness and complete irresponsibility asserted itself. He had no head for liquor, which his cronies knew only too well, and he loved to become the centre of attention by ostentatiously making some foolhardy wager. Any evening when the mood was on him, and the onlookers were applauding his daring, he would throw dice for a hundred pounds a time, toss a coin with anyone in the room for a £50 note, or cut a pack of cards at random, and seemingly with only the most casual interest, for £200 a cut.

One evening, playing hazard at Crockford's, he won over £10,000. Encouraged by this success, he returned the next evening to lose £20,000 without any outward signs of emotion, whether of chagrin or resentment.

Florence tried to reason with him, but he would not listen. She tried to stop him drinking, but he refused to alter his habits. He was not unkind to her, in that he never beat her or ill-treated her. He was far too weak and amiable to commit any act of physical violence. But he was selfish, and unobservant, and he paid little attention to her when she was obviously distressed. He must often have wondered why she had married him. It was evident that she found him sexually attractive, unlike Henry Chaplin, who had never been physically acceptable to her. In the first few months of their marriage, she had fussed over him and gently reprimanded him, expecting that he would, in his turn, make an effort to reform himself. When he had refused and had continued to pursue exactly the same way of life as previously, she had at first become tearful, and then resentful. She was loyal and remained protective, realizing that she was dealing with someone who was fundamentally little more than a child—but a spoilt, exasperating and stubborn child who could neither be cajoled nor disciplined.

She must have realized, quite early in her married life, that she had made a terrible mistake. The glamour, the physical ardour and the crusading fire of her honeymoon soon burnt themselves out. It was not long before she began to think with affection and deep regret of the man whom she had so sorely wronged.

The fact that Florence began to make overtures to Henry Chaplin within a relatively short time of her marriage is not to condemn her. Such overtures were made with modesty and discretion. At first she did little more than to reveal to him that her former affection and admiration for him were by no means dead. Later she began to write pathetic notes to him in which she spoke of the wretchedness of her life with Harry. In her final state of humiliation she was forced to borrow money from him; but this was yet to come.

Henry Chaplin, for his part, showed no bitterness towards her, but he also showed no evidence of his former spontaneous admiration and ardour. He had ceased to love her and he had ceased to find her beauty irresistible. When they met socially and exchanged a few casual and non-committal remarks, the impression which he gave was that he still had affection for her, because of the past, but that his predominant feeling towards her was one of pity. Many men would have shown a certain satisfaction at her plight after having been jilted so shamelessly. Henry Chaplin showed no such attitude. He was not a person to indulge in any form of recrimination. But he made it very clear that the past was past. No matter what might happen to Harry Hastings, he would never again look upon her with love and adoration.

Harry may or may not have realized that his young wife was already beginning to make discreet and timid overtures to the man whom she had betrayed; and he may or may not have appreciated the fact that Henry Chaplin no longer loved her. If he *did* appreciate this fact, it must have increased his resentment towards his rival. It is a bitter thing to deprive your rival of something which he values highly and then to discover later that he no longer attaches such great importance to it. But whatever Harry's reactions, he continued to live an extravagant life of uncurbed dissipation, and to make every possible effort to outdo Henry Chaplin on the turf. In this he was certainly successful during the racing season of 1866.

In this year he also began to challenge Henry Chaplin in a sphere which the Squire of Blankney held to be very much his own. This was the hunting field, with all the prestige which attaches itself to the Master of a famous hunt. In this sphere Harry suffered from one great disadvantage, for he was not a natural horseman or hunt-lover; but he enjoyed one major advantage in that he was considerably richer than Henry Chaplin. Being the Master of a hunt costs a great deal of money; and it often proved more than Chaplin could afford.

The blow which Henry Chaplin suffered when Florence eloped was such that he momentarily seemed to lose his interest in hunting. There could have been no clearer indication of how grievously he had been stricken. In 1863, when his friend, Lord Henry Bentinck, had resigned the Mastership of the Burton Hunt, Henry Chaplin had first of all bought all his hounds, and then all his hunters, but the loss of Florence, followed by his trips abroad with Sir Frederick Johnstone, made it impossible for him to be an efficient Master, and the pack was taken over by Lord Doneraile. But by 1866 Henry Chaplin had regained all his old enthusiasm for hunting and was once again back as Master (Lord Doneraile had found the Mastership very costly and had been glad to be rid of this financial burden).

Henry Chaplin was now a happy young man again. The wound had healed, as Lord Henry Bentinck had forecast it would, once Henry had faced up to the facts, and now he settled down to an ordered, if extravagant, way of life. In the summer he raced his horses, played a prominent part in the London season and visited Cowes. In the winter he hunted. He kept four packs of hounds and hunted his own pack twice a week. He himself hunted six days a week. Moreover he undertook to hunt the country very largely at his own expense. This way of life alarmed many of his friends. He had no great expectations of inheriting any further money, and he was already spending his existing capital at an alarming rate. His racing interests, in particular, were a considerable drain on his resources. It was clear to them that the Squire would soon be in need of something in the nature of a substantial windfall if he was to keep up his existing standards.

Not the least of his financial problems stemmed from the need of entertaining the Prince of Wales, who was a frequent visitor to Blankney during the hunting season. Hounds would meet outside the Green Man on Lincoln Heath, and the Prince and Henry would be surrounded by a delighted retinue of local followers. The Prince, at this stage in his life, had not fully developed the expensive tastes which helped to ruin so many of his friends in the years to come, but Henry's income, liberal though it was, could not encompass the many demands made upon it. He, too, must have begun to realize by 1866 that a windfall of some description would sooner or later become imperative. He was quite prepared to match Harry Hastings in the fearlessness of his wagering; but although he knew far more about horses than Harry, he did not know so much about betting. And Harry was the shrewder judge of form.

The news of Henry Chaplin's prodigality at Blankney and his prestige and popularity as the Master of the Burton Hunt, irritated Harry Hastings considerably. He probably felt that Henry Chaplin was beginning to grow pompous and self-important, and that it was time someone set out to eclipse him. There may have been other considerations which prompted

Harry to accept the Mastership of the Quorn in 1866. His father, the second Marquis, had lived only for hunting. 'His son,' wrote 'The Druid', 'cared for none of these things. Still, he could not bear to see the Quorn without a Master, and he stepped boldly into the breach when Mr Clowes resigned in 1866.'

This may be a flattering assessment of Harry's motives. The Quorn had a long association, it is true, with the house of Hastings. Under Hugo Meynell, of Quorndon Hall, the Quorn had more or less monopolized Leicestershire, but in 1834 Harry's father, the second Marquis, had approached the then Master, Mr Holyoake, and had been granted permission for the Donington area to be hunted separately by the Marquis's own pack. This arrangement had continued until 1851, when the district was handed back to the Quorn. There had therefore been a close understanding between the house of Hastings and the Quorn.

The Quorn was one of the most famous hunts in England, and Leicestershire was the most famous of the hunting shires. Thus if Harry wished to outdo his rival, Henry Chaplin, he could hardly have chosen two better spheres than the turf and the hunting field. He may have been influenced by his family traditions and by the problems facing the Quorn and accepted the Mastership because of them; but it seems probable that he also accepted this honour for more selfish reasons.

But one may well ask what the members of the Quorn were about when they offered him this distinguished position. They must have been well aware of his lack of interest in hunting and his casual and dissipated habits; and they must therefore have realized that, as Master, he could only prove to be casual, unpunctual and ineffective. Mr Clowes had resigned in March, and *The Pall Mall Gazette* had shrewdly observed at the time that what the Hunt needed was 'neither a millionaire nor a kind of head huntsman, but the payment of subscriptions to one of their own class who will command the affections of his neighbours and the confidence of all the country'.

The Quorn country had some unusual features, and these added to the cost of running the Hunt. There had therefore been a tendency in the past to elect a Master who was very wealthy and was willing to bear most of the financial burden himself—often with the result that other members of the Hunt were able to evade some of their own commitments. What was really needed by the Quorn in 1866 was a practical approach to these problems, uninfluenced by self-interest, and with a determination to see that everyone made his fair contribution. But the temptation to take the easy way out, and to solve the problem simply by choosing a wealthy Master, was not easy to resist; and they did not resist it. When Harry Hastings announced his willingness to accept the post, everyone concerned with the Hunt breathed a sigh of relief and applauded his magnanimity. 'The Druid' wrote:

> He wore the horn at his saddle bow for conformity's sake, but he never blew it, and he let the field go its own way, and hunted the country on no system. A bit of a gallop, a check, and then trotting off to sift a favourite gorse for a fresh fox jumped much more with his humour than an old-fashioned hunting run, where hounds had to puzzle it out. Often, when his hounds had reached the meet, ten or twelve miles away, he was hardly out of bed, and he would turn up 'on wheels', and occasionally from London by special train, and give Wilson the word to draw when half the field had gone home. No wonder that caricatures were drawn, and squibs flew gaily about, and that even Leicestershire said it would rather be bled in the purse-vein than have the country hunted gratis in such fashion. Satirical verses failed to sour him. He took the sting out of their tail by reprinting them at his own private press, and posted them far and wide.

How different is the picture of Henry Chaplin at the same time, Master of the Burton Hunt and Lord of the Manor of Blankney, and a man both able and willing to face all responsibilities and to cope with all difficulties. Harry was despised by nearly all the members of the Quorn, but the members of the Burton Hunt looked up to their Master and happily accepted his leadership. There had been trouble in the district, and poison, barbed wire and traps were causing bitter quarrels between the hunting and non-hunting fraternity. Lord Henry Bentinck, with his peppery manner, had been unable to subdue these quarrels, but Henry Chaplin's charm of manner, and the universal respect in which he was held, smoothed out many of these differences.

The most popular poem which was circulated about Harry Hastings at the time was one entitled 'Who Can Tell?' and it found its way into many a country house in Leicestershire, where it was sometimes posted up in a gun-room or billiards-room for the edification of the guests. It ran as follows:

WHO CAN TELL?

When will the Marquis come?
   Who can tell?
Half-past twelve or half-past one?
   Who can tell?
Driving at an awful rate
As if afraid that he is late,
What cares he how long we wait?
   Who can tell? Who can tell?

Shall we have to wait again?
   Who can tell?
In the wind and in the rain?
   Who can tell?
While the Marquis, snug and warm,
In the hall where toadies swarm
Leaves us to the pelting storm?
   Who can tell? Who can tell?

Where will he draw, by way of lark?
   Who can tell?
Gartree Hill or Bradgate Park?
   Who can tell?
Sport regarding as a jest,
North or south, or east or west,
Which will suit his fancy best?
   Who can tell? Who can tell?

Where, oh where is Tailby's horn?
   Who can tell?
Why came I with this cussed Quorn?
   Who can tell?
Marquis, this is not a race,
Can you look us in the face
And say you really like the chase?
   Who can tell? Who can tell?

There was also a famous sketch of the Master, which pictures him standing still on his horse and surveying the disorganized field, while Sir Frederick Johnstone, beside him, is saying urgently, 'They're wrong, Harry! Blow your horn, for God's sake!' To which Harry replies, 'I can't. I should be sick if I did!'

The depths of dissipation to which Harry Hastings was now rapidly sinking is illustrated by a comment made by Lord Rosebery, and referred to in the Marquess of Crewe's life of the fifth Earl. He says that Lord Rosebery was always very interested in the career of Harry Hastings, although he never actually met him. But from all he heard of him, he always assumed that Surtees must have based the character of Sir Harry Scattercash in *Mr Sponge's Sporting Tour* on Harry until he discovered that the book was published in 1853, when Harry was only eleven.

If Harry *did* closely resemble Sir Harry Scattercash, then he must have sunk very low. The portrait is satirical, of course, but the underlying description suggests a truthful observation of a real person.

'Sir Harry was a tall, wan, pale young man with a strong tendency to delirium tremens,' wrote Surtees. 'That, and consumption, appeared to be running a match for his person.'

It is hard to imagine a description at once more pungent and pathetic, and the reference to Sir Harry's friends is equally astringent. 'They were a sad, debauched-looking set, some of them scarcely out of their teens, with pallid cheeks, trembling hands, sunken eyes, and all the symptoms of premature decay.'

A photograph of Harry at this period does much to substantiate the rate of his deterioration. Gone is the slim young man with the sensitive face and the forlorn and waif-like expression whom Tilt had painted. Instead there is a raffish, dissolute man in a seedy and indolent pose, gazing blankly and almost without expression at the camera.

'Thormanby', in *Kings of the Turf*, gives another description of Harry Hastings at this period—only this time in the summer, and playing in one of the many cricket matches which it was Harry's delight to arrange. Country-house cricket was one of the rural delights of the Victorian and Edwardian era, but with Harry the game became a travesty, staged simply to flatter his ego. 'Thormanby' wrote:

> I have seen Lord Alfred and Lord Berkeley Paget seated in high-backed chairs, each with a lady beside him, when they were supposed to be fielding. About every ten minutes the Marquis would raise his hand, and the game would be stopped in order that an adjournment might be made to the great tent for refreshment. And professional bowlers were always bribed to bowl loose balls to his lordship.

Lord Berkeley Paget was Florence's younger brother, so the rift caused in the family by her elopement with Harry did not extend to the cricket field. The Pagets found Harry a convivial companion and a generous host, although they must have sometimes resented the casual way in which he treated Florence.

These cricket matches established not only how vain Harry had become, but how childishly incapable he was of perceiving the elaborate stratagems which were resorted to in order to ensure his success at the wicket. 'Thormanby' goes on to describe the farce to which Donington cricket often descended.

> I remember in this connection on one occasion overhearing a sharp altercation between the Marquis's Majordomo and two Nottingham professionals. The professionals had been promised half a sovereign each if his lordship made the biggest score for his side. I was playing in the Marquis's team, for which a young tailor from Ashby-de-la-Zouche had made nineteen, and that modest score was the highest any of us had made against the straight and deadly bowling of those professional Notts bowlers. The young tailor had the office 'to stop run-getting and let the Marquis score'. So his lordship swiped away in the clumsiest yokel style whilst the tailor kept his wicket up. But unfortunately, just as the Marquis was one run short of the tailor's total, in his eagerness to smite a wide ball he knocked it into his wicket. The Major-domo refused to pay the bowlers their promised half-sovereign on the ground that one of them had bowled the Marquis out before he had headed the score. The professional indignantly replied that he had bowled his lordship a ball three feet off the stumps, and that if the Marquis was so clumsy as to knock it into his wicket, that was no fault of the bowler, who ought not therefore to suffer. A compromise was made by the presentation of five shillings to each of the bowlers. This trifling incident will serve to show in what an atmosphere of adulation the Marquis lived.

Yet Harry could still, at this time, retain much of his old charm, and also his own special brand of courage, as he revealed in his complete indifference to the blows of fate, and to his winnings and losses on the turf. That he also retained his sense of sportsmanship is shown by another story told of him at this period.

There was a card party at Donington Hall, and the game was poker. A young Scottish lord of limited means, who had just left Oxford, was trying to ape his seniors by betting heavily and adopting the same attitude of bored indifference when he lost. Other members of the house party who were standing round the table were having side bets on the result of each hand as it was played. At one point the young Scot and Harry Hastings found themselves left alone in the bidding, the others having fallen out. The stakes were raised by first one player and then the other until there were several thousand pounds in chips on the table, and the young peer began to look white and apprehensive. But at this moment Harry threw in his hand with a typical gesture of good-humoured acceptance and remarked that his opponent had frightened him into submission. A friend who had backed Harry separately to win lost £25. To him Harry remarked in confidence afterwards, 'I held an almost unbeatable hand, but I threw it in. I could not have slept if I had taken his money. Whatever else we do, we have no right to hawk that sort.'

He offered to refund the 'pony' which his friend had lost on the side bet, but the offer was refused. Thus Harry, for all his weakness of character, still retained a certain code of honour.

He divided his time between London and Donington, entertaining lavishly wherever he was and drinking to all hours of the night. In the summer of 1865 he had ordered a yacht to be built and had called it *Ladybird*. It was luxuriously equipped, and in it he entertained ostentatiously when at Cowes (it provided a further way of triumphing over Henry Chaplin who, although an enthusiastic yachtsman, could not afford a comparable craft). *Ladybird* also enabled Harry and Florence to go cruising in the Mediterranean or to visit the Northern capitals of Europe when the fancy took him.

He had also spent money freely on Donington Hall but since he was largely without taste, the changes he made were only for the greater comfort of himself and his cronies. The magnificent library did not interest him, but he had the floor of the dining-room pulled up at considerable cost and a sunken bathing pool laid beneath. In the winter of 1863, as the final act of his coming-of-age celebrations, he had inaugurated the Castle Donington Steeplechase Course, which he had laid out in the flat meadows on the far side of the Trent, opposite Kings Mills, and the races held there continued to attract a mixed crowd of racing enthusiasts and rogues, who successfully ruined the tranquillity of this lovely stretch of the river. Harry also built a gallop for his horses which ran from the Coppice Lodge entrance along the wooded slopes above the Trent and dropped down through the Lime Grove beyond the Hall and on to the East Entrance. It was a fine track, and in summer it must have looked superb; but the beauties of nature meant little enough to Harry, who seldom glanced down at his ancestral home, surrounded by its magnificent trees and with its 'small and swan-loved pond'. This lovely home, nestling in the heart of the hunting country, which had furnished his father with all he had ever asked from life, gave Harry little more than a building which, because of its two hundred or so rooms, could provide accommodation for a host of boisterous friends, their servants and their horses.

One further anecdote of Donington Hall throws an interesting sidelight on Harry's character at this period, and his transformation from an innocent youth to a shrewd owner of racehorses. Donald Shaw was one of Harry's cronies, and in his book, *London in the Sixties*, he speaks of the insight which he was given to training methods whilst visiting Donington Hall and watching Harry's horses being exercised over his private gallops. The fact that they were private meant nothing, for the touts were everywhere, and so it became necessary to deceive them, so that the information which they were transmitting to their masters in the betting ring should prove inaccurate. Thus a blood-stained handkerchief would be given to a rider before taking the favourite for some local handicap for a gallop, and at the end of the trial the horse's nose would be wiped with the handkerchief in such a way that the hidden watchers would believe that it had broken a blood-vessel. At other times, tricks would be used whereby a horse would appear to be lame, when in fact it was perfectly sound.

Harry was by no means exceptional in adopting such stratagems to outwit the touts. The acknowledged master of such trickery was Henry Chaplin's trainer, Captain Machell, who would even scribble down fictitious lists of weights carried by his horses in trials, then drop them 'by accident' and spend a long time searching anxiously for them, knowing full well that he had been observed and that the scraps of paper would be retrieved the moment he left the spot.

The point is made not to emphasize Harry's unscrupulousness, for in his battle against the touts he was fighting a highly unscrupulous enemy, but rather to prove once again that, in matters concerning racing, Harry was by no means such a fool as he looked. Drunk or sober at Donington Hall, he was fully capable of throwing dust in the eyes of all those who were trying to discover stable secrets.

Thus Donington Hall remained for Harry no more than a place for exercising his horses and a weekend home for the riotous entertainment of his many profligate friends. He probably had little real affection for the place, and perhaps the only serious emotion which Donington Hall aroused in him was—oddly enough—a fleeting sense of apprehension. There was a legend that if the head of the Hastings family, while sitting at the head of his own table, twice heard the sound of a carriage driving up to the main entrance when in fact no carriage had arrived, then he knew that his doom was at hand, and that he would die before the year was out. Harry scoffed at the legend, but he was too nervous and highly-strung an individual to ignore it completely. At the back of his mind was probably the thought that in old age the legend might come to haunt him.

Thus Harry Hastings, in 1866 and at the age of twenty-four, was already a degenerate rake, who had lost his youthful looks and much of his youthful charm. But if 1866 was a year of rapid deterioration for him physically, it was by no means an unsuccessful one for him on the turf.

The spring of 1866 brought him both good and bad luck. He gained several gratifying successes, some of them at the expense of Henry Chaplin. In April, at Newmarket, his colt, King Hal, beat Chaplin's Bertie (named after the Prince) in a match. The Duke, now fully recovered, showed his well-being by winning the very next race with ease, and a fortnight later, also at Newmarket, The Duke won three races in as many days, concluding with a convincing win over Chaplin's Breadalbane at level weights, which suggested that had The Duke been able to run in the Two Thousand Guineas and Derby of 1865 he would certainly have always finished in front of either of Chaplin's representatives.

However, it was on the Thursday of the Meeting that Harry gained his greatest triumph until that time, when he won the second of the season's classic races, the One Thousand Guineas, for fillies only. He had bought Repulse, a bay filly by Stockwell out of Sortie, from a Mr Jackson during the previous winter, and now, running for the first time in his name, she justified favouritism by winning a hard-fought race by a head at 2 to 1 on. Harry backed her substantially but, with Cannon riding in place of Fordham, the result was in doubt until the last few strides. In retrospect, he was able to express the view that the fillies of 1866 were a poor lot, and that Repulse was herself of only moderate ability; indeed she never won another race. However, she did all that was asked for her on that April afternoon at Newmarket, landed Harry Hastings a heavy gamble and won for him what was destined to be his only classic race. So he had good reason to look back upon her with affection.

But his luck failed him for a second time in a race which he had always set his heart upon winning—the Chester Cup. For this very open and competitive handicap he entered his old favourite, Redcap, and backed the five-year-old down to favouritism in a field of seventeen. Opposed to him in the race, and substantially supported in the market as second favourite, was another five-year-old named Dalby, the property of a notoriously lucky owner named W. G. Bennett, a wealthy young man whose racing career was almost as meteoric as that of Harry's. The two owners had opposed each other in the same race in 1865, when Harry had entered Ackworth and Bennett had entered Dalby, and Dalby had won.

Harry Hastings sauntered into the Ring at Chester with his usual air of casual indifference—'as nonchalantly as if it had been a garden party', to quote a contemporary comment. He was at once surrounded by a crowd of eager bookmakers, who began to shout the odds for all that they were worth the moment they saw Harry plunge his hand in his pocket, presumably for his betting book. But Harry only smiled indulgently as he removed his hand to reveal his cigar case, from which he selected one of the small 'whiffs' which were then very much the vogue. But having lighted one and inhaled luxuriously he turned to the bookmakers and began to back Redcap as though defeat were out of the question.

After two miles had been covered on the circular course, it was clear that both Dalby, ridden by Hibberd, and Redcap, ridden by Tom Cannon, were certain to be concerned in the finish. Cannon was riding with his usual elegance and judgment, but Hibberd, on Dalby, was going so easily that Harry's confidence must even then have been waning. In the end, Dalby ran on to win unchallenged, leaving 'lucky' Bennett to lead in his winner for the second year in succession, and Harry to light a second, ruminative 'whiff'. He was the first, as always, to congratulate his opponent, and as they stood together in the unsaddling enclosure there must have been many present who envied them their affluence, their good humour, and their success.

They need not have done so, for the writing was on the wall for both these backers. Before the end of his lifetime, 'lucky' Bennett was destined to walk the streets as a beggar and to count himself fortunate to obtain work as a bus conductor.

No blame attached itself to Tom Cannon, a young jockey in whom both Harry Hastings and John Day were placing an increasing reliance. Tom, born at Eton in 1846 and therefore scarcely out of his teens, was not then the equal of George Fordham, who was nearly ten years his senior and a rider of far greater experience and guile. But Cannon was a youngster of considerable promise, with a more elegant style than Fordham, and one who shared the senior jockey's tenderness and understanding towards young horses. John Day had been so impressed by the lad, both as a jockey and a man, that he had allowed him to marry his daughter. It was essential to both Day and Harry, and indeed to all the Danebury stable, that their horses should be ridden by jockeys in whom they could place an implicit trust. Both George Fordham and Tom Cannon were the soul of honour, and incorruptible in an age when corruption was rampant on the turf.

The Derby of 1866 was of no interest either to Harry Hastings or to Henry Chaplin. It was won by Harry Custance on Mr Richard Sutton's Lord Lyon—rather desperately, for Lord Lyon, who was an odds-on favourite, only won by a head in the last few strides. Harry Hastings ran his bay colt, Blue Riband, and Henry Chaplin had Vespasian in the race, with the short-sighted Harry Grimshaw in the saddle, but neither was placed, although Blue Riband was in the lead for a short time approaching Tattenham Corner, and Vespasian did contrive to finish sixth. Richard Sutton had for a time hunted a portion of the Quorn country and was well known to Harry, who no doubt had a good bet on the winner.

On the following day The Duke ran in a match against The Clown for the Epsom Cup, and won by a length at the prohibitive odds of 30 to 1 *on*, having won on the first day of the Meeting at 5 to 2 on, when he gave Breadalbane a thrashing over the Derby course, but over a distance short of the Derby itself. Henry Chaplin accepted the defeat with good sportsmanship, and was heard to remark that The Duke would certainly have finished in front of Breadalbane had they faced each other in the Derby of the previous year.

But Henry Chaplin could afford to be magnanimous. Hermit, his thousand guinea purchase of the previous summer, had been beaten on his first appearance on a racecourse, in a race over half a mile at the Newmarket Spring Meeting, but at the Bath and Somerset County Meeting in May he had triumphed over a large field of promising two-year-olds, and had run well to finish second at Epsom to Colonel Pearson's very promising filly, Achievement, in the Woodcote Stakes.

Harry Hastings must have viewed this success with some alarm, for the colt which he might so easily have bought at Mr Blenkiron's sale at Eltham was beginning to look a real Derby prospect. Both young owners went on from Epsom to Ascot with the knowledge that this meeting could tell them much of what the future held for them.

Ascot, in 1866, produced its usual crop of surprises and sensations. The weather was fine, and the Prince and Princess of Wales were present on all four days. In the race for the Gold Vase on the first day, The Duke was soundly beaten by Mr Sutton's colt, Elland. Harry had backed The Duke down to favouritism, as was his custom, and looked momentarily almost put out by the result. Then in the very next race, the Ascot Biennial Stakes, Hermit, ridden by Custance, ran really well to beat a good field; and in the race following, Breadalbane won by twelve lengths. Chaplin's luck was clearly in, and Harry continued to look disgruntled.

The most remarkable race of the meeting, however, was that for the Gold Cup, when the curious combination of the half-blind Grimshaw and the crippled Gladiateur gave one of their more eccentric performances. Neither appeared to make any effort during the earlier stages of the race, and were nearly a hundred yards behind the other runners when they passed the stands for the first time, but in the end Gladiateur won by fifty yards. Harry Grimshaw's failing eyesight ultimately brought about his death, for the pony-trap in which he was riding ran into an obstruction on the road one dark night, and he was thrown out and killed.

The Goodwood Meeting of 1866 produced further successes for both Harry Hastings and Henry Chaplin and also further excitements. Broomielaw ran in a handicap plate on the Wednesday and won it with some ease. He was ridden by Custance and showed his usual bad temper in the paddock before the race. However, his success had been so easily gained that Henry was encouraged to bring him out again on the following day to see if he could win the Chesterfield Cup with him. In view of the colt's obvious dislike of being saddled, however, permission was asked of the Stewards for Broomielaw to be mounted at the start, which was some considerable way down the course. As Henry was himself one of the Stewards whose permission was sought, it was not difficult to have this request granted.

Harry Custance therefore walked nearly a mile and a quarter down the course in the blazing sunshine, while Broomielaw was led up in the rear. But the moment Custance took off his coat and revealed his racing colours, Broomielaw charged at him like a bull. The coat was at once thrown over his eyes, and he then became calm again; but as soon as Custance was in the saddle, and the coat was removed, the horse went mad again and dived sideways through some furze bushes and into a cornfield, where he started to savage the ground. The starter, Mr McGeorge, sent his assistant, a certain 'Squirt' Norton, to help lead Broomielaw back, but Norton knew how savage Broomielaw could be, having witnessed the occasion when he had bitten off a man's thumb, and he refused to go anywhere near him.

After half an hour, Mr McGeorge's patience gave out, and he shouted that he could wait no longer. So Custance told Norton to hit Broomielaw as hard as he could below the hocks, and then to crack his whip. This Norton did, and the horse charged back on to the course like an infuriated bull. Mr McGeorge, showing more presence of mind than was customary with him, promptly lowered his flag and sent the field on its way. Whereat Broomielaw charged after them, surged through their midst like a juggernaut and was up with the leaders within a few strides. But he was then shut in on the rails, and might have remained so had not Sammy Morden, the jockey on the horse in front, realized who was behind him and hastily moved over. Broomielaw passed him with his mouth open and won the race in a canter, but stopped within twenty yards of the winning post and tried to dislodge Custance and to savage him.

It was 'Broomie's' last race. He was sent to Brighton soon afterwards, but he kicked his horse-box to pieces on the journey and injured himself so badly that he never ran again. He was in many ways a tragic animal, who might have achieved greatness if the secret of his ill-temper could ever have been discovered.

But if Broomielaw disgraced himself at Goodwood, The Duke really came into his own by winning the Goodwood Cup over two and a half miles. This was much more of a prestige race than a handicap such as the Cambridgeshire, which Harry had won with Ackworth, and only horses of quality were entered for it. The Duke, ridden by George Fordham and backed by Harry down to hot favouritism at even money, won by a length—whether easily or not few could say, for Fordham's 'kidding' usually resulted in a close race, and few except the stable ever knew how much he had in hand. He came from just behind and he finished just in front. That was Fordham's method of racing, so that even the horse itself was sometimes in doubt as to whether or not it had been given a hard race.

Not long afterwards The Duke won the Brighton Cup over two miles, when Fordham, finding the rest of the field quite unable to go with him, had the unusual experience for him of winning a race by some fifteen lengths, and before August was out The Duke had also taken the Cleveland Cup at Wolverhampton. He had proved his ability to run and win over all distances, and in the season of 1866 alone he won eleven races.

In every way now, Harry Hastings was a changed man from the slim lad who had first appeared on the grey cob at Newmarket in 1862. He was master in his own home, and master in his racing stable at Danebury. Florence had no means of controlling him. He refused to drink less and eat less, although over-indulgence was fast ruining his never robust constitution, and he continued to surround himself with worthless and dissipated companions. He took no interest in his private life at Donington, or in his Mastership of the Quorn, and his financial affairs were in a hopeless state of confusion, for he would never attend to business matters, other than those connected with the turf, and would never trouble to pay his bills.

John Day, at Danebury, now found his young master an autocrat in all things appertaining to the running of Harry's horses. It was not that Harry had lost his old charm of manner, or that he ever appeared dominating or dictatorial. It was simply that he now made up his mind on everything, decided when and where his horses should run and then instructed his trainer accordingly. And those instructions had to be observed, without question. By the autumn of 1866 John Day was in financial straits himself, having been called upon to meet a dishonoured bill of several thousand pounds to which he had unwisely signed his name, and thus he was in no position to quarrel with his wealthiest patron, even had he wished to do so. George Fordham, quiet, shy and retiring, was the last person to argue with his master, and so Harry Hastings pursued his own way without advice or interference. A sudden major disaster at this time might have served as a warning shot across his bows, but no such disaster occurred. On the contrary, he was about to engineer the most successful betting coup of his career.

By the early autumn of 1866, Harry was seriously in debt. His creditors were beginning to press him, and he was being constantly advised by those who were brave enough to do so that he would have to practise stringent economies or else start selling his assets. It was impossible for him to go on living at his existing rate of expenditure. He could not, even on his income, continue to bet wildly, live extravagantly, run a yacht *and* be Master of the Quorn.

Harry's reply to these dismal warnings was to remark that if debts had to be met, then the Ring might as well be made to settle them on his behalf. The time had come for him to stage a major coup upon the turf.

His wife was horrified at the suggestion, and so were his advisers. To try to recoup himself on the turf could only make the position far worse than it was already.

But Harry was not to be put off. He surveyed his string of horses and assessed them with his customary shrewdness. One of them had to be made the medium of a gamble. Which of them should it be?

Equally important was to choose the right race. It had to be one of the big handicaps, which attracted a large field and therefore constituted a very strong betting market. He had already staged a successful coup in the Cambridgeshire. He now began to estimate his chances in the first of the big autumn handicaps which were run at Newmarket. This was the Cesarewitch a punishing long distance race over $2\frac{1}{4}$ miles in which stamina was the predominating factor.

There was in the Danebury stable at this time a rather under-sized three-year-old colt, by Colsterdale out of Algebra, named Lecturer. Harry had bought this little horse in the winter of 1865 from Alfred Day, who had never won a race with him. Harry himself had been more fortunate. Lecturer had won for him first time out at the Newmarket Craven

Meeting in the spring of 1866 and had then won again at the Bath and Somerset County Meeting in May. Following this, the little horse had been the cause of no little confusion at the same meeting on the following day, when Harry had backed him down to odds-on but had lost his money because Lecturer, ridden by H. Day, had failed to reach the start in time for the 'off' and had taken no part in the race. He had later failed in a big field at the Epsom Derby Meeting, after which he had been rested throughout the summer.

Just how good was 'little Lecturer'? Harry, with his curious facility for weighing up a handicap, decided that even with 7 stone 3 pounds in the saddle, which was considered then to be a prohibitive weight for a three-year-old, Lecturer might yet prove to be a good thing for the Cesarewitch. He discussed the matter with John Day, who shook his head in doubt. For answer, Harry took a folded piece of paper out of his pocket and casually tossed it across the table to his trainer. It gave the details of a trial which Harry wished his trainer to stage over the Danebury gallops. There were two horses to be concerned, and they were to run at level weights. One was Lecturer, but the name of the other is uncertain. It was either The Duke or Ackworth.

The suggestion that little Lecturer could take on either of these two, one of which was a four-year-old, the other a five, seemed unthinkable to John Day. He opened his mouth to protest, and then shut it again. He knew that one did not argue with Harry Hastings. If Harry said that he wished something to be done, then it was best to do it at once, without demur. And so Day arranged the trial.

Because it was a highly secret trial, no one has ever known for certain what was the outcome. Rumour had it afterwards that it was The Duke who raced against Lecturer and was beaten by him—at level weights. Whatever the outcome, and whoever was Lecturer's opponent, the trial satisfied Harry that Lecturer should become the medium of his biggest gamble on the turf and the means of freeing him from his financial worries.

His backing of Lecturer from then on was greatly facilitated by the fact that Admiral Rous, handicapper to the Jockey Club, dictator of the turf and its self-appointed reformer, did not like Harry Hastings or anything about him. It was for this reason that he had deliberately given Lecturer 7 stone 3 pounds in the Cesarewitch and had then let it be known that as far as he, Admiral Rous, was concerned, this would put the little horse quite definitely out of the race. Indeed he openly announced that if Lecturer won, he would be happy to eat his hat. Admiral Rous was proverbial for announcing his willingness to eat his hat and had on more than one occasion been required to eat his words, if not actually his headgear, but on this occasion he seemed to be speaking with good reason. And so, when Harry Hastings began to back his little horse, the Ring showed its willingness to accommodate him. From the outset, Admiral Rous had suspected that a Danebury coup might be in the offing, and he felt satisfied that the weight he had given to Lecturer would ensure its failure. The Ring agreed with him.

Harry Hastings could afford to smile enigmatically. He knew they would have changed their tune quickly enough had they known what he knew. However, it would not do for the Ring—or Admiral Rous, for that matter—to become aware of the truth, and so it became necessary to throw a little dust in the eyes of his opponents.

And so Harry made a show of protesting over the weight allocated to his little horse, announced his probable intention of scratching him and even went through some complicated stratagem of seemingly renouncing the ownership of Lecturer, who in fact ran in the race as the property of a 'Mr H. Wilkinson'; all of which revealed that Harry Hastings was by no means such a fool as he looked and an expert in the ways of throwing a little dust.

It was the custom in those days for owners and bookmakers to assemble at the Subscription Rooms in Newmarket on the night before a big race and for the card to be called over—with the prices then on offer usually longer than they were likely to be on the afternoon of the race. On the Monday evening before the Cesarewitch, Harry Hastings had dinner at the rooms, accompanied by his usual circle of cronies. In the betting before the dinner, 10 to 1 was freely laid against Lecturer and as freely accepted by Harry, who pencilled his numerous bets in his notebook. After dinner, towards midnight, when tongues had been loosened by wine, and the general mood was expansive, the card was called over again; and again Harry backed Lecturer with a dozen different bookmakers, although the best price then available was 9 to 1. And it was '100 to 30 the field, 9 to 1 Lecturer' that the Ring were shouting when the field for the Cesarewitch cantered out on their long journey across the Heath to the start of the race on Tuesday, 9 October.

Lecturer moved down easily, with an unfashionable lightweight jockey named Hibberd on his back, while in the stands Harry Hastings viewed the scene with his customary serenity. His bland indifference to the situation astonished even those who knew him best. There might only have been a few hundreds at stake.

By the time the field had reached 'the bushes' on their return journey, there were only four horses in the race. One of these was little Lecturer, who proceeded to gallop resolutely up the hill 'to win cleverly', as *The Times* observed, by half a length.

Harry strolled down to the paddock to welcome his little colt, whilst from outside on the course the familiar shout was going up from his loyal supporters—'The Markis—Gawd bless 'im!' They had won their handful of shillings, or maybe a sovereign or two, over Lecturer's victory and were wildly delighted. Harry admitted to winning over £70,000.

In fact he probably won more, but he had dined so well the night before that the notes entered in his betting book had become illegible long before midnight, and many of those who had betted with him were aware of the fact and never came forward to pay what they owed. Even so, Harry Hastings had dealt the Ring a tremendous blow. It seemed that his troubles were over.

Harry's critics were momentarily silenced. Even Florence could say little to admonish him when he had thus proved his ability to extricate himself from financial disaster. As for the bookmakers, they were beginning to believe that if Harry ultimately ruined himself, as they all felt he must, it might not be by racing after all but only by the extravagance of his way of life. As a backer of horses, he had to be feared. He was shrewd and he was lucky. No one, they kept telling each other, had ever broken the Ring. It was impossible. Lord George Bentinck had tried, and so had John Gully—but they had failed. Yet here was a dissolute and seemingly scatterbrained young peer, who looked a fool and was not, making the most extraordinary bets and then winning them. The inevitability of his downfall did not seem now quite so certain as it had done before.

But Harry, despite this remarkable triumph, was still not a happy man. For a time he basked in the affluence and admiration which Lecturer's victory brought him, but his satisfaction was marred by a sinister and persistent rumour which he was now encountering on every side. This was to the effect that Hermit, the colt which was owned by his rival, Henry Chaplin, and the one for which Harry had been the underbidder at Mr Blenkiron's sale, was being whispered as a great horse in the making and the probable winner of the Derby of 1867.

Harry had won the Cesarewitch with Lecturer, but he did not have to be reminded that there was no comparison between even the most popular of Newmarket handicaps and the Derby at Epsom. The name of little Lecturer, and of his owner, would be forgotten when the name of the Derby winner was still written large in the annals of the turf. In a hundred years' time racing men would speak with reverence of Blink Bonny and William I'Anson, of Thormanby and Mr Merry, but not of Ackworth or Lecturer, or of Harry Hastings who had won a fortune over both of them. And if Hermit *did* win the Derby of 1867, then he, too, would be remembered for as long as there was racing over Epsom Downs, and so would his owner, Henry Chaplin.

It could not happen. It must not happen. It was a nightmare come to torment Harry in his dreams.

He became increasingly jealous of Henry Chaplin, and this jealousy began to fester within him as the year of 1866 drew to its close. His jealousy took on many forms. He resented Henry's self-assurance, his self-importance, and his way of life. Harry even began to resent Florence, because she had once loved Henry, and because he suspected that she still retained a secret affection for him.

But finally, and worst of all, Harry allowed this mounting jealousy to become concentrated into one single obsession. It was not Henry Chaplin, but his colt, Hermit, whom Harry now began to hate. He could not bear to hear Hermit's name spoken in his presence and least of all in connection with the Derby. As a result, he began to allow prejudice to cloud his judgment. Because he could not contemplate the thought of Hermit winning the Derby, he began to persuade himself that such a victory was impossible. And so he turned bookmaker and began to lay *against* Hermit. Whenever the colt's name was mentioned, Harry spoke slightingly of his chances and offered to lay liberal odds against Hermit carrying off the Blue Riband[1] of the Turf.

[1] The phrase was coined by Disraeli, as he subsequently described

Henry Chaplin was surprised by this hostility towards his colt, and even went so far as to caution Harry and to advise him that he was being unwise in his assumption that Hermit could not win. This only hardened Harry's resolution. By the beginning of 1867, Harry Hastings had only one wish for the coming racing season. It was that he should go to Epsom and there see Hermit defeated in the race for the Derby.

in his biography of Lord George Bentinck. During the Goodwood meeting of 1846, Lord George suddenly decided to dispose of all his racing interests and devote himself to the service of his country, although he had failed to achieve his life's ambition by winning the Derby. Amongst the horses which he sold was a yearling named Surplice, which won the race two years later for its new owner, Lord Clifden. Shortly afterwards Disraeli discovered Lord George in the library of the House of Commons, and tried to comfort him, whereat he gave a sort of superb groan.

' "All my life I have been trying for this, and for what have I sacrificed it?" he murmured. It was in vain to offer solace. "You do not know what the Derby is," he moaned out.

' "Yes, I do, it is the Blue Riband of the Turf."

' "It is the Blue Riband of the Turf," he slowly repeated to himself; and sitting down at a table, he buried himself in a folio of statistics.'

CHAPTER EIGHT

THE CRISIS—1867

HARRY HASTINGS began the racing season of 1867 with an ever-deepening resentment against Hermit. Henry Chaplin began it with an ever-increasing optimism about him. Both were thus at a disadvantage, for to be prejudiced against a horse in racing is as harmful to judgment as to be biased in his favour. Both are the outcome of personal sentiment, and both are the enemy of a detached assessment.

Yet Henry Chaplin had good reason for his optimism. His plans were being carefully laid, and his 'team' was a strong one. As trainer, he had Old Bloss, at Bedford Cottage, a man who understood the well-being of horses and who could be relied upon absolutely to attend to all their needs. As manager, there was Captain Machell, a man who understood all the intricacies of the racing scene. A Newmarket man who was already a part of Newmarket life—shrewd, knowledgeable and up-to-date in his methods. Machell realized that he had a potential Derby winner in his care and he understood exactly what that entailed. There could be no rest, and no relaxation in stable vigilance, until the Derby was past, and months and years of arduous preparation had been brought to their fulfilment. Trainers have grown old and grey with worry in the months before delivering a Derby favourite to the post, but if Captain Machell was not the type of young man to age prematurely, he was also not the one to take a single unnecessary risk. The touts, the betting Ring and the nobblers were his enemies, to be watched and studied at all times. The ultimate prize was wealth, fame and immortality on the turf.

Then there was the jockey. Harry Custance had been signed on as first jockey to the stable at an annual retaining fee of 500 guineas, a large sum for a jockey to earn in those days. He was young, he rode with dash and brilliance, and he had already proved himself to be an Epsom jockey by his success in the Derbys of 1860 and 1866. He was honest and intelligent, and whereas his honesty would prevent him from being bribed, his intelligence would convince him of the need for doing his utmost for an owner who was known to be grateful and generous to those who served him well.

Custance was a strong and determined rider, and this was at once his virtue and his failing. With a lazy horse, who was reluctant to give of his best, Custance was seen to great advantage, but he lacked the gentleness and sympathy of a man like Fordham. A nervous horse could be frightened by Harry Custance; and a high-spirited one could resent this domination from the saddle.

Finally, there was Hermit himself, the pride of Bedford Cottage and the colt in whom Chaplin, Machell, Old Bloss and most of Newmarket itself began to place their hopes by the spring of 1867. By this time he had grown and thickened into an impressive animal of unmistakable class—a rich, red chestnut with just a trace of white about him, on his forehead, and standing a little over 15·2 hands. His hindquarters suggested all the power that characterized the Newminster stock, and his action was light and easy, although in his slow paces he was apt to move with a rather listless air, as though indifferent to exertion unless it contained the urgency of speed and conquest. His legs were short and clean. He had a long, lean head set on a straight, clean neck, fine loins and great haunches, but his thighs, though big, were rather short. His notable feature was that the point of the quarter came down in a line with the point on the hock.

His temperament was amiable and gentle, honest and proud. But he was apt to become excitable before the start of a race and, being headstrong and determined, he resented restraint when eager to give of his best.

He had style and class; and what Charles James Fox used to refer to in the Latin term, *argutus*, suggesting as it did the poetry of grace in motion.

Not all great horses *look* great. Some have been awkward, slovenly and ungainly, and have only revealed their greatness in a moment of supreme effort and unflinching courage. But some great horses have quality stamped indelibly upon them. Hermit was such a horse.

But handsome is as handsome does, and none knew this better than Captain Machell and Henry Chaplin. They had first 'asked Hermit a question' early one cold December morning in 1865, when, as a yearling, they had galloped him over Newmarket Heath by Bury Hill. They had matched him then against a filly, also by Newminster, named Problem, whom

Chaplin had bought at the Eltham sale at the same time as he had bought Hermit. She was thought to be useful, and they had set Hermit to give her 35 lb over a distance of half a mile. He had won that trial by two lengths, and it was in that moment, in the cold and misty air of mid-winter and with the Derby still a year and a half away, that Henry Chaplin had begun to hope. There was still much to do and many obstacles to overcome. But the class was there, and the touch of greatness. In a year and a half it could be brought to splendid fruition.

Moreover they had to decide just how good was this filly, Problem, whom Hermit had beaten so convincingly. She was therefore entered for the Brocklesby Stakes on the first day of the Lincoln Meeting, which opened the season in 1866 on 20 February. There was a large field of useful two-year-olds, and her performance was watched with anxiety by both Machell and Chaplin. She ran splendidly and won convincingly. It was only by a short head, it is true, from the favourite, Jeannie Deans, but the rest of the field were outclassed.

Before this race Machell and Chaplin believed that Hermit might be a very good horse. After it, they knew that he was one for certain.

It was from then on that they began to back Hermit in earnest. The ramifications of these Derby wagers of theirs are hard to disentangle. Each was for ever on the look-out for a prospective layer who would oblige him by offering attractive odds. It was a period in which a great deal of betting was still carried out between gentlemen, without recourse to the Ring. This, in theory, had the advantage of being a gentleman's agreement and therefore sacrosanct, but in fact, the members of the Ring often proved more reliable in settlement than the young bucks of the gentry and aristocracy.

During Hermit's two-year-old season, in 1866, not long after the success of Problem in the Brocklesby, Captain Machell was drinking with some racing friends in Long's Hotel, one of the several fashionable meeting places of the sporting fraternity in the Bond Street area. Taking advantage of the prevailing mood of jovial expansion, Machell took out his betting book, and invited any sportsman present who was in the mood for a gamble to lay him 20 to 1 against Hermit in the Derby and suggested a bet of 20,000 to 1,000. After some hesitation, the bet was accepted.

At this moment the young Duke of Hamilton, who was fast

following in Harry's footsteps and making a name for himself by foolhardy wagering, entered the hotel and pushed his way to the front of the little circle surrounding Machell. He was a little drunk and in a mood of defiant bravado.

'Pooh,' he said, 'you don't call that betting! I will lay £30,000 to £1,000 against Hermit. I will lay it once. I will lay it twice. Three times—four times—five times—six times!'

There was silence in the room for a moment, and then Captain Machell, who only a few years before had been an unknown and penniless subaltern, opened his betting book again, and speaking very quietly, replied, 'I will take you. I accept £180,000 to £6,000 against Hermit in the Derby.'

Later in the evening, the young Duke began to grow more sober and more alive to what he had done. Swallowing his pride as best he could, he approached Captain Machell quietly and offered a payment of £1,000 just to cancel the bet altogether. Machell at first refused. Then he relented. The bet was made void, without forfeit, and the young Duke of Hamilton left Long's with his tail between his legs.

Hermit had run six times as a two-year-old, in 1866, and had won four of these races. In his first race he had been opposed by Marksman, Lot 28 at Mr Blenkiron's sale at Eltham in the previous summer, and the horse which had immediately followed him into the Sale Ring. Mr Merry's colt by Dundee was known to be highly promising, but although he and Hermit were backed to the exclusion of the remainder, neither won. It was a muddling and scrambling sort of a race in which Hermit finished second and Marksman fourth; the winner, by three-quarters of a length, being a filly of Lord Stamford's named Cellina. Three weeks later Hermit met her again at Bath and this time beat her by a neck.

Racing, to inexperienced two-year-olds, is often a confusing affair in which, at first, they do not quite understand what is being expected of them. By now, Hermit was beginning to learn, and to enjoy himself. But it was in this race at Bath that he first showed unruliness at the start. He was ridden by H. Covey, a jockey of no great experience, and when Mr McGeorge, the starter, ordered the field to line up, Hermit became fractious and awkward. This was really no more than an indication of his excitement and his eagerness to get into his stride, but there were those who wrongly interpreted his behaviour, amongst whom was Mr McGeorge, who formed the opinion that Hermit might turn out to be a rogue.

In the middle of May 1866, Hermit was introduced to the Epsom racecourse for the first time, when he was sent to run in the Woodcote Stakes. It was also the first occasion on which he was ridden by the stable's first jockey, Harry Custance. Custance had been warned of Hermit's misbehaviour at Bath, and he determined to show the colt immediately who was master. Custance, writing later in his memoirs, recalled only that Hermit was restive at the start and 'bored his head'. He ran gamely enough, however, and although he was beaten comfortably by a filly named Achievement, there was no disgrace in the defeat, as she was known to be a potential champion.

As first jockey to the stable, Custance rode Hermit in all his remaining races as a two-year-old. He was a good jockey, but Hermit never liked him. The history of the turf is full of anecdotes about horses which have run kindly for one rider but not for another. Horses have very long memories, and they never forget harsh treatment, especially when it is administered when they are young and inexperienced. Broomielaw, who was admittedly something of a savage, always hated Custance. Hermit probably did not hate him, but he seems always to have feared him. This fear and resentment may have been originally aroused on this their first appearance together on a racecourse, when Mr McGeorge was struggling with the runners and warning Custance that Hermit was a difficult horse who had given trouble at Bath and had to be controlled. Custance may therefore have shown an unwise aggressiveness on this occasion, for which Hermit never forgave him.

A month later, Hermit paid his first visit to Ascot, and here, against the background of elegant fashion and trim green lawns, he won the Biennial Stakes by a neck from a good field.

At the Bibury Meeting in mid-June he beat the Duke of Beaufort's Vauban, ridden by Fordham, by a neck. Two days later he ran at Stockbridge and won again, in a race in which the Duke of Newcastle's Julius finished third and Vauban was unplaced.

Thus by the end of the summer of 1866 the pattern for the Derby of 1867 was already beginning to develop, and the chances of the principal contenders were being discussed and assessed. Marksman, Vauban, Julius and Hermit were each looked upon as the possible winner. Then in the autumn at Newmarket, in the valuable Middle Park Plate with its prize-money of 1,000 sovereigns donated by Mr Blenkiron, Mr

Pryor's colt, The Rake, put up an impressive performance by beating Achievement by three lengths. This was certainly a notable Derby Trial, and The Rake was substantially backed throughout the winter as a result of it.

Much, of course, may happen in the interval between a colt's two-year-old and three-year-old season. A brilliant youngster may lose his form in the course of the winter which intervenes; and a slow developer may suddenly begin to show unsuspected promise.

Hermit was not entered for the first of the classic races of 1867, the Two Thousand Guineas, and after much consideration it was decided not to give him an outing in public before the Derby. The same decision was made over the Derby favourite, The Rake.

But if a horse is not raced in public, it is extremely difficult for the trainer to gauge his form accurately. He must rely on the opposition which he provides in private trials, but these trials may prove misleading. Hermit was first of all raced against a colt of Henry Chaplin's named Target. Target was not good enough, and Hermit beat him easily. He was therefore provided with more formidable opposition, in the person of a four-year-old named Rama, who had beaten Ackworth in the Doncaster Cup the previous autumn. Rama, older and stronger than Hermit and very fast, beat him easily, usually by running him off his legs in the first few furlongs. Hermit was game and resolute, but this treatment discouraged him, and he began to lose confidence in himself.

Some trainers, such as John Day, might well have argued that he was learning the hard way, and that such harsh treatment was good for him, but Machell was wiser. Rama was discarded, and Target was brought back. Hermit was greatly encouraged and soon rediscovered his old zest.

Meanwhile Hermit's chief opponents for the Derby were beginning to show their paces in public. Their first really important race was the Two Thousand Guineas. Hermit was not entered for this, but Captain Machell had a very useful colt of his own named Knight of the Garter, which he decided to run in order to get a line to the classic form. Once he knew how good Knight of the Garter was in relation to Vauban and Marksman, he had only to try him secretly with Hermit to discover just how good Hermit was in relation to them also.

The Two Thousand was run on Tuesday, 23 April, and was won by the favourite Vauban. Knight of the Garter was second, beaten by two lengths, and was himself just in front of Marksman. Julius was fourth.

Here, then, was the key to the whole situation. Hermit would have to be *better* than Knight of the Garter in order to beat Vauban and win the Derby, but if he was as good as him, he should still be able to beat Marksman and Julius. A two lengths victory in racing is generally considered to be the equivalent to a 6 lb superiority in a handicap. Thus Hermit would have to carry at least 6 lb more than Knight of the Garter in a trial and then beat him, if he were to have a chance of beating Vauban. Captain Machell decided to ask the chestnut colt to carry 10 lb more, so that the issue could be clearly decided, one way or another. With these weights, which were unknown even to the jockeys who were riding, he staged a secret trial at Newmarket early one morning. As Machell and Chaplin watched the two colts go down to the start for this trial, they realized that the events of the next few minutes would either confirm their faith in Hermit or else destroy their hopes for his success in the Derby.

Hermit, running with all his inimitable ease and enjoyment, beat Knight of the Garter without undue effort. Thus they knew that on Guineas form Hermit was the best three-year-old in England and a worthy favourite for the Derby. It now only remained to deliver him fit and eager at the post for the efforts of eighteen long months of preparation, and the hopes of a lifetime, to be crowned with a glorious success.

For Henry Chaplin, there was now an added interest in Hermit's success. Henry's extravagant way of life, his liberality and the cost of running the Burton Hunt and of himself hunting six days a week during the season were making a considerable inroad into his capital. He was living beyond his means, and he could not go on doing so. Unless something happened to change his financial position, he would have to consider giving up his support of the Burton Hunt, and cutting down on his entertaining; and he might even have to consider the selling of Blankney itself. He could not continue to buy and race horses as he had been doing since Florence's elopement, nor could he continue to enjoy the expensive life of leisure indulged in by the Prince of Wales' set. In short, 'Magnifico's' grand way of living was ruining him, and the most drastic retrenchment was becoming necessary if the Squire of Blankney was to survive.

Hermit's victory in the Derby could change all this. It was

not simply a matter of the stake money to be won, nor even of the money accruing from betting, although both he and Machell had backed their colt substantially. It was also the question of stud fees. A Derby winner at stud could bring in a handsome income to his owner for a number of years after the race. Therefore if Hermit should win the Derby of 1867, Henry Chaplin knew that his financial problems would be solved, and that the continuance of his existing way of life could be assured for ten years at least.

Harry Hastings was in a similar financial predicament, but without a prospective Derby winner in his string to save the situation. He was drinking more, gambling more and taking increasingly less interest in what either Florence or his business advisers implored him to do. Debts were mounting, and the money won over little Lecturer was rapidly disappearing. He was now obsessed with racing and betting and could think of nothing else. He attended every meeting and bet on every race.

But above all else, he was obsessed with the conviction that Hermit could not win the Derby. On this point he scarcely seemed sane. 'Harry is laying against Hermit as though the horse were already dead,' wrote Florence in a letter to one of her friends, and although she tried her utmost to prevent him from committing himself in this way, he took not the slightest notice of her. The very suggestion that he was being foolish in making what is known in racing terms as 'a one horse book', and concentrating on the failure of one single runner, was sufficient to make him offer even more generous odds against Hermit than he had done previously. He derided Hermit—he scorned him. And although the news of what Hermit had achieved in his trial against Knight of the Garter did begin to filter through to the racing world, he refused to believe that such a trial had taken place, or declared that, if it had, it had proved nothing. The Two Thousand Guineas, he argued, was run over a mile. The Derby was run over a mile and a half, and also over a vastly different course from Newmarket. Harry knew all about Vauban, who was trained by John Day at Danebury, was owned by one of Danebury's staunchest patrons, the Duke of Beaufort, and was to be ridden by Fordham. There was the highest confidence behind Vauban at Danebury, and John Day had no fear of Hermit. Moreover there was also The Rake to be considered. This was the colt who had beaten the brilliant filly, Achievement, in the Middle

Park Plate in the previous season, and Achievement had already won the One Thousand Guineas in a canter and was certain to take the Oaks as well. Hermit, as far as Harry was concerned, had little or no chance. He doubted very much if Chaplin's horse could get into the first three at Epsom.

The betting market reflected this assessment to some extent. When the card was called over at Tattersall's, at Albert Gate, a fortnight before the race, Vauban was a warm favourite, The Rake was second favourite, and Hermit was on offer at 8 to 1.

The Derby was to be run on Wednesday, 22 May. Captain Machell, pondering the problems of bringing Hermit to peak condition on this day, but also on the need of discovering just how good Hermit was, decided upon the traditional pre-Derby trial, which it was the custom to stage in those days a week or so before the great event. The day for this trial was fixed as Monday, 13 May, and the distance was to be the full one of a mile and a half. Captain Machell was not superstitious, and the thirteenth of the month seemed as good a day as any other. Harry Custance travelled to Newmarket by the mail train on the Sunday evening in order to attend a discussion at Bedford Cottage with Captain Machell and Old Bloss, and the final plans were made.

Henry Chaplin, to his intense disappointment, could not be present. He was a big man, who throughout his life suffered from the handicap of increasing weight, and now a heavy fall had strained the cartilages in both knees. He remained therefore in his rooms at Park Lane, but gave instructions that the moment the result of the trial was known, a messenger should be sent to give him all particulars.

The course chosen for the race was that by the side of the Ditch to the Cambridge Road, with the finish by the Old Duke's Stand. The trial was to be between Hermit and Rama —the colt who had previously proved too fast for him and had threatened to break his spirit. It was decided to ask Hermit to carry a stone less than his older opponent, who was known to be very nearly the equal of Lord Lyon, who had won the Derby the previous year. If Hermit could beat a horse the equivalent of a Derby winner, a year older than himself but giving him a stone in weight, that would be a fine trial. It should justify stable confidence and the big bets which the stable had already taken about him.

If he failed in this trial, then the stable could take advantage of this secret knowledge to 'hedge' some of these bets in the Ring, and therefore rid themselves of some of their liabilities. Captain Machell was a shrewd backer. He had no intention of committing himself too heavily unless Hermit proved himself, in this final gallop, to be a truly live proposition for the Derby.

Rama was ridden by one of the stable lads belonging to Bedford Cottage. He was responsible for 'doing' Rama and could be relied upon to obey his instructions implicitly. Custance was to ride Hermit and he was put in charge of the trial. It was he who put the weighted cloths under the saddles of the two horses. He thus knew what each was carrying. The lad on Rama had no idea at all.

They hacked down to the start, leaving Captain Machell and Old Bloss by the Duke's Stand. On reaching the old stables by the Ditch, which is a part of the ancient fortifications of Newmarket Heath, the two horses turned and Custance gave his final instructions to the lad. Rama was lazy, and there was a danger that the trial might be run at a false pace. Custance told the lad that if this should happen, he would shout out, and the lad could then show Rama the whip in order to make him increase his pace.

Hermit was on his toes and looked a picture; a perfect example of a thoroughbred racehorse. In the past, Rama had gone too fast for him, but on this all-important occasion Hermit seemed determined to show what he could do. After a few furlongs, Rama began to lag behind, and Custance thought that he was being lazy and not giving of his best. So he shouted to the lad to show Rama the whip. This he did, but still Hermit was travelling far the better of the two. It was then that Custance realized just how good Hermit was. The Derby must surely be at his mercy.

After a mile had been covered, Hermit was still pulling for his head and full of running. The watchers in the stands looked on in delight and admiration. Then disaster struck. Hermit was seen to stagger suddenly in his stride and to cough. Blood began to pour from his nostrils. It flaked across his chest and covered Custance as well. Custance at once brought him to a halt and dismounted. Hermit stood there, weak, unsteady and badly frightened, and with the blood still pouring from his nostrils. What a few seconds before had been the picture of the perfect racehorse was now a tragic figure with all the fire and zest gone out of him.

Custance led Hermit slowly back to the stands where Captain Machell and Old Bloss hurried forward anxiously to meet them. Hermit was still bleeding, and they gently sponged his nose and mouth, and then took him slowly back to Bedford Cottage.

Little was said, for each knew only too well what had happened. Hermit had broken a blood vessel in his nostril; and his chance in the Derby had vanished in that one, catastrophic moment.

As soon as they reached Bedford Cottage, Old Bloss took Hermit away to care for him and comfort him as best he could, while Mr Barrow, the veterinary surgeon, was summoned urgently from the town. Custance followed Captain Machell into the house, where the Captain sat down to write a letter to Henry Chaplin, telling him exactly what had happened. A decision had to be made as to whether the horse should be scratched immediately from the race. Meanwhile, they decided that an attempt should be made to keep the tragedy secret. But it was useless. The news was known all over Newmarket within a few hours.

Meanwhile, Harry Custance hurried back to London to see Henry Chaplin. In the train he met Captain Hawkesley, an associate of Mr Pryor, the owner of The Rake, one of the favourites for the Derby. Hawkesley was sympathetic but practical. He said that as Hermit now appeared to be a certain non-runner, Custance would find himself without a mount. He offered him the ride on The Rake.

Custance replied that he could do nothing until he had seen Hermit's owner; and the moment he arrived in London he took a cab to Park Lane and was at once shown into Henry Chaplin's study.

Henry read Machell's letter slowly, then turned to his jockey. 'We must scratch him at once,' he said.

But Custance advised him not to be too hasty. There might still be just a chance that Captain Machell could patch the colt up so that he might be brought to Epsom. Chaplin pointed out that the race was little more than a week away; but in the end he agreed to postpone any definite decision until he had seen Captain Machell and had received a full veterinary report.

Not that Custance had any reason for wishing the horse to run now. He was the stable jockey and Chaplin had first claim on him. But the moment Hermit was scratched, and he was officially released from his obligations, there would be offers in plenty to ride another favoured entry for the race. This was shown by the speed with which Mr Pryor had acted in order to get Custance to ride The Rake. Jockeys received substantial rewards for riding Derby winners; and no one would wish to be claimed for a broken-down colt such as Hermit when the chance was offered to ride the probable winner.

The bets involved over Hermit were immense; and no one was more heavily committed than Harry Hastings. For six months and more he had been laying against Hermit 'as if he were dead'. He had been warned repeatedly that he was being most unwise, and even Henry Chaplin himself had cautioned him, and told him that Hermit's chance was an excellent one and that he might well win. This had only strengthened Harry in his unreasoning prejudice against the horse.

Chaplin himself had backed his horse with Harry Hastings. He stood to win some £20,000 from Harry if Hermit won. But this was only a part of Harry's commitments over the colt. A victory for Hermit at Epsom on 22 May would deprive him of nearly £120,000, and this at a time when his debts were rapidly mounting and his financial position generally becoming desperate.

The news of Hermit's collapse in his final trial must therefore have come as a sudden relief. Harry, by this time, had realized in his heart that Hermit was a fine horse, and that his continued antipathy to the colt was quite unjustified, but his pride would not allow him to admit this. Now the whole situation was changed for him. If Hermit was scratched from the race, Harry would automatically win around £10,000, for the bets which had been struck with him had been 'ante-post' and would therefore be lost if the horse did not run. But even if Hermit did now run, the position for Harry was saved, for it would be simple for him to lay off his commitments, because Hermit's price would rapidly lengthen to 50 to 1 or 100 to 1 now that his chance of winning had virtually disappeared.

All Harry's problems were therefore solved, once the news became known that Hermit had broken a blood vessel in his final trial. He wrote a note of sympathy to Henry Chaplin, which had a hollow ring to it. Yet Harry was not without genuine sympathy for Hermit and his owner. No one knew better than he how deeply mortifying was the break-down of a horse in which the highest hopes had been placed. The Duke had fallen ill at the beginning of his Derby year and Harry had been bitterly disappointed. Now Henry Chaplin was suffering the same misfortune.

Their rivalry for the Blue Riband of the turf could therefore be postponed for another year; and already Harry was beginning to look forward with growing confidence to the Derby of 1868. He had in his string at Danebury a filly whose ability seemed limitless. Day by day, in her gallops, she was showing herself to be endowed with potential greatness. This was Lady Elizabeth. She, also, was worthy of the term *argutus*. At Danebury it was being whispered that they had found another Blink Bonny.

Henry Chaplin said goodbye to the hopes which he himself had entertained of winning a fortune on the Derby and immortality on the turf. In all, he had stood to win some £140,000. Hastings' contribution would have amounted to £20,000, and Chaplin had taken many other bets on Hermit as well. He had also had a side bet of a level £50,000 with old Sir Joseph Hawley that Hermit would finish in front of The Palmer; and another side bet with Mr Merry of £10,000 that Hermit would finish in front of Marksman.

Custance, although he advised against scratching the horse immediately, quickly lost interest in Hermit as a desirable mount for the Derby, and both he and Mr Pryor, the owner of The Rake, begged Henry Chaplin to release his jockey from his commitment. Henry Chaplin, always a fair minded and generous man, agreed to this suggestion, although it was hard for him to have to relinquish his claim on the best Epsom jockey of the day. The Ring, having heard firstly of Hermit's accident and then of the release of his jockey, knocked the colt out in the betting at first to 20 to 1, and then, when the news seemed to grow worse, to twice that figure.

But during all these alarms, with their repercussions upon the betting for the race, there was one man who kept his head and still hoped for the best. This was Captain Machell. It was really he who persuaded Henry Chaplin to stay his hand when Chaplin was so anxious to scratch Hermit, and now he set about the task of patching up the invalid as best he could. Aided by Old Bloss, he began to cosset and coddle the colt like a baby. Old Bloss had already been sleeping in Hermit's box for weeks past, on a little iron bedstead which was just small enough to be squeezed into the corner, and now he administered to the colt with an ever-increasing devotion. Captain Machell stood to win a fortune if he could get Hermit to the post, but Old Bloss had never made a bet in his life. He stood to lose nothing by Hermit's collapse, but this in no way affected the devotion which he lavished on the horse. His child was ill and must be comforted.

Hermit was allowed very little hay, and was covered with a light rug in order to keep him as cool as possible. His collapse had taken place on the Monday. Within two days he was back in light work, and something of his old spirit seemed to revive within him. But he was a nervous horse, who did not forget, and the memory of his accident stayed in his mind. He had been badly frightened by the loss of blood which he had suffered, and in some way he connected this in part with his jockey, Custance. Had Custance ridden him in these slow gallops which he was now undertaking, Hermit might well have shown a disinclination to make any effort, but now that Custance had been released and no substitute for him had yet been found, Hermit was ridden by one of the stable lads, who treated him gently. His eagerness came slowly back, and although he looked weak and sorry, he was fit enough in himself for Captain Machell to decide to give him a canter or two up the Rowley mile at Newmarket on the Saturday before the Epsom meeting. He was never fully extended, but the former glory of his action had come back to him. Once again there was a touch of *argutus* about his performance.

Captain Machell and Old Bloss accompanied Hermit back to Bedford Cottage. To them it seemed that a miracle might be taking place.

Henry Chaplin was still in London, and still almost too lame to walk. He had not visited Bedford Cottage, or seen his injured colt, for several weeks.

The Derby, according to ancient tradition, was due to be run at three o'clock on the Wednesday afternoon. Hermit travelled to Epsom on the Sunday, and it was decided to follow a further racing tradition by giving him his final winding-up gallop over a part of the course on the Tuesday morning, the day before the race.

Meanwhile The Rake continued to give every satisfaction in his home gallops, and Custance had reason to congratulate himself on being offered so good a substitute for Hermit. He was riding in the French Derby on the Sunday, and left for Paris at the weekend.

The news which greeted him on his return quickly altered his views. Exactly the same thing had happened to The Rake as had happened to Hermit. He had broken a blood-vessel in his gallop on the Friday morning, and although he was still a runner, his chances seemed to have disappeared as surely as had those of Hermit. So The Rake was also knocked out in the betting, and Vauban was installed a hot favourite. Danebury were jubilant. Their chief rival had been virtually eliminated, and they had backed their own contender at a very much better price than could now be obtained. Harry could afford to smile. Things were going well for him.

The final gallops held on the Derby course on the Tuesday morning were watched with more than usual interest, for both Hermit and The Rake were to be given their last chance to show their well-being. This was also Custance's first introduction to his Derby mount, whom he had never ridden before. He rode in one of the first trials of the morning and, mounting The Rake, was sent on a three-quarter-of-a-mile canter by the horse's trainer, Joseph Dawson. Whatever hopes he still held of winning the Derby now vanished completely. 'Of all the Derby horses I have ever ridden, this is the worst,' was the report which he gave to Dawson when he pulled up. He dismounted gloomily, and then paused for a few moments by Tattenham Corner to watch some of the other Derby runners being put through their paces. Suddenly he realized that one of these was Hermit. The colt was looking very different now from the vigorous and vital animal which he had ridden nine days before at Newmarket, and Custance was shocked to see how Hermit's coat had lost its lustre, and how listless he appeared.

Hermit had the usual rather timid and inexperienced lad on his back, and as he approached Tattenham Corner, he took hold of his bit and rounded the corner at top speed. The weather had been cold but dry for days, and the course was very hard. The going at Tattenham Corner was like concrete, and the majority of runners had rounded it warily, afraid of jarring themselves. But to the astonishment of Custance and his friend, Chris Fenning, who was standing with him, Hermit rounded the bend like an express train.

'Be jabers,' said Fenning in amazement, 'I never saw a horse go like that!'

Custance remained silent. He could scarcely believe his eyes. As far as he knew, it was the first serious work that Hermit had done for more than a week. It was incredible.

Old Bloss was so delighted that he at once sent a telegram to Henry Chaplin, begging him to travel down to Epsom at once. Chaplin seized his crutches and answered the call.

Old Bloss's report to his master was full of optimism. Hermit, he said, had squandered the trial tackle they had put against him. And, at the end, had breathed so quietly that he would not have blown out the proverbial candle.

Now a major controversy developed. Chaplin, delighted with the news and the assurance that Hermit was almost back to his best, was eager to regain the services of Custance, whom he had relinquished to Mr Pryor. Custance, in view of what he had seen, and of his experience when riding The Rake that day, was equally anxious to revert back to his original commitment.

But Mr Pryor was adamant. He refused to give up his claim to Custance, maintaining that his horse, The Rake, had also fully recovered and was in excellent health, and would probably win the Derby. He therefore insisted that Custance should ride for him.

The argument became heated, and in the end the matter had to be referred to the Stewards of the Jockey Club. Unfortunately Chaplin had relinquished his claim in writing, and Mr Pryor was able to produce the letter. The Stewards sympathized with Chaplin, but in view of this letter they reluctantly agreed that Mr Pryor still had first claim on the services of Custance.

Thus Hermit, now partly restored to health and with an outside chance of still winning the vast sum in bets which his victory could bring to his owner and trainer, was left on the evening before the race without a jockey.

By now all the best riders had been signed up for the fancied runners, and no experienced substitute for Custance was available. The search went on all evening, but without success. No suitable jockey could be found.

The morning of Derby Day, 22 May 1867, dawned grey and bitterly cold. As the day wore on, biting winds, sleet and finally flurries of snow swept across the Epsom Downs. The huge crowds which normally flocked to the course from London were reduced to a trickle, and *The Times*, in its subsequent report of the scene, referred to the inclement weather 'which froze the general current gaiety of the holiday-makers'. There was a forest of umbrellas on the course and in the stands, and the racegoers slapped their hands for warmth as they watched the horses parading in the paddock.

Henry Chaplin arrived in the Prince of Wales's party, but he was soon forced to leave it in order to continue his now desperate search for a jockey for Hermit. Harry Hastings arrived debonair and smiling with Florence, who was muffled up against the cold in furs and looked drawn and tired.

Harry had his colt, Uncas, in the race, but Uncas had done little to justify any support. Danebury were behind Vauban to a man. The Duke of Beaufort's colt held an outstanding chance, and Harry Hastings had gone for a big win over him. With Fordham riding, and Harry in the mood to bet on this Danebury 'pot', the Ring were in an ungenerous mood, offering Vauban at no more than 6 to 4. Hermit was being laid at 66 to 1 and even at 100 to 1. Uncas was at double this price. The only runners being seriously backed to beat Vauban were The Palmer, Vam Amburgh, The Rake and Marksman—Mr Merry's purchase at the Blenkiron sale.

Hermit himself was led down the course by Old Bloss, who was comforting him as best he could. Because of the supposed need to keep him cool, he was without any covering at all, although it seemed hardly possible that he could be in any danger of becoming over-heated in the miserable conditions which prevailed. He looked lifeless and utterly dejected. His coat was staring with cold, and his tail was tucked in between his legs. He walked slowly and heavily, and there seemed no life in him.

Meanwhile the search for a jockey continued. The official racecard had no jockey's name against that of Hermit, and it seemed unlikely that any rider of experience would be found at this late hour, when all the top jockeys had been booked. Finally it was Lord Coventry who suggested to Henry Chaplin that he might do worse than employ Johnny Daley, who had often ridden in the Coventry colours. He was only twenty, a Newmarket lad and the son of a trainer, and had ridden his first winner at the age of ten, when he weighed only 3 stone 10 lb. He had been popular enough as a lightweight, and had won the Goodwood Stakes and the Stewards' Cup, but no other race of any importance. His weight had increased as he grew up, and he had lost favour with most of his former owners. In short, he was not a 'fashionable' jockey; but he was honest and intelligent, and could be relied upon to obey orders.

Chaplin and Machell were in no position to be selective. They ascertained that Daley was available and booked him on the spot. Captain Machell led him to a corner of the paddock and instructed him on the tactics he was to pursue. Hermit, he emphasized, had fine finishing speed and abundant stamina.

Daley was therefore to wait with him approaching Tattenham Corner, but to keep in touch with the leaders. Once into the straight, Daley was to come with one long, sustained run on the outside to overhaul the leaders—if he could. Hermit was to be handled gently and was not to be punished unduly; and if he showed any sign of breaking a blood vessel he was to be pulled up at once. He had courage and would give of his best without being driven.

The terms on which Daley was to ride were simple and generous. Machell himself would give him £300 if he finished in the first three, and a further £3,000 if he won. To this Chaplin would add £6,000 in the event of victory. Daley listened and nodded his head, but said nothing. He could scarcely believe his ears.

He had arrived at Epsom on that Wednesday morning with but little hope of finding a mount at all, let alone one in the Derby itself. Indeed he had been booked for only one ride during the whole of the three-day meeting, and that was on Baron Rothschild's filly, Hippia, who had only an outside chance in the Oaks on the Friday. Until this moment his financial hopes for the meeting had amounted to, at most, a few guineas. And now he found himself, shortly before three o'clock on this bitter afternoon, in a position in which he might enrich himself for life.

His introduction to Hermit was the first obstacle to be met and this was successfully overcome. The colt had shown a readiness in trials to give of his best for a stable lad, but had demonstrated a growing aversion to the strong handling of Custance. Now Johnny Daley, far quieter and less forceful in personality, was able to strike up an immediate sympathy and understanding with the horse.

Not that Hermit was in any condition to show anger or resentment. He shivered miserably in the biting wind, his tail was tucked even more firmly between his legs, his head hung down and he presented a picture of misery. Old Bloss walked him slowly round and round, comforting him as though he were a sick child. An observer of this scene was heard to remark that Hermit would not fetch £15 at a fair.

The Downs were sparsely covered with shivering spectators, sheltering for the most part under umbrellas, the stands were only half-filled and there were only a few people standing round the ring as the runners were paraded before the race. Henry Chaplin watched in company with the Prince, Captain

Machell and Sir Frederick Johnstone. Harry Hastings stood not far away, while Uncas was saddled and then mounted by Salter. His stable companion, Vauban, as is the custom with Derby favourites, was surrounded by a little group of acolytes led by John Day and what *The Times* referred to as several 'Danebury *attachés*'. George Fordham, who was to ride him, stood watching these preparations, outwardly calm but inwardly nervous and apprehensive. The last Derby favourite which he had ridden had been Lord Clifden, and he had run a poorly judged race then and been beaten by a neck. They were still saying that he was not a Derby jockey. Now was the chance to prove them wrong. He, too, was shivering with cold, and he felt sick and ill. He could have wished that it had been a brighter day.

They saddled 'poor Hermit', as he was now being referred to, in a corner of the paddock where a thorn bush offered some slight shelter from the biting wind. He trembled as he was mounted, and plodded slowly and miserably forward to join the rest of the field as they threaded their way out on to the course. Gone was his old swagger—gone, too, all suggestion of *argutus*.

Henry Custance sat resignedly astride The Rake. He had been assured that the colt was only lazy and would give a good account of himself once the race was reaching its climax, but he reserved his opinion. He was *not* impressed by his mount's chances. But at least these chances were infinitely better than those of his former ride, 'poor Hermit'.

As Henry Chaplin and Captain Machell passed through the Ring on their way back to the Stands, they were joined by Harry Hastings, who had come to make a final bet on the Danebury 'pot', Vauban. Henry Chaplin paused for a moment to speak to him.

'I think Hermit still has a chance, Harry,' he said. 'You can easily cover your bet with me by taking the odds which they are offering now.'

Harry Hastings gave his old, disarming, half-condescending smile.

'Thank you, Henry—but I will not trouble. I fancy that Vauban is the only one that need be seriously considered.'

He moved away to join his Marchioness in the stand. Chaplin and Machell watched him go. A bookmaker standing close to them touched his cap.

'Do you fancy 1,000 to 15 against Hermit, Squire?'

Henry Chaplin nodded and accepted the bet. It was an act of defiance—not one of confidence. Captain Machell followed suit. He took £3,000 to £45.

Snow and sleet were still blowing across the Downs as the riders assembled at the start to hear the customary lecture given to them by the starter, Mr McGeorge. They were to come into line quietly, he warned them, and without jostling, and not to anticipate the dropping of his flag. They were not to argue, swear or shout abuse.

Even so, there were ten false starts. Hardcastle on Master Butterfly, Payne on Fitz-Ivan, and John Grimshaw on Marksman, each lost his temper, ignored Mr McGeorge's instructions and tried to anticipate the dropping of the flag. They were sternly admonished, and another attempt was made. Meanwhile, D'Estournel stubbornly refused to come into line. There were a few derisive catcalls from the crowd, but the cold froze their normal powers of invective.

In the stand, Henry Chaplin watched Mr McGeorge's efforts in company with the Prince of Wales. Harry Hastings surveyed them with an air of bored indifference from his private box, and gave orders for the opening of yet another case of champagne. Florence shivered in the cold and pulled her furs about her. She prayed that it might soon be over.

At his eleventh attempt, Mr McGeorge was satisfied with the start, and the field—all except for D'Estournel—streamed away up the hill towards Tattenham Corner, whilst the starting bell in the stand clanged out mournfully to announce that the eighty-eighth renewal of the Derby Stakes was now in the process of being decided. Harry Hastings paused in the act of sipping his champagne, but showed no outside sign of excitement. Henry Chaplin became tense and strained. Captain Machell focused his glasses on the runners and watched their progress across the sky-line.

The crucial moment in any Derby is that at which the field rounds Tattenham Corner. A horse must hold a good position at this point if he is to have a reasonable chance of winning. Ideally, he should be in the first half-dozen. To be in the rear is generally fatal.

Now, as they rounded the famous corner, it was seen that Fordham was in the lead on the favourite, Vauban. With him were Wild Moor, Marksman and Julius. Behind these leaders were The Rake, Van Amburgh, Corporal, The Palmer and Hermit. The remainder were already trailing.

Into the straight they came and the stands and the winning post were in sight. Vauban was still in the lead, but a groan went up when it was seen that Fordham was feeling for his whip. Vauban was joined by Marksman and Van Amburgh, and he faltered as they drew level with him.

With a furlong to go, Grimshaw forced Marksman into the lead. Van Amburgh was done with now and dropped back, but Vauban struggled on.

It was then that Daley, obeying his instructions to the letter, brought Hermit with a long run on the outside. Vauban, he realized, had hit the front too soon and was visibly tiring; but Marksman was still full of running. Now John Grimshaw on Marksman was watching Fordham closely. He knew only too well how Fordham loved to 'kid' his opponents and to keep something up his sleeve for the last sudden burst of speed on the post. Grimshaw saw Fordham falter and drop back, but he still watched for that sudden burst. And on his right, and unnoticed, Daley was bringing Hermit up to challenge.

Now, at last, the chestnut threw off his misery. He forgot the cold in his bones and the fear in his heart that there might be another sudden rush of blood in his nostrils. Racehorses are sensitive to the mood of a great occasion, and now the cheering, and the waving of hats and umbrellas, galvanized him into life. He was being brought from behind, and that is a great challenge. He lengthened his stride, as do all great horses when they are under pressure, and power surged back into his weakened body and forced him forward. His jockey was not driving him mercilessly but was yet conveying to him the desperate need for one final, magnificent effort. A tired horse tends to swerve as he struggles forward. Hermit was tired, but he ran on straight and true. It was the moment in which he sought for greatness and found it.

In its last hundred yards the Epsom course slopes sharply upwards to the winning post. It is this final rise which can break the heart of a horse that has given of his best and is nearing exhaustion. But the great Derby winners of the turf have breasted this final slope with resolution, refusing to give in. They find within themselves a hidden strength to carry them forward.

Hermit found it now. He passed Vauban and reached Marksman's quarters, but the winning post was almost upon them. Daley, still cool and quiet, asked him for the final, supreme effort, and he gave it unflinchingly. In the last few strides they were locked together; but in the final stride Hermit was in front.

The judge gave his verdict. Hermit—by a neck. Marksman second. Vauban third.

There was a moment of stunned incomprehension in the crowd. In his box, Harry Hastings lowered his glasses and went pale, but his usual smile remained on his face. Then he turned to his wife.

'Hermit has run a great race. I must go and see him unsaddled.'

She said nothing. There was nothing to say.

In the royal box, the Prince and his friends were laughing and shouting and thumping Henry Chaplin on the back. Captain Machell was smiling, his hands trembling a little with excitement. But Henry Chaplin remained mute and incomprehending. He had never really convinced himself that Hermit could win. It had been in his mind no more than a dream. He could not now believe that the dream had materialized. He had won an immense fortune; and he had done more than that. He had found immortality on the turf.

By the unsaddling enclosure, Old Bloss wiped the tears from his eyes, and his simple, honest face was red with emotion. For eighteen long months he had watched devotedly over the chestnut colt, had slept in the stable with him, groomed him, fondled him and talked to him. Now the long months of strain and worry were over. His child had repaid him in full. The name of Hermit would never be forgotten.

Henry Chaplin led Hermit from the course into the little unsaddling enclosure, still too bewildered to speak. Daley slipped the saddle from Hermit's back, and Hermit stood steaming and exhausted, his body played out with fearful effort, the cold already beginning to numb his bones. He shivered and hung his head.

Then the ranks of the crowd of top-hatted watchers were broken, and Harry Hastings pushed forward and came forward to pat Hermit on his sweat-flaked neck. He turned to Henry Chaplin.

'A great horse,' he said. 'A truly great horse.'

A few minutes later Harry Hastings was seen to leave the course with his wife and a party of friends. They were bound for a dinner party in Richmond, and no one, watching Harry at this moment, would have believed that he had been almost beggared by Hermit's success. He was laughing and talking with the utmost gaiety—even speaking of Hermit's victory with enthusiasm. He took no thought for the morrow—or for the settling day that was to come.

On the course, and in the stands, the inquests were being held. Many thought Marksman had won. Others, including his owner, Mr Merry, were saying he *ought* to have won. John Grimshaw was downcast. Fordham had 'kidded' him, even in defeat. Had he not been so obsessed by the need for watching the Danebury wizard, he might have seen Hermit's challenge earlier. Thus Danebury's own jockey had contributed to Hermit's victory.

Vauban, they said, had been brought to the front too soon. Fordham, with his fear of Tattenham Corner, had rounded it in the lead, where he could be clear of all danger. Yet no horse can be expected to win the Derby by making all the running. Fordham himself was conscious of his lack of judgment. He was not well, and the bitter cold, allied to the consciousness of failure, added to his misery. He left the course early and went home miserably to bed.

Mr Merry was left to his own thoughts. It was not only the defeat that rankled in his mind. It was the memory of that June afternoon at Mr Blenkiron's sale, among the laburnums at Eltham, when he had bought Lot 28 and not Lot 27. And now the one had beaten the other by a neck. It was the irony of racing.

Many at Epsom on that dismal afternoon found the victory of Hermit incomprehensible. Yet the person who was most astonished by it was Henry Chaplin. He had backed himself to win an immense fortune over the colt, and yet he had never really believed that such a fortune could ever be credited to him in the bank. Now he faced a clear profit on the race of £140,000—and there was the further regular income to be earned by Hermit when he went to stud. All his financial problems were solved. The cost of Blankney, of entertaining the Prince and of running the Burton hounds—all these things were no longer of any concern. Hermit had solved all these problems for many years to come.

Captain Machell remained quiet and undemonstrative. A secretive man, it was difficult to assess how much he had won. The whisper had gone round that he had long since hedged his major bets on Hermit and was no great winner over the race. But Machell was a professional gambler, and professional gamblers discuss neither their winnings nor their losses. *The*

*Tim*es, on the following day, announced that he had won £63,000, but years later chroniclers of the turf such as the Honourable George Lambton were to maintain that his calmness at Epsom was a façade to hide the bitterness of his feelings at having let an immense fortune slip through his hands.

No one can say for certain. The probability is that Captain Machell *did* make a great deal of money over Hermit, although not so much as he might have done. But he had the profound satisfaction of knowing that it was his faith in the colt, and his refusal to allow him to be scratched prematurely, which had won the day for Henry Chaplin.

As for Henry Custance, he was left to ponder on the mutability of human affairs. He had deliberately forsaken the ride on Hermit, and lost a fortune as a result.

Hermit himself could not speak, but perhaps, if he could, he might have added his own footnote to this remarkable race. He might even have added that it was the breaking of the blood vessel which had really won him the race. He always feared Custance, and he never really gave of his best when Custance was in the saddle. It was because of the broken blood vessel that Custance gave up the ride and Daley took his place. And secondly, Hermit might have added that even Captain Machell and Old Bloss himself were making the mistake which Old John Day so often made and were driving Hermit too hard in his final gallops. He was becoming stale and overtrained. The breaking of the blood vessel gave him a week's rest at the exact moment when he was sorely in need of it. It allowed him to rally his energies.

These are the imponderables of racing. Horses cannot speak, and no one can know what are the causes of their unexpected moments of triumph and disaster. It is probable that Hermit would have won the Derby without breaking a blood vessel, and with Custance on his back; but it is intriguing to consider that what, at the time, appeared to be a disaster might in reality have been a stroke of good fortune.

When Henry Chaplin finally awoke to the realization of what he had won, he showed characteristic generosity. Daley he rewarded as he had contracted to do, but Old Bloss, he knew, was worthy of special attention. He had not known until after the race that the old man had slept in Hermit's box for so long before the race. Now, when he was told of this, he sat down and wrote out a cheque for £5,000. Old Bloss, who had never had a bet in his life, and to whom shillings, and not pounds, were often a sign of unexpected prosperity, was overwhelmed by this generosity.

A week after the race Henry Chaplin went to Newmarket to see his Derby winner. The weather, as so often happens in England, had changed suddenly and was now warm and bright. Hermit was brought out from his box by Old Bloss for his master's inspection. The colt stood proudly in the sunshine, his coat now burnished and shining, his head held high, his ears pricked and enquiring.

'He looks much better in his coat than he was at Epsom,' said Henry Chaplin to his trainer. Old Bloss looked at Hermit and then down at his own figure, now clothed in a fine new suit. 'Yes, and so do I, too, Squire,' he said simply.

The press, of course, made the most of the Derby and were not slow to comment on its ironies and its moral. *Punch*, with the ponderous humour of the period, referred in a heading to the 'Pious Uses on the Turf' and went on to remark, 'Who, after this year's Derby, will dare say that Racing is a sinful amusement? Think of the money carried off from a Rake by a Hermit for the benefit of a Chaplin?' Other comments were more pointed. 'This was the animal who half destroyed a Marquisate, enriched a Commoner beyond his wildest dreams of his ambition, and attained immortality himself in the pages of Weatherby,' was one description of Hermit's victory.

To the puritanical element in Victorian England, now coming rapidly to the fore with the emergence of a prosperous and complacent middle class, there was a satisfying moral to the whole affair, although there may have been some who found it surprising that the Almighty should have used the eighty-eighth renewal of the Derby Stakes as an implement for divine retribution.

Not that Harry Hastings showed any outward evidence of despondency or dismay as he sat down to dine at Richmond on the evening of the Derby. To the gambler there is always 'the getting-out stakes'. There is always another race, and a further opportunity to recover losses already incurred. So to those who asked Harry at his dinner party at Richmond how he would meet his commitments over Hermit, he replied that he would do as he did when temporarily impoverished in the past; he would make the Ring settle his debts for him. The future, he declared, was full of promise. On the following day his filly, Lady Elizabeth, the pride and joy of his heart, was due to run and could not be beaten. On the Friday another filly, Colonel

Pearson's Achievement (who had greatly endeared herself to Harry by beating Hermit at Epsom the year before), was equally certain to win the Oaks. And so to Ascot, with the winnings over these two good things safely in the bank, to recover the whole—if not more—of the losses resulting from Hermit's Derby. Therefore let them eat, drink and be merry, for tomorrow was another day!

So he returned to Epsom on the following afternoon, where Lady Elizabeth, with Fordham up, was opposed to an outstanding two-year-old of Mr Pryor's named Grimston, who had already won on the first day of the meeting.

A desperate and hard-fought race resulted and ended in a dead-heat. Neither Harry nor Mr Pryor was willing to allow the matter to rest there. The issue had to be decided, one way or another and so the pair were asked to race again at the end of the afternoon. Once again both ran with the utmost courage and determination, but this time Fordham's brilliance in the saddle (and he was always at his best in a match consisting of only two runners) brought victory to Harry Hastings, when Lady Elizabeth just won, by a head. Harry returned to London well satisfied. Lady Elizabeth returned to her stable exhausted.

On the Friday, Achievement ran in the Oaks. Backed by Harry Hastings and many others as though defeat were out of the question and ridden by Custance, she seemed to have everything in her favour. The afternoon was less cold than on Derby Day, and the crowd larger. A filly of brilliant speed and abundant stamina, she needed a fast-run race to establish her superiority. But having frightened away nearly all the opposition by her brilliance, the field was the smallest within living memory for the Oaks, and there was no one to make the running for her. They set off at a miserable pace, crawled for the first mile and reduced her to fretful impotence. When she did strike the front, she had lost her enthusiasm, and Daley, imitating his tactics on Hermit exactly, came with a long, smooth run on Hippia and beat her on the post.

For Daley, it was an incredible week. Jockeys, like owners, strive throughout their lives to win a classic race and often fail. Daley had never won a classic race before, and now he had won two within two days of each other. It was a remarkable performance and was loudly cheered. He was the hero of the moment, and his services were at once in demand. But with his quiet and unassuming manner, and lack of 'fashionable' appeal, his great feat was soon forgotten. He slipped back into comparative obscurity and never won another classic race.

Harry Hastings was now tasting the bitterness of defeat. He had lost £120,000 on the Derby, and what little he had regained of this great sum by backing Lady Elizabeth on the Thursday had been swallowed up by his losses over Achievement in the Oaks. Honour demanded that his racing debts should be settled in full, and how could he raise £120,000 by settling day on the following Monday? The bookmakers would not take kindly to a member of the Jockey Club who defaulted in his wagers, and they could be expected to show scant mercy towards a man who had deprived them of £70,000 over Lecturer and had gloated over them when he had done so.

If he *was* to save his honour, only three courses remained open to him. Firstly, to sell everything in goods and property that was readily realizable. And secondly, to turn for help to the shadow who was always by his side—his friend, the moneylender, Henry Padwick.

And thirdly? *Thirdly*, he could ask for time to pay from the only one of his creditors who would be likely to grant it to him. This was Henry Chaplin.

Nothing is more typical of the Hastings story—and nothing is more typical of the characters of its two main participants—than what happened in the days immediately following the Derby of 1867. In fact it was not Harry Hastings who went cap in hand to Henry Chaplin. It was Chaplin himself who, with admirable tact and consideration, sent Berkeley Paget along to see Harry on his return from Epsom with the suggestion that Harry might find it convenient to wait for a few weeks before paying what was owing over Hermit.

Harry's reply was casual and characteristic. He accepted the offer, but with no particular evidence of gratitude, although it must have come as a great relief to him. His note was undated and read as follows:

MY DEAR CHAPLIN—I can't tell you how much obliged I am for your kindness to me. I would sooner cut off my hand than ask anybody to do such a thing, but as you say it will not inconvenience you, I shall take advantage of your offer for a short time. But you may depend upon my doing my utmost to repay you as soon as possible though you know as well as I do that however well off a man may be, to get £120,000 in twenty-four hours is rather a hard job. I am just off to Paris as I am sick of being pointed out as a man who has lost such a sum. If you do not particularly want the 'Sister to The Duke' at the Hampton Court sale I should much like to buy her, but I am afraid it is useless opposing you now.

With very many thanks, yours very sincerely,

HASTINGS

Its most remarkable feature is in the last few lines. Harry is asking his rival to refrain from bidding for a horse which he wants himself, and is not above implying that this rival, being now so much richer, should not use his wealth unsportingly. That he had no right whatsoever to be even considering buying expensive racehorses at a time when he was unable to meet his debts does not appear to strike him at all.

Henry Chaplin, of course, agreed to this request and did not oppose Harry when the filly in question was put up at the Hampton Court sale. Harry finally bought her for 750 guineas, a price which at that time he could not possibly afford.

Henry Chaplin's letter in reply is equally characteristic, and is of interest because it confirms that he had no real expectation of seeing Hermit win. It was written from 9 Dover Street, Piccadilly, and dated 'Sunday'. It ran as follows:

MY DEAR HASTINGS,

I got your note last night. I ought to apologize for having ventured to ask Berkeley if he thought he might mention the subject, but I hope that considering how perfectly immaterial an immediate settlement was to myself, and that under the circumstances it really might be a convenience to you, you would not think it impertinent on my part.

I am only sorry my success should have been so disastrous to you, but certainly nobody in the world, after what had happened, could possibly have foreseen the result of the race. I give you my word, when I was standing by you just before it, I had no more expectation of seeing Hermit win on that morning than even you had yourself.

I am, very truly, yours,

HENRY CHAPLIN

Thus Henry Chaplin continued to behave extremely well over the matter, and Harry Hastings continued to behave very badly. He did not ask for pity, it is true; nor did he forsake for one moment the mask of casual indifference to the calamity which had befallen him. But at the same time there was no suggestion of remorse or self-criticism. The position in which he found himself was not simply due to a gambler's bad luck, or to an understandable miscalculation of racing form. On the contrary, he knew enough about racing to appreciate that Hermit's chance *before* his breakdown was an excellent one; and that the lengthening of the odds *after* he had broken the blood vessel offered a wonderful opportunity to 'hedge' all bets for a very small outlay. There was no reason why Harry should ever have lost money over Hermit's Derby, other than the fact that he was prompted by an ignoble and unreasoning spite.

Finally, if his pride was such that it prevented him from ever showing any emotion, then it should also have prevented him from accepting charity from his rival.

It can only be recorded, therefore, that Harry Hastings continued to behave like a cad; but also that he continued to preserve his gaiety, his courage in the face of adversity, and his unfailing charm. It became increasingly difficult for his friends to excuse his conduct and increasingly difficult for them to dislike him.

He ignored his wife's growing alarm at the financial position in which they found themselves and offered her little comfort in distress. But she was a Paget, and so she remained loyal to him.

So also did his admirers amongst the common crowd. To the riff-raff and blackguards of the racing world, the East End Cockneys living in their poverty and squalor, and to the trollops of London's night life, Harry Hastings was still a hero. He had lost more money over Hermit's Derby than they could ever dream of, and he had done it with a laugh and without complaint. And so they still raised their glasses to him in the dives of the Ratcliff Highway and Temple Bar, and the toast to him was still the same.

'The Markis—Gawd bless 'im!'

CHAPTER NINE

THE FINAL RECKONING

WHEN Harry Hastings entered the Ring at Ascot a fortnight later, the bookmakers raised their hats to him and cheered him loudly.

They had good reason to do so, for Harry had met his commitments in full (except for those owing privately to Henry Chaplin). In the words of 'The Druid', 'Before the Monday the bankers and solicitors had consulted, and the whole of the Marquis's losings were found for him. Thus panic was averted from "The Corner",[1] but the fair lands of Loudoun passed from his hand.' The shadow behind him—the money-lender, Henry Padwick—had also played his part. Estates had been sold, and the treasures of his ancestors had been bartered, or put in as security, but Harry had settled in full. So the Ring cheered, and the crowd applauded 'the Markis' for his gameness and his refusal to be beaten.

It always seemed, throughout the Hastings story, that Fate had a sneaking regard for Harry Hastings, for no sooner had it beaten him to the ground than it allowed him to get up again. Moreover Harry's courage, and his defiance, were never so marked as when he appeared to be on the brink of destruction. This was another of his virtues as a gambler. He never accepted final defeat as inevitable.

A bad Ascot, following so quickly upon a bad Epsom, could have destroyed him there and then. Instead Fortune chose to smile upon him. He went to Ascot almost at the end of his resources. He left it with a large proportion of his Hermit losses regained. At Ascot, in 1867, he bet as if he were riding the crest of the wave, and as if he could do no wrong; and his winnings were sensational and astonishing. His actions showed unbelievable folly, but they also revealed an undeniable courage. It took a great deal to put Harry Hastings down, and to keep him down.

---

[1] The first Tattersall premises were built on Lord Grosvenor's estate at Hyde Park Corner in 1766. Thus Tattersall's, where all bets were settled, became known as 'The Corner'.

'Luck,' said Mr John Oakhurst once, 'is a mighty queer thing. All you know about it for certain is that it's bound to change. And it's finding out when it's going to change that makes you.'

Harry Hastings had probably not encountered Bret Harte's inscrutable gambler at this time, but their minds were in tune. Sooner or later, luck must change. Then, when it does...

The fact was that Harry Hastings had bought a number of yearlings in the previous season in order to add to his already large string, and that several of these, now that they were two-year-olds, were beginning to show remarkable form. Indeed it is doubtful, in the long history of the turf, if any owner has ever found himself, by the middle of a season, with a stronger hand in two-year-olds than did Harry Hastings in 1867. They comprised three two-year-old fillies—Lady Elizabeth, Athena and See Saw—and a two-year-old colt, The Earl. They were destined to win thirty-two races between them before the season ended in November, by which time it seemed reasonably certain that one, at least, would win a classic race in 1868, with the very real possibility that they might even sweep the classic board between them.

Of these four, the best—and in Harry's mind, by far the most beautiful—was his exquisite bay filly by Trumpeter out of Miss Bowzer whom he had named Lady Elizabeth. He believed, and with justification, that she might prove herself to be one of the greatest fillies of all time. And indeed Edward Moorhouse, writing in his history of the Derby fifty years later, was to refer to her as 'probably the most brilliant two-year-old that ever trod the Turf', whilst Theodore Cook, in his great history of the English Turf, was to refer to her as probably the best two-year-old ever bred. In the twentieth century, only Sceptre and Pretty Polly can be looked upon as her equals.

She had begun her racing career at Northampton at the beginning of April, when she won in a canter by five lengths. Brought out the next day, she won again with ease. The riding of her was entrusted to Fordham, and Fordham alone, for his gentleness with two-year-olds made him an admirable tutor for the bewildered and inexperienced little creature that she then was. She then won at Salisbury and at Bath, each time cleverly, with only a very little in it, and then triumphed at Epsom after her initial dead-heat with Grimston. It was a testing initiation and, had it not been for Fordham's restraint and patience, her youthful eagerness might well have been blunted at this early age. It was not the policy of either John Day or Harry Hastings to keep a horse idle, and youth was considered no excuse for inaction. They believed a racehorse was best occupied in racing and not in resting.

On the same day as Lady Elizabeth won at Salisbury, Harry won with another of his two-year-old fillies, Lady Barbara. On the following day he ran her again, in the Stonehenge Plate, in which she dead-heated with Henry Padwick's filly, Hue and Cry. They promptly decided to run a deciding heat, and again the two game fillies dead-heated. Lady Barbara had now run three testing races in less than twenty-four hours. However, Harry demanded that she must run yet again, in a final heat, and this time she won. At Newmarket, later in the summer, he ran her on the first day and then twice on the second day.

But Harry, after his tiring exertions at Epsom, felt urgently in need of a rest, and he retired to Paris, where the dissipations of the town offered a variety of interests not to be encountered in the stews of the Charing Cross Road. He was preparing himself for Ascot, for it was at Ascot, as he well knew, that his fortunes could be revived, and his losses over Hermit recouped.

The importance of Ascot lay in the size and quality of the fields. Then, as now, a gambler who wished to back heavily had to rely on a strong market—that is to say, a field of a dozen or more runners, with large sums of money being invested over each. The Ring is then in a position to show a strength and boldness in laying the odds which it cannot do in small fields at minor meetings. Thus Ascot presented Harry with the ideal opportunity for heavy wagering, and since he had been able to meet his commitments over Hermit in full (except for his debt to Henry Chaplin), his credit was good in the Ring. He had four days in which to win back lost ground, and he had the horses with which to do it.

The spearhead of his attack was to be launched on the Thursday—and in consecutive races. Little Lecturer was to run in the main event, the Gold Cup, and immediately afterwards Lady Elizabeth was to be asked the most difficult question of her short career when she faced a formidable field of two-year-olds in the New Stakes—a race that has always been considered to be a reliable guide to the classic races of the following year.

There was no need for a secret Danebury trial to be held in

order to discover how good little Lecturer might be. His courage and determination were known to every racing man in England. But it was essential to find out what chance Lady Elizabeth really held. Harry Hastings therefore arrived at Danebury after the weekend, and instructed John Day as to what he should do. A trial was to be run on the nearby Stockbridge racecourse in which Lady Elizabeth was to be opposed by the Duke of Beaufort's Lord Ronald, who was three years her senior and a recent winner of the Salisbury Cup; by a three-year-old of Mr Porter's named Challenge (which Harry had once owned and esteemed highly) and by Harry's own five-year-old veteran, Pantaloon. From Lord Ronald she was to receive some ten pounds in weight, but from the other two very little.

By modern calculations, a two-year-old racing against a five-year-old over six furlongs in June would be in receipt of nearly three stone. Thus Lady Elizabeth was given some thirty pounds *more* in weight than she might have been expected to carry against Lord Ronald. At the time, it must have seemed an impossible task.

In fact, Lady Elizabeth won comfortably by no less than two lengths. To quote Theodore Cook again, it was probably one of the best two-year-old perfomances ever done in private.

For Harry Hastings and the Danebury stable the implications were hard to believe. It seemed that Lady Elizabeth was a racing certainty for the New Stakes and could confidently be made the medium of a tremendous gamble. And if little Lecturer could win the Gold Cup immediately before, then the winnings over him could be played up on the filly. The prospect was alluring.

The weather at Ascot was not good. The cold winds that had ruined the Derby persisted, but the Danebury contingent were in no mood to be depressed when, led by Harry, they arrived on the course on the afternoon of Thursday, 6 June.

The first round went to the bookmakers, when Harry's filly, See Saw, was beaten into second place in the race preceding the Gold Cup. A little chastened but still indomitable, Harry began to back little Lecturer in the two-and-a-half mile race for the Gold Cup which was, and still is, the most coveted prize of the Meeting. Lecturer had not failed him when Harry had plunged so fearlessly on him in the Cesarewitch. Now Harry was confident that his gallant little horse would rescue him once again.

Lecturer was opposed by Hippia, the filly on whom Daley had won the Oaks, by Rama, the horse who had partnered Hermit in his trial gallops at Newmarket before the Derby, and by Regalia, a mare of great courage and stamina. It was a severe test.

Almost throughout the race it seemed as though Regalia must win, but as the final hundred yards was reached Fordham came with one of his inspired late challenges on the rails, and drove the little horse past the winning post in front.

Lecturer's victory was received with the loudest cheers of the day. On the free part of the course Harry's followers shouted his colours home with enthusiasm, but it was also in the grandstand and the fashionable enclosures that his success was warmly greeted. As *The Times* was to observe the following day, they cheered Harry 'as being one of the most plucky of speculators, and bearing his losses bravely, as an English gentleman should, there was considerable satisfaction felt at his success.'

Even the Ring gave him a cheer. He had paid his Derby debts in full, and they could afford—for the moment—to be magnanimous.

They remained silent half an hour later, however, when Lady Elizabeth, carrying one of the heaviest investments that even Harry Hastings had ever made on a racehorse, justified his confidence in her by spreadeagling her field in the New Stakes. With Fordham finding it unnecessary even to come from behind, she stormed down the course to win by fully six lengths. The trial on the Stockbridge racecourse had not been misleading. Here, it was very evident, was a truly great horse. And before she had returned to the paddock, the Ring were making her favourite for the Derby of 1868.

Hermit's victory was forgotten. Harry had won back from the Ring nearly all of what he had lost to them over the Derby. He had been cheered as a sportsman and a gallant loser when he arrived at Ascot, and now he was cheered again when he left it because he had fought back with a smile and refused to accept defeat. The bookmakers were the enemy of the man in the street. They still are. They always will be. He loves to see them humbled. So the cockneys and costermongers cheered Harry as he drove away from the course.

'The Markis—Gawd bless 'im!'

On the day following, Harry brought out Lecturer again for yet a further effort. It might have been supposed that the little horse had done enough, and more than enough, by winning a punishing race for the Gold Cup, but Harry and John Day called upon him once more—this time in the Alexander Plate over three miles. Again Harry backed him as if defeat were out of the question, and again this great-hearted little champion gave his all and won convincingly. But as he was led from the unsaddling enclosure after this second victory, he walked slowly and sadly, with a heavy tread. They cheered him, as they cheered his owner, but he was too tired to heed them. All he wanted to do was to go away and rest.

But Harry had little thought for Lecturer. He had recovered his losses over Hermit and deprived the Ring of most of their winnings, but there was one thing he could never do. He could never deprive Henry Chaplin of the immortality which he had achieved by Hermit's success. Hermit had won the Derby— the Blue Riband of the turf. Therefore Henry Chaplin and his colt would always be remembered.

Harry could never rob him of that honour—but he could equal it. More than that, he could eclipse it. Hermit had won by a neck. It had almost been a fluke. So Harry determined that *his* victory in the Derby would be achieved with far more glory and honour. *He* would win it with the finest filly of all time. And when Lady Elizabeth stormed past the post at Epsom in 1868, many lengths ahead of her field, they would cheer her as they had never cheered Hermit, and they would acclaim her as the greatest Derby winner in turf history.

In the past year he had been obsessed with one idea—that Hermit could not win at Epsom. It was a petty obsession, and perhaps Harry now became conscious of that. But now—*now* —he had a far deeper and nobler one. It was that Lady Elizabeth was to be the instrument for attaining all that he had ever asked of life. She would make the name of the fourth Marquis of Hastings remembered by racing men for ever.

It was not an unreasonable obsession, as his dislike of Hermit had been. Her trial on the Stockbridge racecourse and her subsequent running in the New Stakes had made it clear that she might never taste defeat.

It was almost a romance. This hapless, wayward and unstable young man had never been truly in love. Florence had fascinated him with her beauty and had flattered him with initial admiration and adoration, but he had never really loved her in return. He was too selfish and too self-centred. Lady Elizabeth could give him all that he could ever ask of a woman. She was beautiful and incomparable, as Florence had been, but she made no demands upon him. All he wanted was to watch her gallop over the smooth turf at Danebury and then to pat her silken nose and her glossy flanks; to gaze on her in all her majesty on the racecourse, and to bask in the reflected glory which she brought him. His whole future was dependent upon her. She had captured his heart.

There was perhaps significance in the fact that he named her Lady Elizabeth. After all, he had previously named one of his fillies Lady Florence, after his wife. Her second name was Cecilia, so he might have called his filly out of Trumpeter, Lady Cecilia. Instead, she was named Elizabeth.

From this moment on, after Lady Elizabeth's success at Ascot, he became convinced that fate had relented, and that now he could gamble without fear of losing. And if he did lose, momentarily, then there was always Lady Elizabeth who could be relied upon to win for him and to regain his losses, and much more besides. Between June and September in 1867 he attended every race meeting and bet on every race. And during that time his successes were numerous and often substantial. In the fortnight between 19 June and 2 July Lady Elizabeth ran in three races and won them all. Considering her ability, the prices against her were not always prohibitive. When she went to the Newmarket July Meeting the young Duke of Hamilton, who had learnt nothing from his brush with Captain Machell at Long's Hotel, had the temerity to believe that his filly, Leonie, could beat her, and he backed Leonie so heavily that Lady Elizabeth started at only a shade of odds on. Leonie was beaten, of course, with Fordham coasting home on Lady Elizabeth without moving on her. By now she had won nine races in succession, and been granted two walk-overs in addition.

But although Lady Elizabeth had now become the centre of Harry's life, he was in the remarkable position of also owning another two-year-old that might well become a live proposition for the Derby of 1868. This was his bay colt, The Earl, by Young Melbourne out of Bay Celia, who had won his first race at Stamford in July and had followed it with two further victories, including the important Gimcrack Stakes at York, in which Fordham rode him to a convincing two lengths win over a strong field.

At the same time, Athena was running brilliantly and winning race after race, and See Saw was also doing well. But even so, Harry's luck on the turf was not invariably good. Alternatively, he was driving it too hard. His horses were winning, and winning frequently, but he could not wait for the 'good things' to come along, but had instead to back on race after race, day in and day out. As the summer drew to a close and autumn approached, things began to go badly for him once again, and finally fate stepped in to give an ironical twist to his fortunes.

The last of the season's classic races, the St Leger, was run at Doncaster in September. Hermit was made a hot favourite, and Harry Hastings decided to forget his prejudice and to back him, and also Vauban, the Danebury 'pot' which they had all thought certain to win the Derby. But both were beaten by the filly Achievement, whose defeat in the Oaks had been such a blow to Harry, following, as it did, so soon after Hermit's victory in the Derby. Hermit finished second. He was not quite the same magnificent creature that he had been at the height of the summer, and he was ridden in the race by Custance and not his Derby jockey, Daley. Even so, his effort was a creditable one, for Achievement was certainly of the highest class.

One might have supposed that one of the first things which Harry would have done, when luck was running his way in the late summer, was to settle his debt of honour with Henry Chaplin, particularly as Chaplin had been so considerate about it. But Harry's resentment of Chaplin continued, while at the same time he was quite willing to play on Chaplin's generosity. Harry was also shrewd enough to realize that Chaplin would never press his claim too strongly because he knew that it would cause added distress to Florence.

In a letter which he had written to Chaplin early in August, Harry had promised to pay £10,000 at once, and to settle in full by the end of the month. He had been only casually apologetic. 'I am awfully obliged to you for having waited so long. If these damned fools of lawyers would get through the sale of my place in Scotland I should have been saved thousands but you know what a time they take.'

Nothing further was done, however, and at the beginning of September Harry retired to Baden for a few days to prepare himself for the exertions of the Doncaster Meeting. Before he left, Henry Chaplin dropped him another note, tactfully reminding him that the whole of the Hermit debt was still outstanding. Harry's reply, from Baden, was for once almost apologetic, and he even went so far as to mark the envelope 'Immediate'. It ran as follows:

> DEAR CHAPLIN—I have just received yours, and I am extremely sorry that you should have been put to any inconvenience by my not paying up at the beginning of last month. But it is not my fault, but my cursed old lawyer, who takes such an infernal time getting the money, though I have done nothing the last month but write and see him about it. However, now I shall go and get the money myself at once, so you may be certain it shall be paid this week, if I have to pay 100 per cent for it, as I hate owing anybody money. I have had a dreadful time since Goodwood but hope we shall do better at Doncaster—Yours in great haste,
> HASTINGS

The excuse that he had had a dreadful time *since* Goodwood may have been true; but he omitted to mention that he had had a remarkably successful time *at* Goodwood, where John Day sent sixteen Danebury horses and won fourteen races with them, whilst Harry himself won with Redcap and Athena.

Nevertheless, the tide had now turned against him; but no matter how bad things had become by the autumn, there was always Lady Elizabeth to rely upon when all else failed. Little Lecturer was beaten at Doncaster and seemed to have lost heart in racing, which was hardly surprising.

Harry determined that he would choose the second autumn meeting at Newmarket as the place for his final stand against the Ring. He had been lucky there in the past with Ackworth in the Cambridgeshire and Lecturer in the Cesarewitch. Now he planned to run The Earl in the Bedford Stakes and Lady Elizabeth in the Middle Park Plate, where there would be a big field and where a strong market was assured. Both races were to be run on the Wednesday, the third day of the Meeting.

In the Bedford Stakes The Earl, ridden by Fordham, ran a dead-heat with Count de Lagrange's Ouragan. There was a deciding heat, and Fordham was beaten by a head. For once his celebrated late challenge was made just too late.

The Middle Park Plate had attracted a strong field of sixteen runners and among these were two fancied candidates from the famous Kingsclere stable of John Porter, in the ownership of one of the staunchest supporters of the turf, Sir

Joseph Hawley. These were the colt, Rosicrucian, and the filly, Green Sleeve, both of whom were already being mentioned in connection with the Derby of 1868. Even so, Lady Elizabeth was rightly installed as favourite at 11 to 10 against, and backed by Harry Hastings to win £50,000 at these odds.

By now, Fordham's confidence in Lady Elizabeth was almost as great as that of her owner's. Her remarkable finishing speed, her tremendous powers of acceleration and her wonderful manoeuvrability, whereby she could take up almost any position at will, made her the perfect ride. If she was temporarily shut in or obstructed, she could be brought out of the ruck at the last moment for one devastating burst of speed that would take her past her rivals.

When he took her down to the start for the Middle Park, Fordham found her fretful and irritable. She had been given a hard season, and, although still immature, she had won eleven races and was still unbeaten. The field was larger than she was accustomed to, and, woman-like, she seemed to take a dislike to some of them. Fordham calmed her as best he could, and decided to keep her back at the start and allow the others to make the running.

But for once he badly misjudged both pace and distance. Also his supreme confidence in her ability to quicken prevented him from becoming alarmed when he found himself behind and boxed in as the last furlong was reached. When he asked her for her final effort, she responded gamely enough, but she had been left with too much ground to make up. At the winning post Green Sleeve was first, a head in front of her stable companion, Rosicrucian, with Lady Coventry third. Lady Elizabeth was fifth.

It was the only time that Harry Hastings ever showed emotion. Now, at last, the mask of casual indifference was dropped, and he could no longer hide the bitterness of defeat from those around him. He was seen to turn pale and to stagger as though he were about to fall; and for a moment his face was so pitiful in its misery that the Marchioness of Aylesbury, who was standing beside him, realized that she must do something to save his self-respect. So she turned quickly to him, thrust her betting book into his hand and asked him to tell her how she stood on the race.

Harry took the book, pulled himself together and examined it carefully. Then he turned to her, and with a note of genuine sympathy in his voice he told her that she had lost £23.

He himself had lost nearly £50,000 on the race and was nearly £60,000 down on the week. He handed the betting book back to the Marchioness and the old air of casual indifference returned. He shrugged his shoulders and smiled disarmingly as he commiserated with her on her loss.

He did not blame Fordham, for Harry was an experienced backer, and he knew how many fine races his jockey had won for him in the past; that he should sooner or later run a bad one was inevitable. But almost worse than his loss of money was the defeat of his beloved filly—the first in her career. This was almost more than he could bear, and so he determined that she must at once retrieve her great reputation.

Accordingly he challenged the Duke of Newcastle to a match of £1,000 a side with his three-year-old colt, Julius; Lady Elizabeth, as a two-year-old, was to carry 8 stone 2 lb, and Julius 8 stone 11 lb.

On the face of it, it was an outrageous proposition. Julius was one of the best staying three-year-olds in the country. He had finished third behind Achievement and Hermit in the St Leger, and had then gone on to win the Cesarewitch under the highest weight ever carried by a three-year-old in that race. Moreover the difference in physique between a two-year-old and a three-year-old is considerable. The two-year-old is still only a baby, its body by no means fully formed, its muscles still undeveloped. Harry should never have suggested the match, and John Day, who, after all, was held to be one of the greatest trainers of the Victorian era, should never have sanctioned it. It is true that, by winning such a match, Lady Elizabeth could at once regain her pedestal and become again the queen of the turf, but the task set her was far too arduous. It amounted almost to cruelty.

Nevertheless, the match was made, and Harry started to wager upon it with abandon. On such terms, Lady Elizabeth could not be made favourite. Everything was to the advantage of the older horse.

The race was to be run over the Bretby Course, which consisted of the last three-quarters of the Rowley Mile, and as Fordham, on Lady Elizabeth and Daley, on Julius, cantered slowly down to the start, they must have pondered on the tactics which should be adopted. Fordham was on his mettle. He had ridden a poor race on The Earl and a very bad one on his beloved filly in the Middle Park, and he knew it. He was being strongly criticized for his tactics, and he knew that also.

For once his gentle and unassuming nature was hardened by an unnatural resolve. He was *determined* to win, come what may. The kindly spirit which made him so reluctant to punish a two-year-old—because he could feel its little heart beating—was for the moment suppressed. He was *determined* to win.

He won. But at what cost! The two runners, locked together from the start and each giving of its best, galloped down the wide, open course and leaving the bushes behind them strode on up the hill to the winning post. A furlong from home they were still locked together. They were still nose to nose a few yards from the post. Then Fordham rode one of his strongest and most punishing finishes and, driving his beloved filly forward inch by inch, he gained the verdict on the post by a short head.

He returned to the unsaddling enclosure with the cheers ringing in his ears. His reputation as a great jockey had been restored. Her reputation as a great filly had also been restored.

But at what a cost! Lady Elizabeth allowed the saddle to be removed from her back and stood panting and sweating, her whole frame heaving with the tremendous exertion which she had just endured. Those around the unsaddling enclosure clapped their hands in appreciation of her great feat, and out on the course they were cheering her success, but she was too spent to care.

At her head, patting her and stroking her neck, Harry Hastings stood proud and smiling. The darling of his heart had achieved her greatest success. She had accomplished what seemed impossible.

But at what a cost! Only the weeks and months ahead were to reveal that!

This triumph had restored her prestige, but it had done little to resore Harry's finances. He had finally lost £49,000 on the week, and it was only with the utmost difficulty that he contrived to settle his debts to the Ring.

A fortnight later he returned to Newmarket for the Houghton Meeting, determined to have one more fling, but he scarcely backed a winner. The Earl was beaten twice, each time at odds-on, and the few other runners he had at the meeting did nothing. Now his situation was desperate.

A few days later Florence wrote a letter to Henry Chaplin. She was now distracted by worry, and he wrote back, comforting her. Her reply showed clearly enough that she was becoming desperate and that her love for Harry was nearly dead.

I could not help crying over your letter, tears of joy at first, at the kindness of its tone, and then bitter, bitter tears of remorse at the thought of all I had caused you to suffer, and of the happiness that I know now was once so nearly in my grasp, and which I so recklessly threw away for a mere shadow. If what I am suffering now is a punishment for the way I treated you, it is indeed a hard one, and I feel at times it is more than I can bear. You don't know, you have no idea how miserable my life is, and for the future it will be nothing but one long regret. What shall I do? I assure you it is positively killing me and completely ruining whatever good there may have been in my nature....

I have tried everything, reproaches, kindness, everything I can think of, and at last utter indifference, which is an awful thing to come to. Nothing does any good, and I feel and know the danger and temptation in which it places me. It is a hard, cruel lot, and all I can do now is to pray to God to give me strength to bear it. I don't want to ask you to do anything the least painful to you, but I would give anything to see you once quietly and have a long talk with you.... Is it asking too much?

The letter can be seen in different ways. To the cynic it may appear to be no more than a cry from one who has backed the wrong horse and is now trying to revert to the right one. Yet if it is assessed simply for what it says and implies, it surely becomes a pathetic and tragic document. It is so easy, when considering this Hastings story, to forget how young the central characters were when these tempestuous events overtook them.

To condemn her for writing such letters seems harsh in the extreme. Her purpose is surely not merely to ingratiate herself again with her old love and to worm her way back into his affections. There is every reason to suppose that she had always had a real affection for Henry, although it may not have been a very romantic or a very physical one. By the autumn of 1867 she was appalled at the thought of what the future had in store. It must be remembered that her early childhood had been clouded with the problems of money scarcity and the threats of creditors, and now she was undergoing the same nightmare all over again. By the autumn of 1867 she was desperate, lonely and afraid; and by the autumn of 1867 she was only just twenty-five.

In October she wrote to Henry Chaplin again. Harry had still not settled his Derby debts to Hermit's owner in full, and now she had taken it on herself to intercede on his behalf. (Or at least one *assumes* that she had. It is quite possible that Harry had told her to do so, for he was not above using her to help him out of his difficulties.) She was evidently seeing Henry Chaplin quite often at this time, under circumstances that permitted intimate conversation, although there was never any suggestion that he ever allowed himself to return to the old romantic association. He was a man of honour and would not take advantage of another man's wife; and he was also a sensitive man who, having been once deeply hurt, had no intention of being hurt again. But his kindness of heart must have influenced him, and he must have listened to her worries with genuine concern. In her letter she wrote:

> You told me the other day that if you could ever help me in any way you would do it. So I am going to take you at your word and ask you to do me a very great favour, which, having already discussed Harry's affairs, I feel less scruple in writing about than I should otherwise have done.
> The truth is I have had a most miserable letter from him this morning acknowledging to me what of course I knew, which is that he is so frightfully hard up he does not know what to do or which way to turn; and to add to all his other troubles he was served with a writ in Liverpool for £3,000, and how to pay it he knows not. Therefore, seeing a letter this morning in your handwriting to him, and guessing it to be about money, I opened it, and I want you as the greatest kindness to me to let me destroy it and to allow the £1,500 to stand over for the present, unless it is a real inconvenience to you. And if it is, I can only say I will do my best to procure the money for you somehow or other at once. I am sure you will forgive me for asking you this favour. I would not have done so had I not been worried and bothered to death, and I do feel so unhappy about Harry. Please send me one line in answer.

He acceded to her request, as he always did. It was also very evident to him that Harry Hastings was now bent on his own destruction, unless Lady Elizabeth achieved the miracle and extricated him from his predicament. Even so, it seemed certain that his health must soon fail, even if his inheritance did not become exhausted.

Harry still took Florence racing with him, but paid little attention to her while he was there. She shared his admiration for the enchanting Lady Elizabeth, but took no great interest in his string as a whole. They were proving themselves the instruments of his downfall, and she had little enough affection for them. At Newmarket, at the last Meeting of the year, she met Henry Chaplin and they watched some of the racing together. He advised her what to back, put the money on for her and succeeded in winning her a few pounds. She acknowledged this in a letter in which she wrote:

> How too awfully kind of you. You don't know how really grateful I am to you, not only for your goodness about Harry, but also for having won me the money. You can have no idea how useful it has been to me. Thank you a thousand times. I shall never forget it.
>
> I had a letter from our agent this morning, telling me that all the racehorses are to be sold at once, the Quorn Hounds to be given up at the end of the season, and we are to retrench in every possible way. God knows, there is no sacrifice I would not make if I could only get some sort of affection in return. How I dread going home and how I dread the winter! You can have no idea. I feel as if I should never have the strength to go through it. But I will do my duty ... for I am awfully worried about his health. What a miserable life mine is! I am quite disheartened.... I am very glad you had such fun at the ball. I wish you had had ladies staying with you and had asked Lady Westmorland and me. I was in hopes from your letter that you were coming to London, and that I should have caught a glimpse of you.

The letter clearly shows that if Harry had ever had any real love for her, it had died by now. Her need for affection must have been acute, for she was a warm-hearted girl but he gave her none. His mind was taken up with other things.

'How I dread going home and how I dread the winter,' she wrote. Harry, too, must have dreaded the arrival of winter. Racing was over, and all that he could do now was to try to silence his creditors.

He had already sold his Scottish estates to the Marquess of Bute for £300,000 and had disposed of all his hunters and hounds. He also sold numerous other securities, and mortgaged the Donington estate. But still he was in debt. Finally there was only one step left for him to take. He had to sell his racehorses as well.

The sale was held at Stockbridge racecourse—that same course where Lady Elizabeth had run her famous trials before the New Stakes at Ascot. Twenty-one yearlings and twenty-four horses in training were offered and sold; but when it came to Lady Elizabeth and The Earl, he could not bear to see them go. He bought in his beloved filly for 6,500 guineas and the colt for 6,100.

But still he failed to raise enough money to meet all his outstanding debts.

There was only one person left to turn to; Henry Padwick, the money-lender of Hill Street, Mayfair, who had remained so patiently and for so long in the shadows, waiting to pluck this ripest of all pigeons. Padwick had been Harry's racing companion, fellow racehorse owner and confidant ever since Harry's Oxford days. He had known from the outset, as the Ring itself had known, that sooner or later Harry must go bankrupt. Padwick was no Crockford, for he had not the old man's flair for usury or downright wickedness, but he had waited. He may have been as cynical as Crockford, but he was not quite so cunning and so cruel. He was in a risky profession, in which there were many bad debts, and in which there was also no place for sentiment; but he, too, loved owning horses and backing them, and he may well have felt a feeling of sympathy, almost of kinship, for Harry. Henry Padwick was shortly to be labelled the villain of the Hastings story, but it is significant that Harry continued to trust him till the end.

When the New Year dawned, and 1868 was ushered in with the traditional singing of Auld Lang Syne and the exchange of good wishes, Harry was still just afloat. He had obtained a large loan from Padwick, but since his assets were now strictly limited, The Earl was put in as part of the security, and it was agreed that the colt should run temporarily at least in Padwick's name and colours.

The Ring were now in full cry. They were asking, and not without reason, how it was that Harry could still remain a member of the Jockey Club, which stood for all that was honourable in racing, when he himself was a defaulter on a very large scale although he owned the winter favourite for the Derby.

It was certainly an extraordinary position; yet there were some bookmakers who saw in Lady Elizabeth not only Harry's salvation, but also their own. If the filly triumphed at Epsom, she would become immensely valuable and win for her owner a substantial prize, quite apart from what he was able to win in bets, and also a regular income thereafter from her fees at stud. If only Harry could be bolstered up to become even temporarily solvent, they might yet get back a large proportion of what was owing to them.

Racegoers as a whole were divided in their opinions about what Harry should do. Some argued that the Ring had already deprived him (robbed him was also a phrase commonly used) of an immense fortune during his short career on the turf, and the bookmakers were condemned for thus demanding their final pound of flesh. Others, led by the Ring itself, declared that whatever he might have lost by his foolish gambling during his life, it was not on horses that the money had been dissipated. They argued, and with some reason, that they had paid out immense sums to Harry, notably over Ackworth, Lecturer and Lady Elizabeth; and that he would have complained quickly enough if they had welshed on their commitments to him. If Harry had been fool enough to lose a fortune gambling with his friends on cards, dice and all the other absurd betting mediums which attracted him, then that was no concern of theirs.

The exact position between Harry and the Ring has always been uncertain. But it is clear that he was far shrewder on the turf than many people realized, and the Ring were not always the winners from him at the end of each year.

Harry, in the winter of 1867–8, was a very sick man. Excessive eating and drinking, coupled with lack of exercise, had severely damaged his kidneys, and he was suffering from what was known in those days as Bright's disease. Yet of all human ills, worry can prove in the end to be the greatest killer. Outwardly Harry did not appear to be worrying, but inwardly his fears were rapidly mounting. It was not so much the loss of wealth that affected him—it was the loss of all that it meant to him. Popular esteem, the reputation of being 'The King of the Gamblers', notoriety and the deference of the Ring would all be lost once wealth was lost. The 'scarlet and white' would no longer be shouted home by the common folk on racecourses as far apart as Epsom and York. For when the Marquis had lost his money, he would be like a great lover who had lost his virility; and he who had basked in the glare of publicity would become a nobody.

Only one thing could rescue him now, and that was the success of Lady Elizabeth in the Derby. On his visits to Danebury, where they now treated him with far less servility than before, he would spend long periods alone with her in her box, stroking the glossy neck and magnificent flanks. His darling could save him when no one else could.

As for Florence, he had little time for her now. Her unhappiness no longer affected him; it had never been of much concern to him at any time. Worry had robbed her of the bloom of youth and the freshness of beauty. The only loveliness in his life was contained in a stall at Danebury, exuding the very fire of youth and energy.

Or was she? There must have been many moments during that winter and early spring of 1868 when Harry Hastings and John Day looked upon Lady Elizabeth with growing anxiety. Outwardly, and physically, she seemed the same. But she had grown strangely irritable and uncertain in her temper, and had lost much of her former joy in striding across the Danebury gallops. She was now nervous and moody, where before she had been confident and even-tempered. She had lost her appetite and had to be coaxed to eat. But if the truth were dawning upon them, they were refusing to face up to it. Lady Elizabeth was displaying all the symptoms of a horse that had been over-raced and was in the process of going sour. Their greed for the money and fame which she had brought to them had been their undoing. They had taken the pitcher to the well too often.

And now a curious psychological attitude developed in those responsible for her welfare at Danebury. A sick man will often refuse to visit a doctor, because he suspects that he is ill and is afraid to have his fears confirmed. So, at Danebury, John Day and Harry Hastings did not subject her to a normal training schedule. That irony which is so often apparent in the Hastings story now becomes apparent in their treatment of the filly, for they who had always been so adamant about the need for punishing exercise for a racehorse now tended to avoid the strong work to which a Derby candidate ought to be subjected. Excuses were found to avoid those informative trials on which they had always depended in the past. Instead they comforted themselves with the oldest of all human assurances; they told each other that it would be all right on the day.

Indeed they did more. They convinced themselves that she was as fit and brilliant as she had ever been.

The public, meanwhile, had adopted her long since as their idol. There is always something more romantic and more intriguing about a great filly than a great colt. Her femininity makes her more enchanting, and her waywardness more endearing. She will often be smaller and less imposing than her male rivals; and the history of the turf has certainly suggested that she will often be endowed with greater courage.

So the racing public of England took Lady Elizabeth to their hearts long before the Derby was run. And since no hint of any loss of form was ever forthcoming from Danebury, from where, indeed, the most glowing stories of her prowess were constantly emanating, the betting man in the street adored her and saw in her his salvation on Derby Day, where she would reward him for his admiration and devotion by storming to victory. Thus the racing world now loved her in almost the same way as Harry loved her.

Mr Punch, in his forecast of the Derby result, reflected the general mood of his readers when he wrote, 'And now place for Lady Elizabeth. I take off my hat to that darling; and if wishes were horses, and beggars could ride, I'm the beggar that would ride her into glory and win the battle of Hastings!'

In the early spring odds of 6 to 1 could be had about her, although she had never been anything but favourite for the race; and as the day of the Derby grew nearer, these odds rapidly contracted.

It should be stated here, for the benefit of those who are not conversant with the turf, that of the five so-called 'classic' races, two—the One Thousand Guineas at Newmarket and the Oaks at Epsom—are open to fillies *only*; but a filly, if she is brilliant enough, can run in all five races, and can indeed win them all. But such a bold course may lead to disaster, for by running a filly in the Derby her owner may not only lose this race, but also lose his chance of taking the Oaks two days later. Normally a filly is reserved for the One Thousand and the Oaks, and is only asked to race against the colts in the final classic, the St Leger at Doncaster. (No filly has ever won all five classic races, but two—Formosa and Sceptre—have won four of them. Neither ran in the Derby.)

Lady Elizabeth was not asked to run in either of the first two classics. Her objective was the formidable double of Derby and Oaks, for both of which races she was favourite.

Whatever else may be said of Henry Padwick, it must be admitted that without his help Harry would never have been able to run his beloved filly at Epsom, and in his ownership. For as the Derby drew nearer the anomaly of Harry's position came more and more under fire from the Ring. He was at once the owner of the Derby favourite and the biggest defaulter on the turf! So an application was made to the Stewards of the Jockey Club by several leading bookmakers, who declared that Harry should be at once expelled, but they need not have troubled themselves, for Harry sent in his resignation, which was at once accepted.

At this moment, some few weeks before the race, his betting liabilities amounted to some £50,000; not in itself such a great sum, considering what had been his position in the years gone by. A friend tried to effect a settlement by suggesting that he should pay £20,000 at once—which he could just have managed—and the remainder in full if Lady Elizabeth won the Derby. But the Ring were in no mood to be merciful, or to take chances over her victory. They demanded settlement in full. The more hostile creditors demanded from Harry ten shillings in the pound, and the rest within three months. But Harry could not pay even this.

Henry Padwick now came forward to bolster up the situation, at least until after the Derby had been run. He was taking a risk, but he was well aware of the profits to be made if Lady Elizabeth won. He was already more deeply involved than he could have wished, but he had ever been a gambler, and the situation appealed to him. It gave him considerable power behind the scenes, and he was able to manipulate the situation to his advantage. Here was no amateur, trying to beat the Ring. Rather was it a skilled professional, playing them at their own game.

Meanwhile at Kingsclere, in Hampshire, and not so far away from Danebury, other plans were being hatched by those who were every bit as clever at their profession as was John Day. It was generally felt that if Lady Elizabeth did not win the Derby, then victory would go to one of Sir Joseph Hawley's trio who were under the skilful hands of John Porter. This trio comprised the two colts, Rosicrucian and Blue Gown, and the filly, Green Sleeve. Both Green Sleeve and Rosicrucian had finished in front of Lady Elizabeth the previous autumn in the Middle Park Plate, whilst Blue Gown had been beaten by a neck by The Earl at Newmarket in April, when the stable had private reason to suppose he had not been at his best, as the farrier had wrongly adjusted one of his shoes.

Although it had always been deemed advisable to run all three, it was imperative for the stable, and above all their wily owner, to know just which of the three was the best; and also (for such are the intricacies of betting and the need for 'laying off') which was the worst. With such knowledge they would be able to manipulate the betting to their great advantage. These problems could only be settled by a trial, but such a trial would have to be kept secret from their sworn enemies, the touts, who were watching their every move at Kingsclere and reporting back to the bookmakers all that they saw, heard or were able to surmise.

The touts knew that the trial was bound to take place; and their intelligence service, which was excellent and was based (as are most intelligence services) on observation, deduction, bribery and intelligent anticipating, had informed them of the probable morning. They were in a strong tactical position at Kingsclere, for there was an ancient toll-house standing on the road between the Kingsclere stables and the exercise grounds on the Hampshire Downs, and the string usually had to pass it. So on the night before the dawn trial, they bribed the toll-house keeper to allow them to hide inside it, and there they bedded themselves down for the night, with a plentiful supply of food and drink, several packs of cards and all the other necessities of life. But Porter's counter-intelligence service made him aware of this strategem, which in turn he countered with a shrewd one of his own, for he instructed one of his lads to put a chain and padlock across the door to the toll-house, and so imprisoned them. The next morning he took a circuitous route to the training gallops, and so his horses were safely back in their stable, with the trial completed, long before the touts had forced their way out of the toll-house.

The trial itself was inconclusive. It did no more than to suggest that Blue Gown and Rosicrucian were nearly equal, and that each was slightly better than the filly, Green Sleeve.

All that the racing public knew was that both Rosicrucian and Green Sleeve had run in the Two Thousand Guineas, but had done nothing, because they had been suffering from 'flu'; and that Blue Gown had been beaten by a neck by The Earl at Newmarket in the early spring. They also knew that Danebury considered Lady Elizabeth far superior to The Earl, and so they strongly supported Lady Elizabeth; but for some curious reason they formed the definite opinion that Blue Gown was easily the best of Sir Joseph Hawley's trio (probably because only the name appealed to them) and so Blue Gown was the only one of his three which they seriously backed to beat their idol.

Further curious activities were also afoot. Danebury had used its knowledge of Lady Elizabeth's superiority over The Earl to lay *against* him in the race, in the certainty that he could not beat her and win. This is an old racing trick, for he who knows that a horse is certain to lose a race is in almost as advantageous a position as he who knows that another is certain to win. So what with secret trials, rumours deliberately spread about to promote confusion, and those created simply by racing gossip; with bets laid and bets withheld; and finally with a Derby favourite who was the idol of the racing world but who had yet never run before that season and had never even been subjected to a strong stripped gallop (although this fact was unknown), the Derby situation of 1868 was as chaotic and confused as it has ever been in the long history of the race. Those who knew nothing, and this included the public as a whole, were certain they knew everything. Those who should have known a great deal had deceived themselves by wishful thinking; and the owner of three fancied candidates was not himself certain which of them was the best, although the man in the street had no doubt.

Derby Day, Wednesday, 27 May 1868, was one of glorious warmth and sunshine. Nothing could have been further from the conditions which had prevailed in the previous year. The sun blazed down on this English carnival, and the crowds flocked to the course in vast numbers and by every possible route.

To Harry, arriving early in the company of Florence, John Day and Henry Padwick, the setting must have seemed ideal for the triumph to come. Hermit had won before an empty house; but *his* Derby winner would enjoy the acclaim of as great a multitude as had ever been seen on Epsom Downs. The house was full, and the curtain was about to rise.

He had good reason to feel elated. A few days before, he had finally settled all his outstanding accounts at Tattersall's, and was no longer a defaulter (except for some money still due to Henry Chaplin) so once again the Ring could afford to cheer him on his arrival, whilst out on the Downs the crowds were sporting his racing colours of scarlet and white and were shouting his name—'The Markis—Gawd bless 'im'—and "'urrah for Lady Elizabeth!'

Epsom on Derby Day! It was a national holiday, when even the House of Commons, by a tradition long since inaugurated by Lord George Bentinck, suspended its sitting for the day, and when a vast concourse of men and women assembled on Epsom Downs to see the race for the Derby Stakes. Old and young, rich and poor—they slowly converged on this historic site as though impelled by some migrating instinct that had drawn them together.

Their vehicles filled the narrow roads, whilst the occupants chaffed and laughed with each other, and children ran from their cottage doors to cheer on the great cavalcade. On a day such as this, when the sun blazed down, the crowds became so vast that progress on the roads was often brought to a standstill. A traffic block might stretch for seven or eight miles back along the roads from Reigate, Kingston and Croydon, and there were halts of half an hour or more while the hot and agitated police tried to sort out the tangle.

There were unwieldy buses and over-filled brakes, wagonettes and coaches with red-coated guards who tooted loud and long their highly polished brass horns while the inmates cheered. There were the carriages and barouches of the gentry, the traps and donkey carts of the common folk, all united together in one long and joyous procession.

This was still the England of old—the England in which rich and poor were united by a common love of sport and could meet together in amity and good fellowship. Here, at Epsom, the old order still persisted. A coster in his cart could still shout a cheery welcome to a Duke in his crested coach, while the handsome young coachman behind, resplendent in braid and cockade, could throw a knowing wink to the young scullery maid who whistled in delight at him from the back of a broken-down pony and trap.

The men were even more gaily dressed than the women. The gentry, of course, wore their long frock coats and shiny top hats, but with a raffish look on this occasion which belied the seriousness of their formal garb, and with the hats beribboned with their racing colours. Even the schoolboys wore their toppers, and, escaped from the restrictions of Eton or Harrow, were drinking ale and champagne with their seniors as though to the manner born—as indeed they were. Here and there was a soldier in his scarlet tunic and pill-box hat, and the cynosure of every kitchen-maid's eye, whilst even the ordinary working man had put on his finest racing toggery for the occasion and sported the brightest of colours and the loudest of checks, with a tie of green or yellow and an oversized flower in the button hole. There were country yokels in smocks, and men in sombre black who looked as if they might have been undertakers, but were in reality business men who had hurried down from the City, from Mincing Lane, Old Jewry and The Poultry. There were thimblemen with their tables and ingratiating patter, religious fanatics with their banners calling for repentance, pickpockets with their sly looks and nimble fingers, the traders who pushed their carts piled high with steaming pies or bottles of ale, the performing acrobats in their white tights, the fire-eaters and the jugglers, the tumblers and the red-nosed comedians, the tipsters in their jaded jockey silks, claiming kinship with Fordham and Cannon, the blind beggars with their tin mugs and faltering steps, the cripples begging for alms, and all the rag, tag and bobtail of the East End of London, come to Epsom for a day to smell the clean, sweet air and forget the mists of the river and the filth and stench of Shoreditch and Wapping.

Then there were the womenfolk, for although this was above all a man's occasion, the men yet brought their wives and sweethearts with them, who gazed in astonishment at the noise, the excitement, the coarseness and the vulgarity—drunkards shouting out the choruses of popular songs, or relieving themselves against the wheels of their own or other people's carts whilst the female occupants shouted at them indignantly or covered their eyes with their hands. The Quality were dressed in the height of London fashion, with their bonnets and plumes and parasols, their crinolines, their laces and their shawls, but the common folk were every bit as bright and gay, the young girls in their white or pink dresses and with their rosy cheeks, plump, giggling and flirtatious, and struggling to restrain their brawny young companions, who had to enter every inn on the route to sink another quart of ale and discuss the chances of the favourite with the red-faced landlord.

There were the gypsies with their dark skins and mystic eyes, sitting outside their caravans and whispering secrets of love and matrimony in store for those who crossed their palms with silver, whilst their men-folk, sly and evasive, sold broken-down nags behind the caravans, or kicked out at the mongrel curs which ran between the wheels and grabbed at any stray morsel they could find.

Finally there were the children—scampering and scuttling like the dogs between the wheels of the carriages and underneath the hooves of the horses, so that the coachmen swore at them, and the horses reared up and shied. Ragged and barefooted, bedraggled and unkempt, their sharp little eyes burning in their deep sunk, hollow cheeks, their skinny little hands begrimed with dirt. Some of the girls held baskets in which were tiny bunches of spring flowers, which they proffered shyly to the great ladies in their crested carriages; and then screamed at each other like starlings when a penny was tossed down to them. As for the boys, they hung on the back axles of the carriages, or fought amongst themselves, swearing and cursing with all the fluency of their elders.

It had been a late spring, and the roads which led to the course were alive with the burning green of the English countryside in May. The white torches still stood proudly erect in the chestnut trees, the hedgerows were bursting into life and the birds were bursting into song.

On the course itself, all was pandemonium and shouting. The immense crowds spilled over the Downs, and across the race track itself. The huge stands were filled to overflowing, whilst on the other side of the course the carriages and drags were drawn up in lines, where their occupants could just see the heads of the horses and the colours of the jockeys. In lines behind them were the elegant marquees of the smartest regiments and clubs, each filled with deferential servants ready to serve every delicacy imaginable, against a background of vats six feet high containing the very best of vintage champagnes.

Behind these marquees, and covering the slopes of the historic Downs, were booths that offered every conceivable attraction to the swarming, excited crowds. There were dancing booths and sparring booths, and booths where the most wildly melodramatic sketches were enacted by simpering heroines and whiskered villains, hissing out their sinster plans with salacious glee. There were roulette booths, and booths where the thimbleriggers and the three-card men plied their dexterous trade. There were booths which staged *tableaux vivants,* and booths which were little more than brothels. And there were booths which dispensed ale from early morning until late at night, and where drunkards shouted and fought with each other or lurched precariously across the path of more sober folk. In the dim interiors of these booths the swells rubbed shoulders with the paupers, had their fortunes told, gazed upon the tableaux depicting Venus or Aphrodite, or groaned in unison with the rest of those present when the immortal scene of the death of Nelson was presented before them, and a haggard figure in tattered uniform croaked the equally immortal lines, 'Kiss me, 'Ardy—I'm wounded mortually'.

The amount of food which was consumed at Epsom on Derby Day was gargantuan. On the course they ate vast pies, cockles, mussels and eels. In the kitchens beneath the grandstand an army of cooks prepared numberless legs and shoulders of lamb, uncountable rounds of beef, lobsters by the hundred, oysters by the thousand, mountains of eggs, basket upon basket of spring chickens, pigeon pies and game pies, lettuces and salads, while immense tubs of dressing were stirred by strapping young women with birch brooms until the sweat rolled off their foreheads into the creamy yellow liquid beneath.

And all the time there was the hubbub and the excitement, the ebb and flow of the jostling crowds and the hoarse shouting of the Ring.

This was Harry's world; and this was the music of his life. Epsom on Derby Day, with everything which it stood for and all the promise that it held out! To own the Derby favourite on a day such as this, with the sun blazing down, and the course more crowded than it had ever been before, was to savour the supreme moment of existence.

From his father-in-law's box in the grandstand, Harry stood looking down upon the seething, sweating and shouting mass of humanity, and the cries from the Ring were borne up to him on the hot summer air.

'Five to four Lady Elizabeth, sixes Blue Gown, eight to one bar! Who wants a wager?'

His colours of scarlet and white were draped nonchalantly around his hat, and all over the course he could see others wearing these same colours, the men with scarves and buttonholes, the women with ribbons, all displaying them proudly to show kinship with their idol and their darling, Lady Elizabeth, and with her illustrious owner. And when they caught sight of him, looking down upon them from the stand, they waved to him, excited and happy, and cheered him again and again.

'The Markis—Gawd bless 'im!'

Behind Harry, in the background, stood his constant companion and shadow, Henry Padwick, smiling and urbane and seemingly as unruffled as Harry himself. John Day had assured them again and again that the filly was in the peak of condition and was ready to run for her life. They had no fear of the Kingsclere trio, nor of any of the other runners. She was in a class by herself.

On the evening before, they had scratched The Earl. It had been Harry's wish, at Padwick's instigation. The news had come as a shock to the betting public, but no one could fancy a stable companion in opposition to Lady Elizabeth, no matter how good it might seem. Besides, it was known that The Earl was due to run in Paris in the Grand Prix in ten days' time, and so the stable were obviously out to achieve a unique double; or treble, for that matter, as Lady Elizabeth would certainly take the Oaks in her stride on the Friday, once the far greater obstacle of the Derby had been safely encompassed.

As for the Ring, they watched and waited and listened, seeking for those tiny signals which whisper of something in the wind.

Meanwhile the Kingsclere confederacy were busily hatching *their* plots. The public had long since decided that Blue Gown was the best of their trio, and this belief had been confirmed by the stable jockey, J. Wells, who—having been offered the traditional choice of mounts—had also selected Blue Gown, which had therefore been installed as a firm second favourite to Lady Elizabeth.

Sir Joseph Hawley did not share this view. He had not earned the nickname of 'The Lucky Baronet' for nothing, for he had already won the Derby three times, and now he was of the opinion that wherever Blue Gown finished, Rosicrucian and his filly, Green Sleeve, would finish in front of him. Indeed he had secretly no very high opinion of Blue Gown, and would probably have scratched him, had it not been for the public's heavy support of the colt. A very heavy gambler, and the man who had taken a cool hundred thousand off 'Leviathan' Davis when Teddington had won the Derby seventeen years before, Sir Joseph was in the happy position of being able to trade at the most advantageous odds over the two he fancied, while ignoring altogether Blue Gown, the one which the public fancied and which they had made second favourite. Rosicrucian the public ignored, because of the news which had leaked out from Kingsclere that the colt had finished last in a trial. The fact that this news had been 'leaked' deliberately, and was all part of the ancient pastime of throwing dust in the eyes of the racing world, was not known to the man on the Downs. He remained simple and gullible, the eternal shuttlecock between trainers and the Ring.

It was all a part of a typical Derby Day, with its rumours, its secret information and its whispered tips. John Porter and Sir Joseph Hawley knew that Blue Gown would not win. John Day knew that Lady Elizabeth would. And the Ring? They were as cunning as anyone, but they still remained in doubt—cautious as hounds who are seeking for a scent, watching with lynx eyes as the chief actors in this strange drama moved amongst them.

The Marquess of Anglesey had invited Harry and Florence to watch the race with him from his box, and somewhat reluctantly had extended the invitation to Henry Padwick. Henry Chaplin, as in previous years, was in the company of the Prince of Wales. He had an entry in the Derby, a chestnut colt named St Ronan, but this was no Hermit, and he had no great expectation of it. On the whole, he was hoping that Lady Elizabeth would win, if only for Florence's sake. But his patience with Harry was wearing a little thin. Harry was being cheered as the man who had met his debts in full—but he had not met them all. He still owed Henry a part of the Hermit debt, and the fact was beginning to rankle.

Shortly before the racing started, Harry, John Day and Henry Padwick had strolled across the Downs to Sherwood's stables, at The Warren, close by the start, where Lady Elizabeth had spent the night. Here, in the peace of the little paddock, so close to all the bustle and excitement and yet seemingly so remote from it, they had watched her being walked slowly round and round. She was sweating with nervous excitement and already showing signs of irritation and fretfulness. Indeed she had become steadily more short-tempered as her training had proceeded, and Harry had finally been forced to approach the Stewards to ask for their permission to excuse her from being saddled on the racecourse, and from being paraded before the race. This permission had been granted and so now she walked round and round in peace beneath the trees, waiting for the call which would take her out to meet the greatest challenge of her racing career.

Satisfied by what they had seen, the three had strolled slowly back across the Downs. Everywhere they had been recognized, and everywhere they had been cheered. To the racing public at large, this was a typical gesture on Harry's part—that he should walk amongst them at this moment, when the ambition of his life-time seemed within a few minutes of being realized. So they made a lane for him, and the women curtsied and tossed him bouquets of flowers from their baskets, whilst the men laughed and joked with him and patted him on the back. He might have been some famous general, reviewing his troops before a battle; and, in a sense, he was. They were all of them about to go into action, and there was much at stake.

Back in the stand, Harry joined his wife and her father, and called for champagne. Florence welcomed him with a smile, but she was pale and nervous. The sun beat down mercilessly, and the dust rose in a cloud from under the feet of the jostling throng and made her cough.

As the time for the great race grew near, the crowd surged across the course in front of the grandstand, so that nothing of the track could be seen at all. The runners emerged from the paddock, and were greeted with cheers. There was disappointment that they could not pick out the scarlet and white, or Fordham's well-known face, but when the news was spread about that their *prima donna* would not be seen amongst them, but would only appear at the start, they nodded their heads sagely and agreed that it was all for the best. They would have loved to have welcomed her, but they had no wish to upset her at this, the most important moment of her life.

So they jostled and shouted in front of the stands, caught a fleeting glimpse of the horses as they moved towards the start, and then turned excitedly to each other to chatter about what they had seen.

From the stands, it seemed as if the course could never be cleared, so dense was the throng, but suddenly a thin blue line of constables appeared as if from nowhere, and they, too, now played their traditional part on Derby Day—moving forward slowly and without aggression, driving the throng before them like sheep-dogs herding their flock towards a pen, until the course was clear and the great multitude had withdrawn to the slopes of the Downs.

Now the carriage folk paused over their luncheon, the popping of the champagne corks was momentarily stilled, and even in the tents and caravans, thin brown hands which had been crossed with silver remained motionless for a moment as silence settled on the watchers outside. Only the pickpockets continued to go about their business, knowing that it was in these precious moments of concentration, when all eyes were riveted upon the start, that nimble fingers could delve into pockets, and the wallets, and even the sovereigns, of the unsuspecting could be deftly removed.

The visibility was perfect. The colours on the sky-line were clearly outlined. To Harry, and to so many others with him, the moment had come.

At the start, George Fordham coaxed and cajoled his bay filly as she hung back, reluctant to join with the others. Summoning all his skill, and with a mental effort that was almost hypnotic in its intent, he tried his utmost to soothe her. She was sweating profusely now, and her lovely neck was flecked with lather.

In the Ring, where every nuance of mood and behaviour was reflected in a change of price, as though some strange prophetic barometer were at work, the odds against Lady Elizabeth were lengthened, while those against Blue Gown grew shorter. The hounds had picked up a scent, and were making the most of it in the short time left to them before the 'off'.

The starter, Mr McGeorge, never more serious nor more self-important than on an occasion such as this, delivered his final warning to the jockeys and told them to come slowly forward into line.

Anxiously he watched Lady Elizabeth, for he knew that he would be lynched by the mob if he were to lower his flag when she was behind or facing the wrong way. Her antics were now becoming more violent, and she reared up in the air, trying to dislodge Fordham from her back. Then, for a moment, she regained her balance, and he coaxed her gently forward. McGeorge dropped his flag and the field sped away, while the bell in the stands tolled out the news. And the shout of 'They're off' was given a greater volume when it was seen that the scarlet and white colours were in the thick of the fray.

So much preparation, so much excitement! And then so much disappointment! For in a few seconds the hopes that had risen so high were dashed on the instant to the ground.

Never, at any moment in that race, did Lady Elizabeth suggest that she could win. Within a furlong her effort was spent; and long before Tattenham Corner was reached her chance had disappeared.

Harry was at least spared the agony of a desperate finish.

But to the crowds who peered anxiously over the heads of those in front of them and strained to catch a glimpse of the scarlet and white, the truth did not dawn upon them until the horses had flashed past them in the straight. In the last quarter of a mile there were only two horses that could possibly be concerned with the finish. These were the outsider, King Alfred, and Blue Gown; and in the last few strides, Wells forced Blue Gown into the lead to win on the post by half a length.

Another Derby was over, and another day was done. The crowds gradually melted from the course as evening drew on, leaving their litter, their beer bottles and their hopes behind them. A few hungry dogs, and a few hungry children, remained behind to scavenge amongst the rubbish for a slice of beef or a piece of pie. A few drunks lurched homewards across the Downs, or lay down in the clumps of bushes on the hill to sleep off the fumes that clouded their brains. The sun dropped slowly down behind the paddock, and the cloud of dust which had hung like a haze all day above the roads which led to the course settled at last.

The Derby was over, and the favourite had been beaten. Well, it had happened before and it would happen again. In a hundred years' time there would be the same tumult, the same excitement and the same high hopes. The colours would flash round Tattenham Corner and into the straight, and the great roar would greet them as they neared the post. But the days of the scarlet and white were almost over. There could be no hope for them now.

There were no more cheers for Harry Hastings. In a way, the common folk felt that he had let them down. Slowly they jogged their way back along the dusty roads to London, disappointed but not downcast. There would be other heroes to discover—and other horses to cheer.

Harry drove back in his open carriage to London, with Florence and Henry Padwick. All chance of re-establishing himself had now gone. He was far too much in debt for any possibility of recovery. Padwick now owned nearly all his worldly possessions, and God alone knew who owned his soul. He had tried to find solace in champagne, but it had been a useless effort. Now he sat, crumpled and bleary-eyed, still making a feeble attempt at an air of bravado for the benefit of those whom he passed on the road. Beside him sat Florence, pale and motionless. But she, too, had her pride. If the carriage was to be open, and the world was to see them, then she would behave as a Paget should in this final moment of defeat. Her eyes were dry and her head was held high.

CHAPTER TEN

THE ROAD TO KENSAL GREEN

After the Derby, the inquests.

Sir Joseph Hawley was left to ponder on the fallibility of an owner's judgment, for he had never fancied the chances of Blue Gown. As for his trainer, John Porter, *he* was left to ponder on the fallibility of secret trials, for in his home gallops Blue Gown had never suggested that he was markedly superior to his two stable companions, Rosicrucian and Green Sleeve.

George Fordham was left with sadness, but no self-criticism. They had said of him that he was no Derby jockey, and now he had failed on yet another Derby favourite. But no one could blame him this time. His mount had never shown with a chance.

But what of Lady Elizabeth? How to explain her extraordinary loss of form?

The controversy raged throughout racing England. Even today there are still those who will argue about it. Why did she run so lamentably?

It is said that beauty is in the eye of the beholder—and those who behold beauty are often blind to its imperfections. Many of those who saw Lady Elizabeth at Epsom on that Wednesday afternoon, and indeed who also saw her at Danebury in the weeks before the race, declared at the time that she looked magnificent. Alexander Scott, in his *Turf Memories of Sixty Years*, recalling the Derby of 1868, wrote:

> On my way down to see the horses in the paddock, I saw the Marquis arm-in-arm with his trainer, John Day, wearing a confident smile of anticipation on his countenance. Anyone with an eye for a good thoroughbred must have admired Lady Elizabeth as she stood there in the paddock. She looked a veritable picture, and did John Day every credit. It certainly was not lack of condition on her part that lost the race. If looks alone could win Derbies, Lady Elizabeth would have won that one....

The attitude of the Ring largely supported this view. It is true that she had not pleased the watchers in her canter on the morning of the race, had sweated a lot and shown evidence of temperament, and that they had 'knocked her out' in the betting from 5 to 4 to 7 to 4, although this may have been due in part to an inspired run of money on the ultimate winner, Blue Gown. Even so, they would have made her price longer had they really had reason to foresee the fiasco that was to come.

Harry was not an expert on horses and could not judge her condition. But his trainer, John Day, was an acknowledged master of his craft. He must have known the exact state of her well-being. So also must George Fordham. It was said by those who were present that the Danebury contingent were dumbfounded by what happened, and that both Day and Fordham were heart-broken at her defeat and utterly at a loss to account for it.

Yet there were others who described Lady Elizabeth on that afternoon as being nothing but 'a dried-up bag of bones'. This was said *after* the race, when she had run as if she were a physical wreck, but most of the evidence suggests that she looked reasonably well on the day. That her defeat was no fluke, due simply to her being off colour on that particular afternoon, was proved by her dismal failure in the Oaks, on the Friday, when running over the same course and distance she was again never in the race with a chance. She was offered at 5 to 1, which suggested that the Ring, at least, had formed their own conclusions, and she was beaten out of sight by the winner, Formosa. Cannon had been substituted for Fordham as her jockey, and—ironically enough—it was Fordham who rode the winner. Admittedly there was a violent thunderstorm before the race, and the conditions were hot and oppressive, but excuses for her could not continue to be made. The saddest comment on the whole affair was that after the Oaks she was booed by a section of the crowd. *Sic transit*....

What really brought the controversy alight, however, and produced one of the most notorious *causes célèbres* in turf history, was the fact that The Earl was sent, as planned, to run in the Grand Prix de Paris on the Sunday week after the Derby, and there, ridden by Fordham, gained a comfortable victory over some of the best horses in Europe.

This really did put the cat amongst the pigeons. The evidence of Danebury chicanery seemed only too apparent to a number of racegoers, who not unnaturally wished to know how it was that a horse which in all probability could have won the

Derby with ease came to be scratched on the night before the race; and how his stable companion, who was a hot Derby favourite, came to run so deplorably. The turf had for long been the breeding ground of rumour and gossip, but this really started the tongues wagging.

At Ascot in the following week, The Earl, still running in the name of Harry Hastings, won 'the Ascot Derby', the St James's Palace Stakes and the Biennial Stakes, whilst Lady Elizabeth put up another dismal performance to finish last in the Prince of Wales's Stakes.

This was altogether too much. Questions had to be asked, and—as so often happens on these occasions—they were asked by someone with more vehemence than discretion. The gallant Admiral Rous, the ruler and dictator of the English turf, stormed into battle with a broadside fired during Ascot, when he was overheard to remark, somewhat injudiciously, that had he taken as much laudanum as had been given to Lady Elizabeth he would have found himself in his coffin. The comment was reproduced in *The Sporting Life* and then quoted in *The Pall Mall Gazette*.

The Admiral was then over seventy. He was a fiery character with a habit of speaking first and thinking afterwards, but the purity of the turf was something very dear to his heart, and he believed that heavy gambling was a curse that needed stamping out. He also believed that money-lenders such as Henry Padwick were largely to blame for encouraging foolish young aristocrats such as Harry in their extravagances. These views were shared by the Queen herself, who was becoming increasingly alarmed by the excesses of the upper classes, particularly in gambling. However, the statement about laudanum was too damaging for him to admit, so he wrote a letter to *The Times* in which he made matters far worse. In it, he said:

My belief is that Lady Elizabeth had a rough spin with Athena in March when the Days discovered she had lost her form—a very common occurrence with fillies that have been severely trained at two years old; that when the discovery was made they reversed a commission to back her for the One Thousand Guineas Stakes at Newmarket, and they declared that Lord Hastings would not bring her out before the Derby on which he stood to win a great stake.

I am informed that when Lord Hastings went to Danebury to see her gallop they made excuses for her not to appear. If he had seen her move the bubble would have been burst.

But the touters reported she was 'going like a bird'. Ten pounds will make any horse fly if the trainer wishes it to rise in the market!

She had never been able to gallop the whole year. Lord Hastings has been shamefully deceived, and with respect to scratching The Earl, Lord Westmorland came up to town early on Tuesday to beseech Lord Hastings not to commit such an act.

On his arrival in Grosvenor Square he met Mr Hill going to Weatherbys with the order in his pocket to scratch The Earl, and Mr Padwick closeted with Lord Hastings.

In justice to the Marquis of Hastings I state that he stood to win £35,000 by The Earl, and did not hedge his stake money. Then you will ask: 'Why did he scratch him?' What can the poor fly demand from the spider in whose web he is enveloped?

> I am, Sir,
> Your obedient servant,
> H. J. ROUS

13 BERKELEY SQUARE, 15 June 1868.

The letter was clearly an attack upon Henry Padwick, who was obviously 'the spider'.

Henry Padwick and John Day therefore both considered that they had been grossly libelled—as indeed they had—and each sprang to his own defence. Henry Padwick, in a long letter to *The Times*, declared that it was Harry who had decided on the scratching of The Earl, and that he, Henry Padwick, had had nothing to do with this decision. He had scratched the horse, but only on Harry's instructions. The Duke of Beaufort, Lord Westmorland, Mr Coventry and Captain Barlow had been others present at Harry's house at 34 Grosvenor Square when the matter had been discussed, and everyone had tried to dissuade Harry from scratching the horse and thus depriving the public who had backed him of a chance of getting a run for their money. But Harry had been obdurate. He had insisted on The Earl being taken out of the race. Padwick concluded his letter with the comment:

> I had no control over, or interest in, the horse, and I was no party to his being scratched. Lord Hastings, in the

presence of the gentlemen I have mentioned, accepted the exclusive responsibility for the act. I beg most unhesitatingly to state that I had not betted one shilling either on or against The Earl for his Derby engagement.

Harry Hastings also rallied to his own defence, in the following letter:

> To the Editor of *The Times*
> Sir: I have read with the greatest astonishment a letter which appears today bearing the signature of Admiral Rous. I can only characterize that letter as a tissue of misrepresentations from first to last. There is no single circumstance mentioned as regards my two horses, Lady Elizabeth and The Earl, correctly stated.
> I wish also to add that so far from being shamefully deceived, as stated in Admiral Rous's letter, The Earl was scratched by my express authority, that I myself wrote to Messrs Weatherby to scratch him, and that no one either prompted me, or suggested to me, to adopt that course.
> I trust that this contradiction will induce Admiral Rous to abstain in future from publishing statements which he would find to be unfounded if he had previously taken the trouble or sought an opportunity of verifying them.
>
> Yours, etc,
> HASTINGS
> 34 GROSVENOR SQUARE, 16 June 1868.

Meanwhile John Day had visited his solicitors, and had instructed them to take proceedings against the Admiral; and an eminent counsel was briefed on his behalf. The Admiral, who was not easily cowed, replied by retaining the Attorney-General to plead his case, and a body of English sportsmen rallied to his aid and started a fund to pay for his defence.

During the preliminary skirmish, Harry Hastings remained the shuttlecock. The tide of legal battle ebbed and flowed over him, but he remained the plaything of fortune. To all those who watched him, during the weeks that followed the Derby, it was very clear that the prophecy which had appeared in *The Tomahawk* magazine could not long be delayed. Harry's carriage was driving forward, with the Devil holding the reins and Death on the rumble seat. Whoever might win in the legal battles that were about to be fought, it was very clear that the certain loser would be the fourth Marquis of Hastings.

He had lost nearly all his old friends now, and even the common people had forsaken him. True, he never now went down into the stews and dens of the East End, but even had he done so, he would have found few inmates there to toast his name. Worse still, he was once again a defaulter, for he had been quite unable to pay his debts over the defeat of Lady Elizabeth. When he went to Ascot that June, his reception from the Ring was very different from the one which they had accorded him a year before, when they had cheered him to the echo. He was booed now, and few would accept his bets. His debts to the Ring alone amounted to £40,000, and he had no hope of meeting them. He offered to pay seven shillings in the pound, but no one expected him to be able to do even this, and in fact he could not.

By now even Florence had lost all her affection for him. She still pitied him, but her love was quite dead. Now, when Henry Chaplin spoke sharply of the fact that Harry Hastings had still not settled his debt over Hermit, she did not intercede on behalf of her husband, but took Henry's side.

Finally, when Harry decided to spend the summer on his yacht, *Ladybird*, cruising in Norwegian waters, in an attempt to regain his strength, she did not accompany him. Probably he did not ask her to; and no doubt she would have done so if he had asked. But Harry wished to get away from it all and to forget Florence, to forget Lady Elizabeth and to forget the turf. He had one last straw at which he could clutch. The Earl was clearly a great horse. He surely had the ability to win the last of the season's classic races, the St Leger at Doncaster, and thereby do something to bring back the glory to the scarlet and white colours. But the St Leger was not due to be run until September, and so, until then, he would rest and try to forget. *Ladybird* stole slowly out of Southampton early one morning in late June, and there were few on the quay to wish her or her owner god-speed.

Florence spent the summer with a woman friend at White Place, near Maidenhead, and from here she wrote Henry Chaplin a number of letters, in which she told him of her unhappiness, her regrets, and her remorse over the evil which she had done to him.

> I was glad to be able to have that talk with you, and to hear the truth, for I have always had such a tremendously

> high opinion of you that I could not bear to think you had done anything to make me alter it. You know the position I am placed in, and that of course in the eyes of the world I am bound to stick to my husband. Therefore, I cannot go boldly about and say I believe *you* in preference to him, but I want to tell you that I do believe you implicitly, and I am quite satisfied with the explanation you gave me, as far as you yourself are concerned.

And in a later letter, she speaks again of her changing attitude towards her husband:

> At first, when I was certainly happy, I don't think I viewed my conduct in the same light I do now (and to tell you the truth I did not think you really cared about me): but now when I am utterly miserable I see my behaviour to you, as I have never seemed to see it before, and God knows how deep and bitter are my feelings of remorse. If I only could have seen the future then as I see it now, how differently I should have acted; how different both our lives would have been.

But a man who is capable of a deep and genuine emotion is also a man who can be deeply wounded; and he does not find it easy to forget, even if he finds it in his heart to forgive, as Henry Chaplin had certainly found it in his.

However, Henry seems to have been willing enough to visit her occasionally and even to have flirted with her in a reserved and respectable way. 'If you had come down,' she says in one of her letters, 'you would have dined with us, for I don't think anyone would be a bit the wiser if you did, would they?' So there was a certain air of secrecy about these meetings. There must have been many times, as she sat with him, when she pondered on how different her life would have been had she never eloped with Harry and had become instead the mistress of Blankney Hall.

'In this world there are no second chances.' It was the philosophy which was to haunt James Barrie in the years to come, and now it came to haunt Florence. Henry was kind to her and helped her in every way he could; but she knew that with him there could be no second chance.

So while Florence spent the sunny hours near Maidenhead and thought of what might have been, Harry must have sat on the deck of *Ladybird* and also pondered on the missed chances in his life. There were so many 'ifs'. If he had only bought Hermit at the Middle Park sale instead of Henry Chaplin. If Grimshaw had only ridden a cleverer race in the Derby of 1867 and had seen Hermit's challenge before it was too late. If only Fordham had not waited so long on Lady Elizabeth at Newmarket. If only Harry himself had only been less avaricious of success and had not subjected his beloved filly to that heart-breaking struggle with Julius. If only....

And now the sands were running out for him—at the age of twenty-six. The increasing feebleness in his body could no longer be ignored, or laughed away. Already he felt, and looked, an old man. One could not go on burning the candle at both ends indefinitely. The day of reckoning had sooner or later to be faced.

There may well have been another thought which troubled him on this journey across the sea. A few weeks before, he had entertained a small party of friends at Donington Hall, in an attempt to revive some of the gaieties of the past. Among the guests had been an old friend of the family, George Gordon, the son of Lord Francis Gordon, and others of Harry's cronies. After dinner one evening, when it was already growing late, Harry had been disturbed by the sound of carriage wheels on the drive outside the Hall and had sent a servant to find out whom this late arrival might be. The servant had gone to the front entrance, but there was no one there. A few minutes later Harry had heard the sound of carriage wheels again and had again summoned the servant and told him to go to the main entrance—but again the servant returned to report that no one was there. It was then that Harry remembered the legend of the Hastings family, that when the master of the house, sitting at the head of his table, twice heard the sound of a carriage outside when none was there, then his death was certain before the year was out.

Perhaps Harry smiled at the memory of this incident, for he had met it with characteristic aplomb. Having explained to his guests what the implications were, he had invited them to lay him odds against the legend coming true, and had then backed himself to survive, remarking with a smile that if he lived, he would win, and if he lost, it would be up to his opponent to recover the wager from his executors.

But if his prevailing mood on this cruise was one of melancholy, there was still one hope which yet remained to him. The year of 1868 might still end in glory for him if The Earl should triumph in the St Leger at Doncaster. This was not the Blue Riband; but it was a classic race, and the winning of it was held to be the final achievement in a horse's classic career.

He returned to England, feeble still and by no means recovered, to find that the controversy over the Derby was still raging. Admiral Rous, having realized that he had been incautious in his previous statements, was now behaving more warily. He was admitting nothing, and no longer allowing himself to be drawn. The reason why The Earl had run at Newmarket in the spring under the name of Henry Padwick, and not of Harry Hastings, had been more or less explained. Because, said Padwick, he had been forced to take the horse in a bill of sale, for otherwise the Sheriff would have seized the colt and sold him to pay Harry's debts. Once Harry had become almost solvent again, as had happened shortly before the Derby, the horse had been restored to him. This seemed reasonable enough. But even so, it was a murky business. It was not easy for anyone at Danebury to explain away the fact that they had held an almost certain Derby winner in their care and had allowed the colt to be scratched on the evening before the race. The public had been betrayed, the colt had been betrayed—even the owner, despite all his protestations, seemed also to have been betrayed.

As for Lady Elizabeth, there were several explanations. She carried a fortune on her back, and it is possible that she may have been 'got at'. This was a great age for nobbling, and she would not have been the first Derby favourite to have been rendered 'dead meat' before ever she reached the post. Even today, the artifices of the horse-doper are not fully known. There are secret drugs which can have a crippling effect, the worst of which is that the horse is never the same again. They can be administered in many ways, and certainly need not necessarily be taken by the mouth. But had this been so, the Ring would almost certainly have known about it and this knowledge would have been reflected in a gradual lengthening of the price offered against her. But no such gradual lengthening took place. It was not until she was seen in her final canter on the morning of the Derby that the Ring began to field against her, and then the lengthening of the price was only a minor one.

The real answer must have lain, as the Admiral pointed out in his original letter to *The Times*, with the fact that loss of form is a very common occurrence with fillies that have been severely trained as two-year-olds. It is not their bodies which suffer, but their minds. They grow sour and sick of racing; and they remember the pain and distress which previous races have caused them and flinch from being subjected to any further such ordeal

Lady Elizabeth may well have been martyred in the cause of Victorian training methods, which were based on the belief that with young animals, as with young humans, the rod should never be spared. George Fordham can be exonerated from all blame. He merely carried out his orders. There was no jockey riding who would have shown greater compassion than he. The Days, Harry Custance, Cannon, Grimshaw and certainly—in the years to come—the great Fred Archer would never have subscribed to the humane view that a horse should not be driven to its utmost powers of endurance when the money was down and the finish was certain to be a close one.

Ladybird sailed back into Southampton late in August, and Harry returned to Grosvenor Square to find Florence waiting for him. He greeted her perfunctorily. His only interest was to learn about the progress of The Earl. The colt was by then a hot favourite for the St Leger, as he had every reason to be. Harry had little enough money for gambling now, but he was able to scrape together some two and a half thousand with which to back his colt. He knew it was his final fling. If this bet went down, he could never place another of a comparable sum. But he was able to trade at odds, grudgingly offered, of between 2 to 1 and 7 to 4. Thus he would win nearly £5,000 if successful. It seemed a fortune to him now.

Hardly had the bets been laid and entered in his betting book, than John Day came post-haste up from Danebury to make his report at Grosvenor Square. The Earl had broken down in training. His case was quite hopeless, and he would have to be scratched at once.

It was the end. Harry had lost his last gamble and without even being given a run for his money. Nothing was now left to him; not even honour.

His debtors crowded around him, baying for their money. They hounded him at every turn. Finally his health broke down completely under the weight of persecution, misery and despair.

The last time the public saw him was at the first October meeting at Newmarket, when—a broken, frail old man of twenty-six—he was wheeled in a basket carriage on to the Heath. The man who had bet to the tune of thousands and had staggered the Ring by his daring and brilliance was now only able to wager a modest 'pony' of £25, and that only after he had been brutally reminded by the bookmaker that settlement would have to be made immediately after the race.

He had come to see his lovely filly, Athena, run in The Grand Duke Michael Stakes. Not that he could any longer call her 'his', for Henry Padwick owned her now, as he owned so many other things which had once belonged to Harry Hastings. She cantered down to the start, with Fordham on her back, and the Ring made her favourite, as they had so often done over Harry's horses in the past.

She won easily, breasting the rise to the winning post with grace and swiftness, and they pushed the basket chair into the unsaddling enclosure so that Harry might pat her silky neck. She had never been to him the equal of his darling Lady Elizabeth, but she, too, had captured a corner of his heart.

He left the course soon after, and as he did so he lifted his hand in a salute to the Ditch, as racegoers have done for generations, in thanks for blessings received and for those to come. It was his farewell to the turf. He was never to see the Heath again.

At least he was spared the final ignominy a month later, when Lady Elizabeth ran in a miserable little race of second-raters and finished third in a field of five. Fordham rode her gently, without driving her hard, and then walked her slowly back to the unsaddling ring. The scarlet and white colours were glimpsed for a moment by the crowd on the Heath before he dismounted, and then they disappeared from view. They, too, had been seen at Newmarket for the last time.

Towards the end of October he paid what was destined to be his last visit to Donington. He was seen 'crawling about on a stick' at King's Cross and at Leicester, 'an old young man—worn out alike in mind, body and estate'.

At Donington they were shocked to see his frail condition; and his pathetic attempts to appear as gay and casual as of old deceived no one. By now he had become morose and moody, and when he drank the effect was only to promote a mood of melancholy and self-reproach. One evening, when he was seated in the great library, surrounded by the portraits of his ancestors who gazed down upon him from the panelled walls, his glance fell on a picture of Henry Chaplin which he had once hung there in a moment of bravado. Now the face seemed to be reproaching him. He took a pistol from a drawer and shot at the eyes. The bullet holes are still there.

He left for London a few days later, and there can have been few at the Hall who expected to see their master again. They, too, looked at him reproachfully, for his downfall was also theirs. At the Hall, and in Castle Donington, there were many who were dependent for their livelihood on the continuing prosperity of the house of Hastings. Harry was dragging them all down to poverty with him.

They realized only too well that the great Hastings era of extravagant living and lavish entertainment had passed away for ever. Yet it was only a little more than five years since they had held the festivities to celebrate his twenty-first birthday, and perhaps they recalled the verses of Mr Adcock, which he had dedicated to the most noble Marquis at the time, and of which the last verse had run:

> *God grant in every true renown*
>   *He daily may increase.*
> *And when he lays earth's grandeur down*
>   *May he depart in peace:*
> *And when this world recedes from view,*
>   *On heaven's thrice happy shore,*
> *May we our song of love renew,*
>   *With him for ever more!*

The world was already receding from Harry's view, but no bright vision of heaven's shore came to comfort the invalid. Harry was losing the gamble between life and death, but he was losing as he had always lost—without self-pity and without complaint. 'The wheels were down' for him, and that was that.

The autumn winds were growing keen, and plans were made for Harry to winter in the sun. The papers announced that 'the Marquis and Marchioness of Hastings intend to leave shortly for Egypt', but there was little enough money left for travelling now. *Ladybird* had been sold, and so, instead of Egypt, they went to Folkestone, where it was quiet and sunny—and cheap. There they spent a few weeks. Then they returned to Grosvenor Square.

Throughout all this time Florence looked after her dying husband with gentleness and devotion. Her love for him may have faded, but the pity which his frail body had always aroused in her was still strong. He had never really bothered to understand her, or to help her, but she had always understood him, although she had sadly miscalculated her ability to reform him. Now that he was losing strength rapidly, and was scarcely able to move from one room to another, her compassion deepened. The courage was still there, and the defiance. It was not for life that he was fighting; this no longer seemed to matter to him. But the mask of indifference had to be maintained to the end. Fate might destroy without pity, but Fate should not be given the satisfaction of watching him whimper in defeat. Thus he remained true to the one fine tradition of his life.

It was nearly all over now. He had little time left for living, and little for which to live. His horses, all save Lady Elizabeth and The Earl, were disposed of, his goods were sold, his money gone and his honour lost. The racing season of 1868, which he had started with such high hopes of retrieving his fortune and winning the Blue Riband of the turf, was now dying in the fog and mist at Lincoln, Liverpool and Shrewsbury; but he was not there to see it die. On Tuesday, 10 November, in the late afternoon, Henry Chaplin won a handicap race at Shrewsbury with a colt by Vengeance out of Typhoon, which he had called Spider. Harry would have congratulated him had he been able to be present. But instead he lay dead, his thin, white hands, almost feminine in their delicacy, spread out above the coverlet on his bed, his wasted body lying motionless beneath. His last words, spoken in a whisper so that they could scarcely be heard, were, 'Hermit's Derby broke my heart. But I did not show it, did I?'

Then he had gone, drifting away into eternity before the grey light of dawn had broken over the roof-tops of London. The news was quickly spread around, and by lunch-time they were already discussing it in the clubs of St James's, and in the taverns around Leicester Square, where there were still a few of his old cronies left to raise their glasses to him in a final toast: 'The Markis—Gawd bless 'im!'

The death certificate, signed by his physician, Dr Arthur D. White, gave the cause of death as 'Disease of the kidneys (Morbus Brightii)', which was but another way of saying that Harry had destroyed himself with dissipation; and it was not for Dr White to add that death had also been due, in part, to a broken heart resultant upon the success of Hermit and the defeat of Lady Elizabeth. Florence was present by his bedside when he died. The end had been inevitable for several days, and did not take her by surprise. She had been married for exactly four years and three months, and was now a widow at the age of twenty-six.

It was decided to bury him at Kensal Green Cemetery—that vast conglomeration of stone and marble, hallowed sentiment and pious text, which, together with Highgate, is the last resting place in London of so much that was Victorian England. Here were the graves of worthy and prosperous folk—revered fathers and much loved mothers, laid down to sleep in solemn requiem and in the certain hope of the resurrection to eternal life.

The funeral cortège left 34 Grosvenor Square shortly before ten o'clock on the morning of Saturday, 14 November. The news of its departure had spread round London, and a large crowd assembled to watch it go. One would like to think it was affection for Harry which had made the people collect, but in truth it was probably only curiosity; and a realization that a symbol of mid-Victorian extravagance was being carried away, and an era of uncontrolled betting on the turf was being brought to an end. Even the man in the street must have known that racing would never see such a gambler as Harry Hastings again.

But for whatever the reason, the people poured into Grosvenor Square and shouted, pointed and stared. There were more than a hundred cabs filling the street, with men, women and boys clambering over the roofs of them in their efforts to gain a better view while the cabbies cursed them and the horses stirred restlessly between the shafts. To many the scene was more reminiscent of Derby Day than a day of mourning, and a ragged cheer went up when the coffin was brought from the house.

The cortège moved forward, and the police cleared a pathway for it with difficulty, while the watchers clustered round, and peered inquisitively into the mourning coaches. The hearse was drawn by four black horses, with black ostrich plumes nodding on their heads, and was followed by nine mourning coaches. The first two contained the principal mourners—Harry's step-father, Admiral Yelverton, Mr Abney Hastings, Lord Mauchline, Mr H. Clifton, Viscount Marsham, Mr Kirwan, Lord Henry Paget, Lord Alexander Paget and Lord Berkeley Paget. In the seven remaining coaches were friends and kinsmen, including Henry Chaplin, Freddy Granville, Henry Padwick and John Day. In the last two coaches were the steward and principal servants of Harry's household. Finally, in the rear, was the private carriage of the deceased and those of the Marquess of Anglesey and the Duke of Newcastle. The widow, accompanied by Lady Constance Marsham and the Hon. Barbara Yelverton, travelled by a separate route to the cemetery; as did the Earl of Westmorland and several others of Harry's personal friends.

It was one of those mild, damp and misty mornings so typical of London in November. The rain dropped slowly from the branches of the plane trees in the Park on to the wet leaves below, and 'The Ladies' Mile' from Apsley House to Kensington was deserted. The fretful hum of London was silenced by the damp cloak that lay upon it, and grey mists swirled across the waters of the Serpentine.

The long cortège, with its black horses beating out a steady rhythm with their clattering tread, moved out of the Square and into Park Lane, and on towards the Marble Arch. Then it turned left into the Bayswater Road, and right up Westbourne Terrace until it reached the Harrow Road. The mourners, sunk deep in the gloomy recesses of the carriages and enveloped from head to toe in black, were scarcely visible to the passers-by, but the men on the pavements raised their hats, while the children stopped to stare.

The journey was made in good time, and if Harry had been travelling in one of the carriages and had been tempted to wager a hundred guineas that they would be late, he would have lost his money, for the procession turned in at the cemetery gates just before twelve o'clock. But Harry lay motionless in his highly polished coffin, with its heavy gilt mountings, its lid that bore his coronet and a plate inscribed with his titles, and his family crest and motto: *Sparsimus quoque tela et nos*. Over it all lay a covering of rich crimson velvet.

The cortège passed through the gates to the cemetery, where another large crowd had collected, and drew up outside the chapel in the grounds. Here the pallbearers carried the coffin up the steps, at the top of which the Rev J. G. Bourne, Vicar of Castle Donington, was waiting to receive it. The mourners filed into the chapel, where the widow, who had arrived a few minutes earlier, was waiting, dressed in deepest black and with a heavy veil hiding her face. The mourners took their seats on the right side of the chapel, and the burial service began.

'I am the resurrection and the life, saith the Lord....'

The gilt mountings on the coffin gleamed under the subdued light, and the crimson velvet took on a deeper colour.

'We brought nothing into this world, and it is certain we can carry nothing out. The Lord gave and the Lord hath taken away....'

The setting was sombre, and the chapel echoed to the muttered responses. Henry Chaplin, his heavy frame squeezed into one of the narrow seats, allowed his glance to stray to the figure of Florence as she sat with her hands folded in her lap and her face pale and expressionless.

'For man walketh in a vain shadow, and disquieteth himself in vain; he heapeth up riches, and cannot tell who shall gather them....'

The rain dropped down on the roof of the little chapel and on the sodden turf above the scattered graves. At the entrance to the cemetery the coachmen had dismounted from their seats and were now standing in little groups at their horses' heads, waiting for the ceremony to end. The horses themselves stirred restlessly, their black plumes nodding and swaying as they pawed the ground, anxious to return to the warm, dry comfort of their stables.

The short service ended and the mourners filed out of the chapel in the wake of the coffin. A brick vault had been made in the ground some fifty yards away, and into it the coffin was now reverently lowered. On top of it was placed a garland of autumn flowers. The mourners stood round in a circle, their heads bowed and still.

'For as much as it hath pleased Almighty God of his great mercy to take unto himself the soul of our dear brother here departed, we therefore commit his body to the ground....'

Harry was weighing out for the last time, his battle over and his distance run. He had fallen at last in the unequal strife.

The earth was scattered on the coffin, and the final prayer was spoken.

'The grace of our Lord Jesus Christ, and the love of God and the fellowship of the Holy Ghost, be with us all evermore. Amen.'

The ceremony was over and the clock above the chapel chimed the hour of one. In the words of *Bell's Life in London,* 'the remains had been interred in the most private manner consistent with the rank of the deceased'.

The nine mourning coaches returned back along the Harrow Road to the West End of London, now moving at a brisker pace. 'The Markis' was no more.

The will, when it was read, contained no surprises. It was dated 17 June 1868, and so Harry must have drafted it soon after the defeat of Lady Elizabeth at Epsom. It was attested by William Boys, describing himself as 'House Steward' to the deceased, and by Samuel James Evans. It appointed as Harry's executors and trustees his step-father, Admiral Hastings Reginald Yelverton, CB, and 'my friend Henry Padwick', of Manor House, Horsham, and gave to each of them £1,000. The income from all his estates and investments he left to his wife during her life; 'and from and after her decease or second marriage, which shall first happen', to his sister, the Viscountess Marsham, during her lifetime and to her children after her death. To Florence he also left 'all the Jewels usually worn by her or usually in her possession and all her paraphernalia'.

The will was proved on 20 November at £90,000, but Harry's liabilities swallowed up nearly all of this. Florence's income from the capital and securities mentioned in the will, however, assured her of an annual income of £2,000. She also inherited Lady Elizabeth and The Earl.

By his death the Marquisate and most of his other honours became extinct. But the Scottish Earldom of Loudoun devolved on his eldest sister, Lady Edith Maud, the wife of a Mr Charles Frederick Clifton, who had assumed the name of Abney-Hastings, and had issue. His three other sisters, Lady Bertha, Lady Victoria Maria Louisa and Lady Frances Augusta Constance, the Viscountess of Marsham, were each alive.

The Victorian Press, as was only to be expected, wrote long obituaries about the deceased, and moralized at length and with unctuous reproof on the rake's progress and his early demise, which several of them suggested was richly deserved. *The Field* wrote:

> There should surely be some moral attached to the career of such a man as the Marquis of Hastings. His was, indeed, a short life and a sad one. In a few brief seasons he contrived to sacrifice 'health, fortune, friends, and fame' by a course of conduct that can only be characterized as utterly reckless. There was something approaching insanity in the

way in which he scattered his means; a suicidal rendering of the *tela sparsimus* which speaks to the honours of his family. And then the return—the great object to be obtained—was so small in comparison with the risk he courted. Let us make the most we can of it, and say he

> '*Blazed forth at once, Newmarket's brightest star,*
> *With knaves of all descriptions popular,*'

and the notoriety of the Marquis of Hastings is at its zenith. He had not even a sportsman's excuse for his prodigality. He had not personal prowess; was no horseman, and cared little or nothing for the hounds he kept for a season or so, for he would leave them in the field on the first opportunity; whilst the thousands he wagered on a plating race might, so far as real sport was concerned, as well have depended on the length of a straw or the colour of a card.

'To describe Lord Hastings as a friend of racing would be impossible,' said *Bell's Life in London,* 'and we fully endorse the remark of a leading Turf authority that "the Marquis of Hastings was the worst enemy to the Turf he ever recollected during the course of his experience".'

Poor Harry! It was then so much the custom to speak eulogistically of the dead that it comes as a shock to read these condemnations of him, written before he was even in his grave. It was generally felt that his influence on the turf had been harmful, and that he had given birth to excesses which would have to be suppressed. Few writers suggested that he was young and inexperienced; and few blamed the Ring, which had led him on to his destruction. Few even found it in their hearts to pity him.

There was only one person who wrote of Harry Hastings with compassion and understanding. Henry Hall Dixon, known throughout sporting England under his pen-name of 'The Druid', contributed an obituary notice to *The Daily News* which they published on 11 November and which *The Times* repeated in full on the following day. It is too long to be given here, but the first part of it can at least be quoted. It ran as follows:

> 'The Earl's year' has reached a sad climax in the death of its leading actor. The Spider and the Fly drama is ended.

That poor coroneted youth who had crowded into six years more Corinthian excitement and weightier Turf cares than many 'fast men' know in a lifetime, has laid down his weary load. He was only twenty-six in July, and he had frittered away two fine family estates. Betting is said to be the touchstone of the Englishman's sincerity, but with the Marquis a craving for the odds had really become a disease. He worshipped chance with all the ardour of a fanatic. His wits were, he considered, worth to him in the betting ring at least £20,000 a year, and he sometimes threaded his way through the mazes of trials and public running with all the sagacity of a wizard. His public *coups* were often so brilliant that it was hardly to be wondered at that he believed in his own destiny and his power to break the Ring. He cared little whether the draining or other improvements on his Donington estate were stopped if he only got fresh supplies for another Newmarket campaign. The Ring, on the other hand, had marked him for their own, and never left him. They would cluster beneath the Jockey Club balcony at Epsom, holding up their hands to claim his attention, and catching at his replies like a flock of hungry hawks. There he would stand smiling at the wild tumult below, wearing his hat jauntily on one side, a red flower in his buttonhole, and his colours round his neck, and cool and calm while 'the talent' made his horse a 'hot favourite' at once, and a few slipped back to the Ring to follow his lead. For a time he was a perfect Cocker; but he fell at last in the unequal strife, and the men who had 'drawn' him most copiously were among those who set their faces most sternly against him when he wished to see the Heath once more.

'For a time he was a perfect Cocker.' It might almost have been the inscription upon his tombstone; but this was being prepared on Florence's instructions, and she it was who chose the wording on the simple stone cross which was placed above his grave—a grave that was to be visited by fewer and fewer mourners as the years went by.

Nearly a hundred years later, the writer of this book made the same journey along the Harrow Road to the Kensal Green Cemetery. He was escorted along the neatly-kept paths and past the forest of marble monuments that were the symbols of Victorian prosperity, until he was led aside into a little clearing near some trees, where the attendant indicated a spot which he felt must be the place. But the head-stones were worn and indecipherable, and the stones at the foot had become discoloured and overgrown, so that it was not possible to discern what was written on them. Having indicated the probable grave, the attendant asked to be excused and withdrew.

I was left to my thoughts and my investigations. The matted grasses could easily be removed, but the grime of a century lay on each worn stone. I took a handful of foliage and started to rub away the dirt on the stone at my feet until a few words became readable:

> Sacred
> To the beloved memory
> of
> Henry Weysford Charles
> Plantagenet Rawdon Hastings

It was June, and the air was warm and still. In the distance the tube trains could be heard as they rumbled their way towards Wembley and Harrow. No other sound came to disturb the silence, for the graves which surrounded me were all of the same Victorian era, and there were no mourners present to look upon them or to lay on them the small bunches of flowers which were scattered over those in other parts of the vast cemetery.

It was quiet and very peaceful. The tombstones which surrounded Harry's were for the most part cumbersome and ornate, with their massive Latin inscriptions and pious texts; but Harry's was simple, with the figure of an angel bearing a cross. Beneath the feet of the angel was a verse from a hymn—Number 264:

> *If thou shouldst call me to resign*
> *What most I prize, it ne'er was mine,*
> *I only yield thee what is thine;*
> *Thy will be done.*

The inscription must have been chosen by Florence; and the poignancy of it must have touched her. What was it that Harry Hastings prized the most in his short life? Honour? Hardly that, because he had been reckless enough of it. Courage in the face of adversity? Perhaps, for only once in his life had he ever dropped the mask of indifference and shown his distress, and that had been after Lady Elizabeth's defeat at Newmarket. Was it Lady Elizabeth herself? It might well have been, for it was certainly not his wife. Was it the Blue Riband of the turf, which Hermit had carried off and Lady Elizabeth had not? Or was it no more than the adulation of the crowd and the cheers that hailed a popular winner? Or was it something that he never quite understood—a secret longing to be loved for himself alone and not because of his wealth and his titles?

He had been the symbol of an era—an era which had largely died with him. An era in which gambling had reached unprecedented heights and had proved the downfall of many men with the wealth and position which Harry had enjoyed. An age of idleness and boredom and irresponsibility. An age in which youth had lacked maturity and judgment, but had seldom lacked courage.

For a time he was a perfect Cocker, and perhaps that was all he asked of life. And when the wheels were down, he made no complaint.

With my fingers I scraped away the dirt on the stone until I could read the rest of the inscription:

*Lord all pitying Jesus blest,
Grant him thine eternal rest.*

I stood looking at the stone, wondering who was the last person who had come to visit that grave and trying to picture in my mind the scene when they had laid Harry to rest in the mists of a grey November day. Now everything was green with the promise of early summer. I turned away and walked slowly along the silent avenues until the vast hum of London came throbbing back as I reached the main gates of the cemetery.

The Harrow Road is not one of London's proud thoroughfares. It is a drab and narrow street between dingy houses, and a phrase from one of the obituaries came back to me. 'It is a strange and mournfully significant circumstance that the Marquis should be buried at Kensal Green.' But he had already by then been branded as 'The Wicked Marquis', and so perhaps there was no place for him to lie amongst the ancient trees of Donington.

I crossed the road to where the wooden hoardings warned of

the dangers of night starvation and extolled the virtues of cigarettes that satisfy, of pale ale and meat pies. The number eighteen 'bus came into sight but, before I boarded it, I bought an evening paper. It was the second day of the Ascot meeting, and the favourite had been beaten in the big race. But there was always tomorrow, with its chance to recover losses.

Plus ça change, plus c'est la même chose. Racing did not change, and neither did the outlook of those who backed horses. Men come and go, but the turf lives on. And chance remains, to make fools of us all.

> *And so 'twill be when we are gone,*
> *The saddling bell will still ring on.*

CHAPTER ELEVEN

EPILOGUE

IT is one of the ironies of the Hastings story that Harry Hastings himself was the only one of its several characters to die young. His life ended at the age of twenty-six, but most of those with whom he was connected lived on into old age, and on into a twentieth century which had long since forgotten the Hastings era on the turf. Henry Chaplin lived to be eighty-two. Florence was sixty-four when she died.

When Henry Chaplin died, on 29 May 1923, not only was Victorianism dead, but so also was Edwardianism. Indeed it could also be said that Chaplinism was long since dead as well, for nearly all that he stood for as a die-hard Tory Squire had been swept away by the winds of change. Henry's political career had started in the year of Harry's death, when he had been returned for Mid-Lincolnshire, and thereafter he largely dedicated himself to the political service of his country, as Lord George Bentinck had done before him. Throughout his long political life he fought to defend the cause of the English farmer, and for a time he was looked upon as the white hope of the Tory Party, for he represented so much of what old-fashioned Toryism implied. But times changed, and Conservatism moved forward in thought, if albeit somewhat slowly. leaving Henry Chaplin trailing in its wake. In the House of Commons he remained stubbornly an amateur politician, who neither understood nor took part in its professional cut-and-thrust. Moreover his prominent place in society, and his close friendship wth the royal family, caused him to be labelled 'a mouthpiece of the fashionable world'.

Yet his sincerity was never in doubt, and the farm labourers of his constituency trusted him implicitly. Throughout his political career he remained resolute and incorruptible. An honest man who was incapable of comprehending dishonesty. A simple man whose intellectual capacity could not grapple with the new forces being aligned against him. Of him *The Times* could write in its obituary: 'No one was ever more entirely free from bitterness or sourness. He had none of the gloom or the spite that so often hangs round the retired politician or the impoverished owner of property. With a sunny humour which no clouds could dim, he enjoyed life till he fell ill and died.'

And during his long life the clouds *did* often threaten that sunny humour, for like Harry Hastings he was at heart a gambler and this, coupled with his extravagance, nearly brought about his ruin.

It might have been supposed that after Harry's death he would have been tempted to resume his association with Florence. She would have welcomed him back and would certainly have come to him with a far greater appreciation of his kindness and consideration. But Henry Chaplin, despite his bluff exterior, was a sensitive man who had been grievously hurt. And perhaps he may never have been deeply in love with her in the first place. But whatever the reason, Henry Chaplin never again became intimately associated with Florence. He met her socially, and befriended her when she was in need; but never again did he love her.

In 1876 he married another Florence—Lady Florence Leveson-Gower, the elder daughter of the third Duke of Sutherland. This was a true love match, and his friends, including the Prince of Wales and Disraeli, were delighted by his choice of a wife. She shared all his interests except racing, and the only point about her husband which worried her was his continuing extravagance and his rapidly decreasing income. He continued to entertain as lavishly as ever and remained master of the Blankney Hunt.

They had three children, a son and two daughters, but the birth of the third child, Florence, on 8 October 1881, coupled with other physical causes, proved too much for Henry Chaplin's young wife, and she died in her husband's arms two days later. Thus his marriage lasted for only five years.

He was left alone to continue his political career, while his financial position grew steadily worse. His good luck on the turf had by now deserted him, and he never owned another racehorse of the calibre of Hermit. but Hermit himself contributed most handsomely to the support of his master. He was an outstanding success at stud, and headed the winning list of stallions between 1880 and 1886. Between 1873 and 1879 his progeny won 846 races, and he begat no less than five classic winners, including Shotover, who won the Derby of 1882, and St Blaise, who won it a year later for Henry's lifelong friend,

Sir Frederick Johnstone. For many years after his retirement to stud, Hermit brought in to his master an annual income of £15,000, and he did not die until 29 April 1890. His skeleton can still be seen in the Museum of the Royal College of Veterinary Surgeons.

By 1892, Henry Chaplin was in serious financial trouble, and he was forced to sell his family seat of Blankney Hall, which was bought by Lord Londesborough. It was his ambition thereafter to buy back the Hall before his death, but this ambition was never realized. His wealth had been sadly dissipated, and he was never able to restore his fortunes. The house itself was demolished in 1961.

'When our Harry is broke, which is only a matter of time, all the crowned heads of Europe ought to give him a hundred thousand a year in order that he may show them how to spend their money.' The words of his old friend, Lord Willoughby de Broke, may have come back to him in these days of hardship. If they did, he must have smiled at the memory. He was broke, and the crowned heads of Europe remained indifferent to the situation. But at least he could boast that he had spent his money freely and had enjoyed the grand way of life. In 1915 he became leader of the opposition to the Coalition Government, and he remained an MP until 1916, when he finally said farewell to the Commons on his elevation to the peerage as a viscount. The House viewed his departure with mixed feelings. He was the last of the sporting amateurs.

In October 1922 he visited Newmarket to see the Middle Park Stakes, and men turned to watch him as he passed and whispered to each other that he had witnessed the first Middle Park that had ever been run—long, long ago in 1866. It was a strange link with the past.

He never went racing again and died the following spring, on 29 May, just a week before the Derby.

Florence, Marchioness of Hastings, had already been dead for sixteen years. Under the terms of Harry's will she had been adequately provided for, with an income of some £2,000 a year. She had also inherited Lady Elizabeth and The Earl. The latter she sold privately, for The Earl had never been a favourite of hers, but Lady Elizabeth she kept, no doubt for sentimental reasons. Lady Elizabeth was sent to stud, but it is one of the ironies of the turf that whereas a great colt often succeeds in begetting progeny that are blessed with his own outstanding qualities, a great filly rarely does so. The peerless

Sceptre and the immortal Pretty Polly were both comparative failures at stud, and so was Lady Elizabeth.

Florence married again, almost within a year and a half of Harry's death. She must have felt lonely and deserted, and the realization that Henry Chaplin no longer loved her must have been a blow to her pride. Even so, her second marriage came as a considerable surprise to her friends, for she chose not only a man seven years younger than herself, but also another compulsive gambler.

On 6 June 1870, Florence became the wife of Sir George Chetwynd, of Grendon Hall, Warwickshire. In some ways her second husband closely resembled her first, for George Chetwynd was tall and slim and a man of great charm. But he differed from Harry in that there was also a calculating and unsympathetic side to his character. 'He was more talked of, more envied and in some quarters more disliked than any man of the fashionable world,' wrote the Honourable George Lambton in his memoirs. The fact that Florence married a second young man who seemed bent on his own destruction does at least substantiate the theory that she was at heart a salvationist, and that her aim in marriage was to rescue and reform a dedicated rake. But she was as unsuccessful with George Chetwynd as she had been with Harry Hastings, so her reforming zeal came to nought.

Hers was not a happy life, nor one blessed with much sense of fulfilment. She had four children by her second marriage— one son, and three daughters. Her son, George Guy Chetwynd, became the fifth baronet on the death of his father on 10 March 1917, and her eldest daughter, Lilian Florence Maud, married her cousin, the fifth Marquess of Anglesey. Florence herself died on 3 February 1907, at Long Walk House, Windsor, after a few days' illness. She was sixty-four. She was buried at Grendon four days later, when there were a large number of wreaths, although there was not one from Henry Chaplin.

After her marriage, little was seen of her in Society and she lapsed into comparative obscurity, although she continued to be present at certain balls and on certain social occasions. Malicious gossip followed her throughout her life, and there was always someone ready to recall that she had been the central figure in the notorious Hastings affair. She paid dearly for her one disastrous act of indiscretion, and there were not many in Victorian Society who were ready to forgive or forget.

Yet all the evidence suggests that Florence was kind, sympathetic and tolerant throughout her life. 'She had an affectionate nature—sometimes impetuously and unwisely affectionate. It gave her no return from the people she gave her love to.' The comment is from a private letter sent to the author while he was compiling this book. It is from a woman whose mother was deeply attached to Florence, and it continues: 'Hers was a defect of judgment, not of character ... she is still to me a person of great charm and goodness.'

The other personalities in the Hastings story need only be dealt with briefly. Albert Edward, Prince of Wales, became King on the death of his mother, Queen Victoria, on 22 January 1901, but before that he had achieved the ambition shared by all connected with the Hastings story by winning the Derby with Persimmon in 1896, amidst scenes of the wildest enthusiasm; again in 1900 with Diamond Jubilee; and finally, when he was King, with Minoru in 1909. He also won the Grand National in 1900 with Ambush II, so he lived to savour the major glories of the turf.

Henry Chaplin's friend, Sir Frederick Johnstone, won the Derby twice, but he, too, ruined himself by gambling. In 1911 he was forced to sell his Westerhall Estate in Dumfries-shire which had been in the family for 700 years. George Fordham, the jockey who could not come down the hill at Epsom, also won the Derby in the end. In middle age he took to drink and was forced to retire from the saddle, but after three years he came back and thereafter rode almost as well as ever. His victory in the Derby was gained on Sir Bevys in 1879—a bad horse, on whom Fordham rode a thoroughly ill-judged race. Captain Machell, Henry Chaplin's trainer, had a brilliant career on the turf, and as an owner won the Grand National three times between 1873 and 1876. But he became quarrelsome and suspicious with old age and made many enemies. He died in 1902, at the age of sixty-four. But he, at least, was never ruined by gambling. On the contrary, he was able to buy back his ancestral home at Crackenthorpe, in Westmorland, after his run of successes in the Grand National.

Henry Padwick, the money-lender, lived on at his house in Hill Street, growing ever wealthier. He never made up his quarrel with Admiral Rous, who died in 1877 and was buried in Kensal Green Cemetery, not far from the grave of Harry Hastings. Padwick, in common with most of the other male characters in the Hastings story, drank and ate too much and ruined his digestion in consequence. Like Captain Machell, he became quarrelsome in old age, due to frequent attacks of gout. He died at Hill Street in 1880.

For a time he was a perfect Cocker. Indeed most of the characters in the Hastings story were perfect Cockers for a time. But Padwick and Machell stayed prosperous throughout their lives because they were professionals.

The nineteenth century staged the war of the gamblers. Backers versus bookmakers. Amateurs versus professionals. The amateurs traced their descent from Charles James Fox, who did not care whether he won or lost. The bookmakers traced theirs from William Crockford, to whom winning was the only thing that mattered. To this struggle there could be only one outcome. Captain Gronow, who observed this gambling war in its opening stages, summed up the issue when he wrote:

'As is so often the case at Lord's cricket-ground, the great match of the gentlemen of England against the professional players was won by the latter. It was a very hollow thing....'

It will always be a hollow thing. But at least it can be said of Harry Hastings and Henry Chaplin that they put up a good fight.

BIBLIOGRAPHY

THE Hastings story is a small part of the Victorian canvas, and while there are some aspects of it which have been dealt with in detail by previous writers, there are others in which the information is only fragmentary and unreliable. For example, there is much to be learnt about the ancestry of both Florence Paget and Harry Hastings. Each had an illustrious grandfather whose name appears frequently in the many books dealing with English history in the eighteenth and nineteenth centuries.[1] But there is little to be discovered about their childhood and adolescence. The reader who wishes to investigate further into this period of their life must be prepared to spend many hours delving into local newspapers for an occasional comment which may, or may not, be accurate.

As soon as the three main characters in the story have entered that phase of their life in which they became prominent figures in the social life of Mayfair, the newspapers and periodicals of the period such as *The Queen* and *The Morning Post* provide some guidance; but here again this is primarily social gossip and therefore not wholly reliable. Once Harry Hastings and Henry Chaplin begin their rivalry on the turf, the vast library of racing histories is open to the student, and all the facts about their successes and failures in racing are readily available. But their private lives still remain largely a matter of hearsay, and the celebrated elopement, although frequently referred to by turf historians, is never dealt with factually.

The only one of these three main characters who can be seen in complete outline from infancy to old age is Henry Chaplin, thanks to the biography of him which was prepared by his daughter, the late Marchioness of Londonderry, and published under the title *Henry Chaplin, a Memoir*, by Messrs Macmillan in 1926. This book deals with his youth and with his

---

[1] The collection of English historical manuscripts in the Henry E. Huntington Library in San Marino, California, USA, has a very large number of Hastings family papers amounting to some 50,000 items, but none that refers to the fourth Marquis or to Lady Florence Paget.

family, political and sporting life; but even this work is brief and uncertain in its account of the elopement. The long obituaries, which appeared in *The Times* after Chaplin's death on 29 May 1923, also give a good picture of him; and two contemporary volumes on politics, *Prophets, Priests and Kings* (Gardiner, Dent's Wayfarer Library, 1917) and *Politicians of Today* (Wemyss Reid, Griffith and Farran, 1880), each have a chapter on him. But, of course, his political career started after the Hastings story was ended.

Lady Florence Paget, as has been noted throughout this book, remains largely an enigma, especially in childhood, due to the fact that her father was under a cloud during this period, and was sometimes even on the run from his creditors. The present Marquess of Anglesey has written a comprehensive biography of the first Marquess under the title *One-Leg* (Jonathan Cape, 1961), and this gives full particulars of her ancestry and frequently refers to her father, the second Marquess, and to the life which he led; but even the author of *One-Leg* can throw little light on Florence's earlier days and her life before she became the idol of society in the early 'sixties. Here again, one must largely rely on paragraphs in topical periodicals such as *The Queen*.

Harry Hastings himself has been described in numerous books on the turf, but seldom in any detail, or with any great degree of accuracy. The majority of writers declare that he ruined himself by backing horses, and only the late J. B. Booth was at pains to point out that Harry was far shrewder and more successful than his contemporaries realized. There is a chapter devoted to Harry in Thormanby's *Kings of the Turf* (Hutchinson, 1898) which also contains a chapter on Henry Chaplin, Admiral Rous, George Fordham, Harry Custance and several of the other characters who appear in *The Pocket Venus*. *Baily's Monthly Magazine* of June 1866, had a profile of Harry. T. H. Bird's *Admiral Rous and the English Turf* (Putnam, 1939) contains two chapters on 'The Spider and the Fly' episode, when the Admiral attacked Padwick in his celebrated letter to *The Times*, and these chapters should certainly be read as they describe the whole incident. Other turf reminiscences which should be consulted when studying Harry's racing career include: *Turf Memories of Sixty Years* (Alexander Scott, Hutchinson), *Arthur Yates, Trainer and Gentleman Rider* (Blunt, Grant Richards, 1924), *Gamblers All* (Sergeant, Hutchinson, 1931), *Old Pink 'Un Days* (Booth,

The Richards Press, 1924), *Bits of Character* (Booth, Hutchinson, 1936), the Badminton Library's volume on *Racing, Life and Times of the Druid* (Lawley, Vinton, 1895), and the Hon. George Lambton's *Men and Horses I Have Known* (Thornton, Butterworth, 1924). The obituaries which appeared after Harry's death are informative, and those appearing in *The Field, The Times* and *Bell's Life in London* should be read. But the longest, the most instructive and the best was that written by Henry Hall Dixon, 'The Druid', which appeared in *The Daily News* of 11 November 1868 and *The Times* of the following day. It can be found in full in *Bits of Character* and *Life and Times of the Druid* which have already been mentioned. As regards Harry's private life, the only writer to mention him frequently was one of his old cronies, Captain Donald Shaw, whose reminiscences, *London in the Sixties*, was published by Everett in 1908 under the pseudonym of 'One of the old Brigade'. Accounts of the celebrations attending Harry's twenty-first birthday are given in the greatest detail in the local papers which covered the event, above all in *The Loughborough Monitor* and *The Leicester Journal* of July 1863. The Leicester Archaeological and Historical Society's booklet, *The Rise and Fall of a Market Town* (Lee, 1956), tells the story of Castle Donington in the nineteenth century, and Donington Park and the Hall have been described in numerous local guide books, the majority of which are out of print and are only to be picked up at random in the district.

The number of books which deal with the history of the turf in general; of the classic races, and of the Derby itself; of Newmarket, Ascot and other courses; and the number of racing biographies, are legion, and the reader is invited to study those on which the author mainly based his researches. *The Racing Calendar* of each year gives the official results of every race run, together with owners' colours, lists of Stewards and members of the Jockey Club, racecourses, etc. The Derby itself is dealt with in *The History and Romance of the Derby* (two volumes, Edward Moorhouse, Biographical Press, 1911), *The Romance of the Derby Stakes* (Macey, Hutchinson, 1930), *The History of the Derby Stakes* (Mortimer, Cassell, 1962), *The Blue Ribbon of the Turf* (Curzon, Chatto and Windus, 1893), *The Classic Races of the Turf* (Logan, Stanley Paul, 1931), *A History of the English Turf* (three volumes, Theodore Cook, Virtue), *The History of the St Leger Stakes* (Fletcher, Hutchinson, 1926), *Newmarket* (Siltzer, Cassell,

1923), *Royal Newmarket* (Lyle, Putnam, 1940), *Royal Ascot* (Cawthorne and Herod, Treherne, 1902), while the full history of the Derby course is given in *Epsom and the Dorlings* (Dorling, Stanley Paul, 1939). The standard works on the training of racehorses during the nineteenth century include *The Race-horse in Training* (William Day, Chapman and Hall, 1880), *Kingsclere* (John Porter, Chatto and Windus, 1896), *The Life of Mathew Dawson* (Humphris, Witherby, 1928), *Racing Life of Lord George Cavendish Bentinck* (Kent, Blackwood, 1892), *Ashgill, The Life and Times of John Osborne* (Radcliffe, Sands, 1900), *Malton Memories and I'Anson Triumphs* (Fairfax-Blakeborough, Trustlove and Bray, 1925) and *Reminiscences of the Turf* (William Day, Bentley, 1891) which also contains an informative chapter on Henry Padwick, the money-lender. As to jockeyship, the best book for this period is Harry Custance's *Riding Recollections and Turf Stories* (Arnold, 1894).

As regards histories of the turf for the general reader, as opposed to the specialist, the following are recommended: *The Turf of Old* (Batchelor, Witherby, 1951), *Racing Romance* (Felstead, Werner Laurie, 1949), *Sporting Spectacle* (Wentworth Day, Methuen, 1939), *The Sport of Kings* (Nevill, Methuen, 1926), *The Turf* (Hislop, Collins, 1958, in Britain in Pictures Series), and *Racing England* (Chalmers, Batsford, 1939). The classic works, of course, are those by 'The Druid', particularly *Post and Paddock* and *Silk and Scarlet*, published last century by Vinton in their Sporting Library series.

As regards the background of Victorian morals, and the expeditions into the East End of London, the author relied chiefly upon the works of Henry Mayhew, *London in the Sixties*, already referred to, *Taine's Notes on England* (Thames and Hudson, 1957), *Sexual Life in England* (Bloch, Francis Aldor, 1938), and—for lighter reading—*The Girl With the Swansdown Seat* (Pearl, Frederick Muller, 1955). The recently published abridged edition of reminiscences, *Captain Gronow* (Raymond, Bodley Head, 1964), provides a great deal of information about upper-class life in Victorian England. The Pelican book, *A History of London Life* (Mitchell and Leys, Penguin Books, 1963), also helps to fill in the background. But to absorb the background of the Hastings story quickly, yet in detail, the reader cannot do better than to pay a visit to the Tate Gallery, and there to stand for a time before Frith's *Derby Day*. So much of the mood and character of what has been written in this book is pictorially presented in this Victorian canvas.

As for fiction, most of the novels of Whyte-Melville, and particularly *Digby Grand*; and of Surtees, and particularly *Mr Sponge's Sporting Tours*, give a good idea of the sporting background to which Harry Hastings belonged. There is an excellent description of a Victorian Derby Day in George Moore's *Esther Waters*, and of Oxford in Harry's day in Thomas Hughes' *Tom Brown at Oxford*. But these are only suggestions. The Victorian era, with all its remarkable contradictions and its many episodes of wild extravagance, is as well documented as any period in English history.

THE END

INDEX

Abercorn, Marquis and Marchioness of, 112
Abney-Hastings, *see* Clifton, C. F., and Hastings, Lady Edith Maud
Adcock, Mr, 255
Adelaide, Queen, 36
Adelberg, Count, 78
Albert Edward, *see* Prince of Wales
Aldcroft, 146, 150
Alexandra, Princess, 73, 112, 174
American Civil War, 60–1
Anglesey, Marquesses of, *see* Paget
Archer, Fred, 100–1, 253
Arnold, Dr, 58–9
Ascot, Meeting of 1864, 110–11; of 1866, 174; of 1867, 212–17; of 1868, 246, 249
Ashby-de-la-Zouch, 35, 38, 51, 62, 73, 168
Aylesbury, Marchioness of, 221–2

Bagot, Henrietta, Marchioness of Anglesey, 22
Bagot, Rt Hon Sir Charles, 22
Barlow, Capt, 247
Barrow, Mr, 193
Batthyany, Count, 146
Beau Brummell, 44
Beaudesert, 20, 31
Beaufort, Duke of, 90, 187, 190, 199, 215, 247
Beaufort House, 154
Bedford Cottage, 152, 183–4, 191–3, 196
Bedford Stakes, 220
Bell's Life in London, 259, 261
Bendigo, 51
Bennett, W. G., 172–3
Bentinck, Lord George, 58, 78, 92, 96, 137, 180, 182 n, 234, 266

Bentinck, Lord Henry, 57–8, 136, 163, 165
Blake, Frederick John, 120
Blankney Hall, 30, 56–7, 66, 73, 107, 114, 115, 117, 126, 136, 163, 189, 250, 268
Blenkiron, Mr, 158–9, 174, 181, 186–7, 199, 205
Bloss, Old, 152, 155–6, 183–4, 191–3, 195–6, 197–8
Blue Riband of the Turf, origin of phrase, 182 n
Booth, J. B., 273
Bourbon family, 25
Bourne, Rev J. G., 258
Bowles, John, 49
Boys, William, 260
Brighton Cup, 176
Brighton Races, 95, 175–6
Bullingdon Club, 54, 55
Burton Hunt, 58, 162–3, 165, 189, 205
Bute, Marquis of, 226

Calais, The, 51, 62
Calthorpe, Lord, 154
Cambridgeshire, The, of 1864, 132–4, 139, 152, 177, 220
Campbell, Eleanora, 22
Campbell, Flora Muir, Countess of Loudoun, 25, 27 n, 28
Cannon, Tom, 133, 143, 172–3, 235, 245, 253
Castle Donington, 34–6, 38–9, 46, 62, 73, 123, 255, 258
Castle Donington Steeplechase Course, 169
Cavendish Square, 37
Cesarewitch, The, of 1864, 132; of 1866, 177–80, 220; of 1867, 222
Chaloner, T., 71
Chaplin, Charles, 30–2, 56–8
Chaplin, Harriet, 57

Chaplin, Rev Henry, 29–31, 56, 57
Chaplin 'Mrs Henry' (wife of above), 29, 56–7
Chaplin, Henry 1st Viscount: ancestry, 29–30; birth and childhood, 18, 29, 31–2, 55–8; character, 16–20, 29–32, 52–64, 107–8; appearance, 28, 52; Harrow, 58–9; at Oxford, 51–60; travels in America, 60–1; friendship with Prince of Wales, 53–5, 105, 110, 115, 147, 163, 267; life at Blankney, 57–8, 61–3, 66; life in London, 63, 65–6, 84, 88; meets Lady Florence, 102, 104; romance with Lady Florence, 105–114; engagement, 112–15; goes big game hunting in India, 108, 136; introduction to racing, 69, 135; registers racing colours, 142; elected member of Jockey Club, 157; buys Hermit, 158–9; mastership of Burton Hunt, 163; wins Derby with Hermit, 181–208; his Derby bets, 195, 205; letters to Harry Hastings, 210; resumes association with Lady Florence, 223–6; sees Derby of 1868, 239; attends Harry's funeral, 257–9; political career, 266–8; marriage to Lady Florence Leveson-Gower, 267; last visit to Newmarket, 268; death, 268; *The Times* obituary, 266–7
Chaplin, John, 29, 30
Chaplin, Thomas, 30
Chester Cup, 172–3
Chester Races, 145
Chesterfield Cup, 175
Chesterfield House, 112, 116
Chetwynd, Sir George, 269
Chetwynd, George Guy, 269
Chetwynd, Lilian Florence Maud, 269
Christ Church College, 40, 44, 46–56, 59–60
Clarendon Hotel, 67
Classic Races, The: history of 143 n, 230, 252
Cleveland Cup, 176

Clifton, C. F. (Abney-Hastings), 260
Clifton, Mr H., 257
Clowes, Mr, 164
Cock-fighting, 38, 50–1, 78, 81
Congreve, Miss, 120
Cook, Theodore, 213, 215
Coote and Tinney's Band, 75, 112–13
Coventry, Lord, 199
Coventry, Mr, 247
Covey, H., 186
Cowes, 76, 88, 163, 169
Cremorne, 82, 109
Crewe, Marquess of, 167
Cricket at Donington, 34, 51, 167–8
Crockford's Club, 161
Crockford, William, 86, 227, 271
Custance, Harry, 143, 145–9, 156, 173–5, 183, 184, 191–206, 208, 219, 253

Daily News, The, 14, 261
Daley, Johnny, 199–206, 208, 216, 219
Danebury, 90–2, 131, 140, 144, 145, 154, 173, 176, 177, 195, 197, 199, 214, 215, 218, 229–33, 244–5, 246, 252
Danebury Confederacy, 85, 87, 91, 93
Daniell, Col and Mrs, 46
Davis, 'Leviathan', 238
Dawson, Joseph, 197
Dawson, Mathew, 137, 159
Day, Alfred, 177
Day, H., 178
Day, John Barham, 77, 91–4, 99, 190, 206, 246, 253
Day, John, 92–5, 97, 99, 101, 116, 130–3, 137, 145, 151–2, 154, 155, 173, 176, 178, 188, 190, 201, 214, 215, 217, 220, 222, 229, 231, 233, 238–9, 244–5, 246–8, 253, 258
Day, Sam, 92
de Broke, *see* Willoughby de Broke, Lord
Derby Day (Frith), 45, 276
Derby Day, general description of, 233–7
Derby, The history of, 143 n; Derby of 1821, 92; of 1835,

278

49; of 1840, 70; of 1846, 92; of 1848, 182 n; of 1851, 238; of 1856, 146; of 1857, 45, 137; of 1860, 143, 183; of 1861, 143, 158, 159; of 1863, 69–72; of 1864, 109, 137; of 1865, 146–51; of 1866, 173, 183; of 1867, 198–206, 251; of 1868, 217–18, 221, 230–45; of 1879, 270; of 1881, 143 n, 149; of 1882, 267; of 1883, 267
Derby, 12th Earl of, 143 n
Derby, 14th Earl of, 44
Disraeli, Benjamin, 181–2 n, 267
Ditch, The, 191, 192
Dixon, Henry Hall, *see* 'Druid, The'
Dodgson, Charles, 47
Doncaster Cup, of 1866, 188
Doneraile, Lord, 163
Donington Hall, 25–8, 31–40, 50–1, 73–7, 89, 107, 109, 123, 169–71, 251, 254–5
'Druid, The', 14, 90, 164–5, 212; Hastings obituary, 261–2
Dunraven, Earl of, 44
Durnford, F. E., 43

Ellice, Caroline Horatia, 29
Ellice, William, 29
Endell Street, 81
Eton, 37, 39–46, 58, 59, 78, 91
Evans, S. J., 260

Faultless's Pit, Endell Street, 79
Faust, 118
Featherbed Lane, 51, 62
Fenning, Chris, 197
Field, The, 260
Fordham George: character and skill, 99–101; Derby of 1863, 70–2; of 1867, 201–5; defeat in Middle Park Plate, 221–2; match with Julius, 222–3; Derby of 1868, 240–5, 253; wins Derby of 1879, 270; also mentioned, 92, 95, 131, 143, 172–7, 184, 187, 190, 199, 208, 213, 216, 218, 235, 251
Fox, C. J., 184, 271
Frith W. P., 45–6

Goater, William, 150

Ghost of Hastings family, 34, 171, 251
Gimcrack Stakes, of 1867, 218
Glasgow, Lord, 96, 110
Gold Cup, Ascot: of 1866, 174; of 1867, 214–15
Goodford, Dr Charles, 41
Goodwood Cup, 176
Goodwood: meeting of 1864, 124; of 1866, 174; of 1867, 220
Gordon, George, 251
Graham, Mr, 156
Grand National, 270
Grand Prix, 245
Grant, General, 61
Granville, Freddy, 78, 109, 120–2, 258
Granville, Mrs, 120–2
Gray's Inn Road, 79
Green Man, The, 163
Grendon Hall, 269
Grey de Ruthyn, Barbara, Baroness ('The jolly fast Marchioness'), 27, 28, 36–7, 39, 46, 56
Grey, Lord, 158
Grimshaw, Harry, 144, 147–9, 155, 173–4
Grimshaw, John, 95, 202–5, 251, 253
Gronow, Capt, 67, 271
Gulliver, Miss, 40
Gully, John, 85, 87, 91–4, 180

Hamby, Elizabeth, 29–30
Hamby, Sir John, 30
Hamby, Walter, 30
Hamilton, Duke of, 78, 79, 81, 186, 218
Hamilton, Kate, 83
Hampton Court Sales, 210
Hardcastle, 202
Harrow School, 24, 39, 42, 58–9
Harte, Bret, 213
Hastings, Bertha Lelgarde (Baroness Grey de Ruthyn), 37, 260
Hastings, Dowager Marchioness (Countess of Loudoun), 25, 27 n, 28
Hastings, Edith Maud (Countess of Loudoun), 37, 46, 75, 120–2, 260

279

Hastings, Lady Flora, 27 n, 35, 40, 55, 69
Hastings, Frances Augusta Constance (Viscountess Marsham), 37, 75, 258, 260
Hastings, Francis, 1st Marquis of, 23–6, 35, 76
Hastings, George Augustus Francis, 2nd Marquis of, 26, 35–7, 164
Hastings, Henry Weysford Charles Plantagenet Rawdon, 4th Marquis of: titles, 16; ancestry, 23–8; family motto, 258; character, 16–19, 27, 29, 37–45, 48–51, 55, 62, 66–7, 81–3; shrewdness, 49, 93–4, 152, 160, 273; birth and childhood, 17–18, 28, 37–9; appearance, 16, 49–50; at Eton, 39–46; at Oxford, 46–56; coming-of-age celebrations, 72–7; his inheritance, 77; life in London, 63, 65–72, 78–89; life at Donington, 31–9, 167–71; cricket matches, 34, 51, 167–8; introduction to racing, 77–8, 90–3; elected member of Jockey Club, 77, 94; racing colours, 77, 95; gamble on Ackworth, 132–4; gamble on Lecturer, 177–81; wins only classic race, 172; meets Lady Florence, 102, 104, 105–6; elopement, 118–30; buys Kangaroo, 141–2; buys other horses cheaply, 151–2; compulsive gambling, 48–9, 161; accepts mastership of Quorn, 164–6, 176–7; resigns, 226; compared to Sir Harry Scattercash, 167; buys yacht, 169; obsession over Hermit, 181–3, 190, 211; letters to Henry Chaplin, 209–10, 220; cheered at Ascot, 212; recovers Derby losses, 212–16; financial situation becomes desperate, 223–31, 248–9; sells Scottish estates and racehorses, 226–7; deterioration in health, 226, 228; resigns from Jockey Club, 231; defeat of Lady Elizabeth at Epsom, 237–43; 'Spider and Fly' controversy, 245–9, 252; final breakdown in health, 251, 253–4; sees family ghost, 251; last visit to Newmarket, 253–4; death, 256; funeral, 257–60; his Will, 260; obituary notices, 260–2; grave at Kensal Green, 262–5
Hastings, Paulyn Reginald Serlo, 3rd Marquis of, 27, 37–9
Hastings Scandal, see Hastings, Lady Flora
Hastings, Selina, Countess of Huntingdon, 34
Hastings, Victoria Mary Louise, 37
Hawkesley, Capt, 193
Hawley, Sir Joseph, 158, 195, 221, 231–3, 238, 239, 244
Hawtrey, E. C., 41–2, 44
Hermit, see under Racehorses
Hibberd, 172, 180
Hill, Lady Alice, 75
Hill, Mr, 132, 247
Hohenlohe, Prince, 78
'House, The', see Christ Church College
Howe, Earl, 36, 39–40, 90
Huntingdon, Francis, 10th Earl of, 24–5
Huntingdon, George, 4th Earl of, 33

I'Anson, William, Senior, 109, 138, 142, 150, 181
I'Anson, William, Junior, 139, 145, 147–50

Jackson, Mr, 171
Jockey Club, The, 44, 49, 77, 94, 142, 157, 178, 198, 209, 227, 231, 262
Johnstone, Sir Frederick, 54, 60–2, 69, 108, 110–11, 136–7, 150, 162, 166, 201, 268, 270
'Jolly fast Marchioness, The', see Grey de Ruthyn, Barbara
Jolly Sailors, The, 80
Jowett, Benjamin, 47

Keate, Dr John, 40–2, 91
Kensal Green Cemetery, 257–9, 262–5, 270

Kent, John, 97, 137, 141, 144, 151
Kilmanseg, Count, 78
Kingsclere, 231–2, 238
Kings Mills, 33, 38, 169
Kings of the Turf, 167
Kirwan, Mr, 257
Knipe, Rev John, 120

'Ladies' Mile, The', 116, 258
Ladybird, 169, 249, 251, 253, 255
Lady Elizabeth, *see under* Racehorses
Lagrange, Count F. de, 98, 143–4, 156, 220
Lake Chaplin, 61
Lake Johnstone, 61
Lambton, Hon George, 206, 269
Leicester Journal, The, 73–4, 123, 274
Leicester Yeomanry, 47, 68
Leveson-Gower, Lady Florence, 267
Liddell, Dean, 47, 53, 59–60
Limmer's Hotel, 67, 78, 83, 106–7
Londesborough, Lord, 82, 268
Londonderry, Marchioness of, 13, 119–20, 158
London in the Sixties, 80, 120, 170
Long's Hotel, 67, 186, 218
Long Walk House, 268
Lonsdale, Lord, 154
Loughborough Chronicle, The, 124
Loughborough Monitor, The, 74–5, 123–4, 274
Loudoun estate, 212, 226

Machell, Captain, 150, 152–5, 156–9, 170, 183–206, 270, 271
'Magnifico', *see* Chaplin, Henry
Maidstone, Lord, 158
Malton, 138–9, 142–50
Mann, John, 150
Marshall and Snelgrove, 119–22
Marsham, Viscount, 120, 257
Marsham, Lady Constance (Lady Constance Hastings), 258, 260
Mauchline, 257
McGeorge, Mr, 70, 175, 186–7, 202, 241
McNair, John, 83
Melbourne, Lord, 27 n, 35

Merry, James, 117, 158–9, 181, 186, 195, 199, 205
Meynell, Hugo, 164
Middle Park Plate (Stakes), 187, 190–1, 220–2, 231, 268
Middle Park Stud, 157, 251
Moira, Earls of, *see* Hastings, Marquises of, and, 24
Moira, village of, 36, 73, 75
Moorhouse, Edward, 213
Moosejaw, 61
Morden, Sammy, 175
Morning Post, The, 115, 119
Morrison's Hotel, 153
Mott's Dancing Rooms, 82
'Mr Henry', 141. *See also* Padwick, Henry
'Mrs Henry', *see* Chaplin, 'Mrs Henry'
Mr Sponge's Sporting Tour, 167

Newcastle, Duke of, 187, 222, 258
New Stakes, 215–16, 217
Nicholson's Quadrille Band, 75
Norton, 'Squirt', 175
North, Lady, 75

Oakhurst, Mr John, 213
Oaks The: history of, 92, 143 n, 230; of 1864, 147; of 1867, 200, 207–8; of 1868, 230, 238, 245
Obituary notices: 'The Druid', 14, 90, 164–5, 212, 261–2; *The Field*, 260–1; *The Daily News*, 261–2; *The Times*, 261–2, 266
Old Bloss, *see* Bloss
One Thousand Guineas: history of, 143 n 230; of 1866, 171; of 1867, 191; of 1868, 239, 246
Osborne, John, 137

Padwick, Henry: career and character, 84–8; sells Kangaroo, 141–2; and is blamed for its failure, 151; underwrites Harry Hastings, 212, 227, 231; at Derby of 1868, 237–43; 'Spider and Fly' controversy and scandal over The Earl, 245–8, 252–3; attends Harry's funeral, 258; executor of Harry's Will, 260; death, 270;

also mentioned, 209, 214, 233, 254
Paget, Lord Alexander, 257
Paget, Lord Alfred, 167
Paget, Lord Berkeley, 167–8, 209–10, 257
Paget, Lady Florence Cecilia: ancestry, 20–3; character, 16–20, 29, 102–4; 128–9, 269; appearance, 17, 102–3; birth and childhood, 17–18, 23, 31; advent in Society, 64, 102–5; visits Epsom, 72; meets Harry Hastings and Henry Chaplin, 102, 104, 105–6; presented to Queen Victoria, 105; betrothal to Henry Chaplin, 113; elopement with Harry Hastings, 118–30; letters to Henry Chaplin, 126–7, 223–6, 249–50; life with Hastings, 160–2; growing estrangement, 223–4, 226, 249–50; remorse over betrayal of Henry Chaplin and resumption of friendship, 249–50; administers to her dying husband, 255–6; attends his funeral, 257–60; benefits from Will, 260; marries again, 269; her death and funeral, 269
Paget, Henry, 2nd Marquess of Anglesey, 20–3, 72, 103, 239–40, 258
Paget, Henry Cyril, 5th Marquess of Anglesey, 269
Paget, Henry William ('One-Leg'), 1st Marquess of Anglesey, 20–3
Paget, Henry William George, Lord Uxbridge and later 3rd Marquess of Anglesey, 20–3, 123, 257
Paget, William, 1st Baron Paget, 20
Pall Mall Gazette, The, 164, 246
Palmerston, Lord, 92
Past Times and Pastimes, 44
Patti, Mlle Adelina, 118
Payne, 202
Pearson, Col, 174, 207–8
'Pocket Venus, The', *see* Lady Florence Paget
Porter, John, 137, 220, 231–2, 239, 244

Porter, Mr, 215
Prince of Wales: at Oxford, 40, 53–4, 62; life in London with Chaplin and Hastings, 65–8, 78–9, 84, 88, 89, 103; first visit to Epsom, 68–72; at the Derby of 1867, 198, 204; and of 1868, 239; at Ascot with Princess Alexandra in 1866, 174; successes on the turf, 270; also mentioned, 267
Pryor, F., 187–8, 193–5, 198, 208
Punch, 207, 230
Pusey, Canon, 47

Queen Magazine, 103, 104, 115, 119, 272, 273
'Queen Mary' blood, 137, 150
Quorndon Hall, 164
Quorn Hunt, 26, 164–6, 173; 176–7, 226

Racehorses:
Achievement, 174, 187, 188, 190–1, 208, 219
Ackworth, 132–4, 139, 152, 172, 176, 178, 181, 188, 220, 228
Ambush II, 270
Athena, 213, 218, 220, 246, 254
Attraction, 97
Bacchus, 153–4
Bahram, 143 n
Bay Middleton, 158
Bertie, 171
Blair Athol, 109, 137, 138, 145
Blink Bonny, 45, 137, 138, 139, 142, 145, 155, 181, 195
Blue Gown, 231–3, 237–45
Blue Riband, 173
Breadalbane, 139–51, 155–6, 171, 173, 174
Breffni, 145
Brioche, 98–9
Broomielaw, 139–50, 156, 174–6, 187
Cellina, 186
Challenge, 215
Clown, The, 173
Consternation, 95, 99
Corporal, 202
Dalby, 172
Defenceless, 158

D'Estournel, 202
Diamond Jubilee, 270
Duke, The, 90, 116–17, 124, 130–1, 140–2, 145–6, 152, 155–6, 171, 173–6, 178, 194
Dundee, 159, 186
Earl, The, 152, 213, 218, 220, 222, 223, 227, 231–3, 238, 245–9, 252, 253, 256, 260, 268
East Sheen, 97, 98
Elis, 96
Elland, 174
Ellington, 146
Fandango filly, 97
Fille de l'Air, 147
Fitz-Ivan, 202
Formosa, 143 n, 230, 245
Garotter, 97
General Peel, 110
Gillie, The, 69
Gladiateur, 143–4, 146–9, 155–6, 174
Green Sleeve, 221, 231–3, 238–44
Grimston, 208, 213
Gustavus, 92
Hermit, 158–9, 174; wins Derby of 1867, 181–208; 219, 233, 251, 256, 264; record at stud, 267–8
Hippia, 200, 208, 216
Hue and Cry, 214
Iroquois, 143n, 149 n
Jeannie Deans, 185
Joker, 149
Julius, 187, 189, 202, 222, 251
Kangaroo, 141–2, 143–52
King Alfred, 242
King Charming, 146
King Hal, 171
Kingston, 157
Knight of the Garter, 189 190
Lady Barbara, 214
Lady Coventry, 221
Lady Egidia, 99
Lady Elizabeth, 195, 207–9, 213, 216–18; defeat in Middle Park, 220–2; match with Julius, 222–3; becomes public idol, 229–30; runs in Derby, 231, 237–48, 252–3; last race, 254; failure at stud, 268–9; also mentioned, 225, 226, 228, 256, 257, 260, 264
Lady Florence, 110–11
Lecturer, 90; wins Cesarewitch, 177–81, 190, 209; wins Gold Cup, 215–17; 220, 228
Leonie, 218
Lord Clifden, 70–2, 201
Lord Lyon, 173, 191
Lord Ronald, 215
Liddington, 117, 131, 143
Macaroni, 70–1
Marksman, 159, 186–9, 195, 199–205
Master Butterfly, 202
Minoru, 270
Mundig, 49
Musjid, 158
Newminster, 158, 184
Odine, 97
Old Fuller, 97
Ouragan, 220
Palmer, The, 195, 199, 202
Pantaloon, 141, 143–4, 215
Persimmon, 270
Pretty Polly, 138, 213, 269
Problem, 184, 185
Pyrrhus the First, 92
Quadrille, 98
Queen Mary, 138, 150
Rake, The, 188, 190, 193–9, 202
Rama, 188, 191–2, 216
Rattler, 72
Redcap, 97, 98, 125, 172, 220
Regalia, 216
Repulse, 171
Rosicrucian, 221, 231–3, 238–44
Roulette, 98
Sceptre, 138, 143 n, 213, 230, 269
Seclusion, 158
See Saw, 213, 215, 218
Shot, 159
Shotover, 267
Sir Bevys, 270
Spider, 256
St Blaise, 267
St Ronan, 239
Target, 188
Teddington, 238
Thormanby, 143, 158, 181

Racehorses—(contd.)
  Tippler, 97, 98, 124
  Tomato, 133
  Trumps, 97, 124
  Uncas, 199, 201
  Van Amburgh, 199, 202
  Vauban, 187–91, 199, 201–5
  Vespasian, 173
  Virago, 87
  Wild Moor, 202
Racing, organization of in nineteenth century, 95–6
Radnor, Countess of, 102
Ratcliff Highway, 79, 211
Rawdon, Elizabeth, 24
Rawdon, Lord Francis, see Hastings, 1st Marquis of
Rawdon, Sir George, of Moira, 24
Rawdon, Sir John, 4th Baronet, 24
Reay Forest, 135
Redesdale, Lord, 43
Robinson, Jem, 92
Rob Roy, 103
Rocky Mountains, 60–1
Rosebery, 5th Earl of, 42, 44, 167
Rothschild, Baron, 99, 133, 200
Rottingdean, 56
Rous, Admiral, 158, 179, 246–8, 252, 270
Roxburgh, Duchess of, 104
Ryhall Hall, 29, 31, 56,

Sait, 71
Salter, 201
Scattercash, Sir Harry, 167
Scott, Alexander, 244
Seafield, Countess of, 104
Shafto, Bobby, 78–80, 82, 109
Sharp, E., 149
Shaw, Capt Donald, 79, 120, 170, 274
Shaw, Jimmy, 82
Sherwood's Stable, 239
Siltzer, Frank, 157
'Skittles', 103, 116, 126
Spaum, Baron, 78
Sporting Life, The, 246
Spye Park, 87
St George's, Hanover Square, 37, 67, 120
St George's Hotel, 106, 119
St Leger: history of, 143 n; of 1836, 96; of 1865, 155–6; of 1867, 219, 222; of 1868, 249, 252, 253
St Vincent, Lord, 70–2
Stamford, Lord, 186
Stevens' Hotel, 67
Stewards Cup, 124, 199
Stewart, John, 83
Stockbridge Course, 215, 227
Stone, E. D., 41
Storey, Rev, 51
Surtees, R. S., 167
Sutherland, 3rd Duke of, 267
Sutton, Richard, 173, 174
Swan and Edgar, 121
Sweep, The, 79
Swinburne, A. C., 135
Symonds, Charles, 85

Tathwell, 30, 73
Tattersall, Edmund, 138
Tattersall's, 191, 212 n, 233
'Thormanby', 167
Tilt, 167
Times, The, 115, 180, 198, 201, 205–6, 216; 'Spider and Fly' correspondence, 246–8, 252–3; obituaries, 261–2, 266–7
Tomahawk Magazine, The, 248
Tomlinson, 153
Touts and their methods, 146, 170–1, 232
'Triple Crown, The', 143 n
Turf Memories of Sixty Years, 244
Turk's Head Tavern, 83
Two Thousand Guineas: history of, 143 n; of 1865, 143–4; of 1867, 188–9; of 1868, 232

Uxbridge, Lord, see Paget, Henry William George

Vaughan, Dr Charles John, 58–9
Vaughan, E. H., 58
Vere Street, 119–22
Vernon, Diana, 103–4
Victoria, Queen, 27 n, 35, 54, 55, 69, 70, 105

Walker, Mrs, 56
Warren, The, 239
Waterford, Lord, 83–4
Weatherby's, 247, 248

Wells, J., 238, 242
West Acre, 58
Westerhall Estate, 270
Westmorland, Lord, 247, 258
Westmorland, Lady, 226
'Weysford, Mr', 77, 95
White, Dr A., 256
White Hart Inn, The, 58
White Horse Inn, The, 51
Whiteley, 145
White Place, 249
Whyte-Melville, G. J., 42, 53, 78
Wilkinson, Mr, 120

'Wilkinson, Mr H.', 179
Willesley Hall, 46
Willoughby de Broke, Lord, 52, 268
Wilson, 165
Winchelsea, Lord, 123
Wolley, Rev Charles, 40
Wombwell, Mr, 120

Yelverton, Admiral Sir Hastings Reginald Henry, 37, 46, 257, 260
Yelverton, Hon Barbara, 258
York Races, 131, 156, 218

SPHERE BOOKS INCLUDE:
(arranged by subject)

BIOGRAPHY & AUTOBIOGRAPHY

A SILVER-PLATED SPOON	Duke of Bedford	5/–
MARLBOROUGH – VOLUME 1	Winston S. Churchill	12/6
MARLBOROUGH – VOLUME 2	Winston S. Churchill	12/6
MARLBOROUGH – VOLUME 3	Winston S. Churchill	12/6
MARLBOROUGH – VOLUME 4	Winston S. Churchill	12/6
MARLBOROUGH – VOLS. 1/2/3/4 in presentation case	Winston S. Churchill	50/–
I'LL COME BACK IN THE SPRINGTIME	Maurice N. Hennessy	5/–

DOMESTIC SCIENCE

GREAT DISHES OF THE WORLD	Robert Carrier	10/6

GENERAL FICTION

THE CONSCIENCE OF LOVE	Marcel Ayme	4/–
SPELLA HO	H. E. Bates	5/–
FLIGHT OF FATE	Vicki Baum	4/–
THE WEEPING WOOD	Vicki Baum	7/6
THE HOUSE IN PARIS	Elizabeth Bowen	4/–
ATLAN	Jane Gaskell	5/–
THE CITY	Jane Gaskell	5/–
THE SERPENT	Jane Gaskell	5/–
THE BLAZE OF NOON	Rayner Heppenstall	4/–
ALL THE CONSPIRATORS	Christopher Isherwood	3/6
RETREAT TO INNOCENCE	Doris Lessing	5/–
TROUBLE IN BURMA	Van Wyck Mason	3/6
CONFESSIONS OF A MASK	Yukio Mishima	4/–
APPOINTMENT WITH VENUS	Jerrard Tickell	3/6
THE DEATH SHIP	B. Traven	6/–
A STANDARD OF BEHAVIOUR	William Trevor	3/6

HISTORY

A SHORT HISTORY OF THE RUSSIAN REVOLUTION	Joel Carmichael	5/–

MYSTERY & THRILLER

THE MAN WHO CHOSE DEATH	Eric Allen	4/–
DEVIL BY THE SEA	Nina Bawden	4/–
THE SOLITARY CHILD	Nina Bawden	4/–
DOUBLE FOR THE TOFF	John Creasey	3/6
HERE COMES THE TOFF	John Creasey	3/6
THE TOFF PROCEEDS	John Creasey	3/6
THE TOFF TO MARKET	John Creasey	3/6
CABLE CAR	June Drummond	3/6
CALL AFTER MIDNIGHT	M. G. Eberhart	3/6
RUN SCARED	M. G. Eberhart	3/6

THE DISAPPEARING BRIDEGROOM	Margaret Erskine	3/6
THE WHISPERING HOUSE	Margaret Erskine	3/6
THE CASE OF THE LUCKY LEGS	Erle Stanley Gardner	2/6
THE CASE OF THE SULKY GIRL	Erle Stanley Gardner	2/6
THE CASE OF THE VELVET CLAWS	Erle Stanley Gardner	2/6
CLUE OF THE FORGOTTEN MURDER	Erle Stanley Gardner	2/6
THE D.A. CALLS A TURN	Erle Stanley Gardner	2/6
THE D.A. COOKS A GOOSE	Erle Stanley Gardner	2/6
THE D.A. GOES TO TRIAL	Erle Stanley Gardner	2/6
THE HOURS AFTER MIDNIGHT	Joseph Hayes	3/6

POLITICAL SCIENCE & ECONOMICS

THE BITTER HERITAGE	Arthur Schlesinger	5/–

REFERENCE & GUIDE

PEARS MEDICAL ENCYCLOPAEDIA	J. A. C. Brown	7/6

ROMANCE

THE MAN BEHIND THE MASK	Patricia Robins	3/6

SCIENCE FICTION

FAR BOUNDARIES	August Derleth	3/6
THE ODIOUS ONES	Jerry Sohl	3/6
THE TIME DISSOLVER	Jerry Sohl	4/–

SELF HELP

YOGA OVER FORTY	Michael Volin & Nancy Phelan	5/–

SOCIAL SCIENCE

THE SECOND OSWALD	R. H. Popkin	4/6

TRAVEL & ADVENTURE

ULYSSES FOUND	Ernle Bradford	4/6
THE SLAVES OF TIMBUKTU	Robin Maugham	5/–

WAR BOOKS

THE FACE OF WAR	Martha Gellhorn	5/–
THE WAR GAME (Illus.)	Peter Watkins	5/–

WESTERNS

DESERT HERITAGE	Zane Grey	3/6
LIGHT OF THE WESTERN STARS	Zane Grey	3/6
PRAIRIE GOLD	Zane Grey	3/6
THE RAINBOW TRAIL	Zane Grey	3/6
RIDERS OF VENGEANCE	Zane Grey	3/6
THIEVES' CANYON	Zane Grey	3/6
WILD FIRE	Zane Grey	3/6

James Clavell
TAI-PAN

Now only 10/6

705 Pages

In this turbulent, panoramic novel of the founding of Hong Kong, James Clavell, author of KING RAT, narrates the saga of how one man, with majestic vision, ruthless will and ingenious grasp of command, guides the development of a colony destined to influence the course of history. It is a masterful re-creation of a momentous epoch in the history of the British Empire.